Modern Critical Interpretations

Modern Critical Interpretations

J. R. R. Tolkien's
The Lord of the Rings

Edited and with an introduction by
Harold Bloom
Sterling Professor of the Humanities
Yale University

CHELSEA HOUSE PUBLISHERS
Philadelphia

© 2000 by Chelsea House Publishers, a subsidiary of Haights
Cross Communications.

Introduction © 2000 by Harold Bloom

Printed and bound in the United States of America

10 9 8 7 6 5 4 3 2

∞ The paper used in this publication meets the minimum
requirements of the American National Standard for
Permanence of Paper for Printed Library Materials,
Z39.48-1984

Library of Congress Cataloging-in-Publication Data

The lord of the rings / edited and with an introduction by Harold Bloom.
        p. cm. — (Modern critical interpretations)
    Includes bibliographical references (p.) and index.
    ISBN 0-7910-5665-1 (alk. paper)
    1. Tolkien, J.R.R. (John Ronald Reuel), 1892-1973. Lord of the
rings. 2. Fantasy fiction, English—History and criticism.
3. Middle Earth (Imaginary place)
I. Bloom, Harold. II. Series.
PR6039.O32L6325   1999
823'.912—dc21   99-052464
                                                                CIP

Contributing Editor: Aaron Tillman

Contents

Editor's Note

My Introduction considers some of the aesthetic limitations of J. R. R. Tolkien's vast prose-romance *The Lord of the Rings*, while acknowledging that its continued popularity is not likely to abate soon.

Hugh T. Keenan traces the appeal of *The Lord of the Rings* to its child-like vision of the struggle of Life against Death, after which Burton Raffel, distinguished translator of Cervantes, analyzes the literary flaws of the trilogy.

Randel Helms, contrasting Tolkien with William Blake, rightly sees Tolkien as being more equivocal about Eros, while Humphrey Carpenter, Tolkien's biographer, gives an account of the composition of the trilogy.

To Jane Chance Nitzsche, Tolkien's "epic" takes its crucial origin from the great Old English epic *Beowulf*, after which Jared Lobdell examines various Edwardian literary origins, including Chesterton, Haggard, and Blackwood.

David L. Jeffrey analyzes the deep meaning Tolkien invests in names, while Rose A. Zimbardo praises Tolkien for revising an older vision of cosmic harmony.

Katharyn W. Crabbe concludes this volume by admiring Tolkien's use of allusions to a variety of languages and cultures in order to distinguish the different peoples of Middle-earth.

Introduction

Roger Sale, Tolkien's best critic, is not included in this volume because the essay on *The Lord of the Rings* from his book *Modern Heroism* is reprinted in full in the volume on J. R. R. Tolkien in the Chelsea House series MODERN CRITICAL VIEWS. I will attempt, rather briefly, to define my aesthetic doubts about Tolkien's trilogy by contrasting them to Sale's shrewd defense of what he regards as Tolkien's and the protagonist Frodo Baggins's heroism.

Tolkien, at twenty-three, went off to the Western Front, was wounded, and lost to the war nearly all his friends in his own generation. For Sale, the trilogy is Tolkien's delayed, ultimate reaction to the Great War, which decimated Great Britain's young men. Tolkien dated his lifelong love of fairy-stories to his turning away from the War, and *The Lord of the Rings* is a vast fairy-story.

Sale accurately observes that the trilogy purports to be a quest but actually is a descent into hell. Whether a visionary descent into hell can be rendered persuasively in language that is acutely self-conscious, even arch, seems to me a hard question. I am fond of *The Hobbit*, which is rarely pretentious, but *The Lord of the Rings* seems to me inflated, over-written, tendentious, and moralistic in the extreme. Is it not a giant Period Piece?

Sale nevertheless makes quite a strong case for the trilogy, and a vast readership implicitly agrees with him. I don't know whether Frodo Baggins breaks free and away from Tolkien's moralism to anything like the extent Sale suggests. Frodo, and Tolkien's deep creation of fairy-lore, are the strengths of the trilogy, in Sale's account.

But there is still the burden of Tolkien's style: stiff, false-archaic, over-wrought, and finally a real hindrance in Volume III, *The Return of the King*, which I have had trouble rereading. At sixty-nine, I may just be too old, but here is *The Return of the King*, opened pretty much at random:

At the doors of the Houses many were already gathered to see
Aragorn, and they followed after him; and when at last he had
supped, men came and prayed that he would heal their
kinsmen or their friends whose lives were in peril through hurt
or wound, or who lay under the Black Shadow. And Aragorn
arose and went out, and he sent for the sons of Elrond, and
together they labored far into the night. And word went
through the city: 'The King is come again indeed.' And they
named him Elfstone, because of the green stone that he wore,
and so the name which it was foretold at his birth that he
should bear was chosen for him by his own people.

I am not able to understand how a skilled and mature reader can absorb
about fifteen hundred pages of this quaint stuff. Why "hurt or wound"; are
they not the same? What justifies the heavy King James Bible influence upon
this style? Sometimes, reading Tolkien, I am reminded of the Book of
Mormon. Tolkien met a need, particularly in the early days of the Counter-
culture, in the later 1960's. Whether he is an author for the coming century
seems to me open to some doubt.

HUGH T. KEENAN

The Appeal of The Lord of the Rings:
A Struggle for Life

Long before *The Lord of the Rings* became popular with children, educated readers began taking it enthusiastically and seriously. But how could mature readers take to the melodramatic incidents, the superficial brotherhood theme, and the one-dimensional characters of the trilogy? Most only hint at the reason, and few reveal themselves as did W. H. Auden, who says, "by the time one has finished his [Tolkien's] book, one knows the histories of Hobbits, Elves, Dwarves, and the landscape they inhabit as well as one knows one's own childhood." This hint from Auden marks the elemental nature of the book, I think. The major appeal of *The Lord of the Rings* grows from its underlying and pervasive presentation of the basic struggle of Life against Death. Tolkien's thematic presentation explores in its course the psychological meaning of childhood, another strong appeal for the mature reader.

But it is not often realized that psychology rather than philosophy or literary merit is responsible for a large portion of this growing esteem. Sober critics have read the novel as a basic conflict of good and evil in moral or Christian lights. They have debated the novel's determinism or free will. They have made the obvious comparisons between Tolkien's trilogy and the novels of C. S. Lewis and Charles Williams. One critic has even compared

From *Tolkien and the Critics: Essays on J. R. R. Tolkien's* The Lord of the Rings, edited by Neil D. Isaacs and Rose A. Zimbardo. © 1968 by University of Notre Dame Press.

Tolkien's theories about the fairy-tale genre to his practice in this story. All of their efforts have been somewhat disappointing, for they have to conclude that *The Lord of the Rings* differs from more than it resembles any of these philosophies, novels, or theories.

Despite their basic differences, three of the critics—Reilly, Sale, and Spacks—agree that the world depicted by Tolkien is amazingly alive. His world includes hobbits, elves, dwarfs, orcs, monsters, and ghosts. The abstracts of Death and Life are personified by the Nazgûls and the treelike Ents. The creatures of this world interact and communicate to a surprising degree. The Rangers, as Miss Spacks points out, "understand the language of beasts and birds," whereas Tom Bombadil "is in the most intimate communion with natural forces; he has the power of 'the earth itself.'" Hobbits, men, and even orcs can talk through a universal language, the Common Speech. Some living creatures do not speak the Common Speech, and others which we ordinarily consider as inanimate in the real world are sentient in the world of the novel. These include the Balrog, the other spirits of Moria, the Eldar beyond the Sea, and the mountain Caradhras. Even stone statues cry out a warning in this gothic land while stones, trees, and blades of grass listen for the advance of an enemy army.

In view of the reiterated fertility-sterility conflict in this world and the absence of a clearly defined deity or religion, the forcing of a vague moral pattern (good vs. evil) on the book's contents is an unpromising endeavor. Something is more important than good vs. evil. This something is life vs. death. Questions of life and death dominate the minds and actions of the inhabitants. As Sale observes in passing, "The world is alive, and the story is the story of the ways in which it is called on to *be* alive when the shadows threaten and darkness grows powerful."

The peculiar achievement of the author is to have created a world which is at once completely (or to a superlative degree) sentient and yet dying, to have presented vividly, objectively, and emotionally the eternal conflict between life and death. The reader of this essay may rightly catch an allusion to Norman O. Brown's *Life Against Death: the Psychoanalytical Meaning of History*, to which this line of argument is greatly indebted. In applying Freudian analysis to mankind rather than to individual man, Brown concludes that

> mankind, in all its restless striving and progress, has no idea of what it really wants. Freud was right—our real desires are unconscious. It also begins to be apparent that mankind, unconscious of its real desires and therefore unable to obtain satisfaction, is hostile to life and ready to destroy itself.

This statement seems equally valid for the fictional world of *Lord of the Rings*.

In Tolkien's trilogy as in the science fiction trilogy of C. S. Lewis (especially the final volume *That Hideous Strength*), man is bent on destroying himself through sociological, technological, and psychological means. Man's technology is the enemy of his humanity. But whereas Lewis' world is heavily Christian and he traces the source of man's perversity to the influence of the Devil, Tolkien's world is almost nonreligious. He traces the perversity of his creatures—in the Shire and outside it—to their own twisted natures. The greed of the dwarfs for *mithril* causes them to destroy their home in Moria by disturbing the Balrog. Consequently they lose much of their skill in metalworking. The exiled Númenor have become practicers of the black arts in their vain search for immortality and so have fallen into sloth. Faramir confesses that even "'Gondor . . . brought about its own decay, falling by degrees into dotage, and thinking that the Enemy was asleep, who was only banished not destroyed.'" The pride of Théoden and his people makes them isolate themselves and ally with Saruman, the tool of the Dark Lord.

In *Beowulf*, Grendel and his mother can be seen as the objectifications (in part) of the flaws of the king Hrothgar and of the faults of his court. In *The Lord of the Rings*, Sauron can be similarly viewed as the objectification of the fears and self-destruction (death instinct) of the inhabitants of Middle-earth.

Frodo, the hero of the trilogy, and his three fellow hobbits overbalance the nine-man fellowship. The question is why are so many representatives chosen from the Shire. To know the answer, we must find out what hobbits are. Then we may be able to understand too why Frodo is made the hero of the novel. Neither he nor his fellow hobbits are daring, handsome, or even clever as heroes typically are.

Exactly what are hobbits? Edmund Wilson, despite what else he says, seems to have a fair answer:

> The hobbits are a not quite human race who inhabit an imaginary country called the Shire and who combine the characteristics of certain English animals—they live in burrows like rabbits and badgers—with the traits of English country-dwellers, ranging from rustic to tweedy. (The name sees a telescoping of rabbit and Hobbs.)

Like rabbits or country folk, the hobbits emphasize family and fertility as manifested by their love for genealogical facts and by their well-populated, clan-size burrows. Their love of domestic comforts is in line with their dual nature. Like children they enjoy birthday parties as frequent as those in *Alice in Wonderland*, the receiving of presents, and the eating of snacks, plus full meals, while they do little work and mostly play. Yet furry and fat like rabbits (or country squires) though they be, they prove to be the human-like creatures most interested in preserving life. The hobbits combine the strongest traditional symbols of life: the rabbit for fertility and the child for generation. They represent the earthly as opposed to the mechanic or scientific forces. Therefore they are eminently suitable heroes in the struggle of life against death.

In the journey to Mordor, these hobbits link the Men of Gondor to the Ents, Gollum, the Rohirrim, the Dwarfs, the Elves, the Barrow-wights, the Orcs, and all the rest of the creatures (except the birds)—even Shelob. Gandalf, whose sole purpose is to preserve the life of the world, acts in a similar capacity, but the hobbits become more personally involved. Gandalf interests himself in the fate of future living creatures. The hobbits Merry and Pippin act for the present. Merry becomes the retainer of Théoden and Pippin becomes the retainer of Denethor, the Steward of Gondor.

What justifies Frodo's being the hero? Here one comes to a paradox. Frodo has the usual rabbit-like and child-like nature of a country hobbit. He enjoys smoking, birthday parties, presents, good food, and good company. But as he journeys toward Mordor, he loses some of this vitality,. He becomes isolated, less humorous, more rational, and even mystical, in contrast to his old emotional, animal self. In other words Frodo grows up; he becomes adult in a human sense. He becomes conscious of his sacrificial duty. He becomes humble as he learns more about the world outside the Shire and as he perceives the pathos of mortality through the passing of the fair and the beautiful.

The sacrificial nature of Frodo brings us to two interesting points. Since the ensuing age is to be that of Men and since hobbits resemble markedly the Men who live isolated lives, prefer war and comfort to learning and beauty, and pride themselves on their sense of duty and honor, there is a strong suggestion that Frodo and his kind represent psychologically the eternal child who must be sacrificed so that the man may live. The national languages of the hobbits and the Men are very close. Douglass Parker puts it in other terms:

> Their [hobbits'] real name, translated as 'halfling' is very significant. Half-fairy, half-man, yet neither, they are a transition-stage from the Third Age to the Fourth, and, in the destruction of the Ring by Frodo, Sam, and the erstwhile hobbit Gollum, they are the efficient causes of the transition itself.

At a more universal level, Frodo is the Child who fathers the Age of Men.

The second point may prove clearer to see. When Frodo reaches the Crack of Doom, he suddenly puts on the Ring and vows to keep it, thus defeating the purpose of the arduous Quest. Why does he do it? Because of the Ring's powers. These include strengthening of hearing, while diminishing sight, preservation of youth if the Ring is kept but not worn (see the cases of Bilbo and Frodo), and invisibility when the Ring is worn, plus permanent vanishing if the Ring is worn too long. But primarily, it grants one the power to rule and to achieve his chief desire. For instance, when Sam puts on the Ring, he has a vision of controlling the world and making it one large garden. As gardening is the *idée fixe* of Sam, for him the promise the Ring gives is the world cultivated as a magnificent garden. Gandalf and Galadriel also experience the power of the Ring; it offers them the chance to achieve their most cherished desires. Fortunately all three individuals refuse this unlimited power. Exactly what the Ring promises Frodo at this moment at the Crack of Doom we do not learn. But we may be assured that this includes the power to rule and to dominate in achieving the desire.

Norman O. Brown interprets such aggressiveness as an extroversion of the Freudian death instinct; in this way people repress the recognition of the existence of death. Sale comes to a similar conclusion about Frodo's mental conflict at this moment. In speaking of Frodo's blindness to the powers and the results of keeping the Ring, Sale observes

> Tolkien does not enforce this irony but he does make clear that the struggle is not so much one of good against evil as of life against itself in its effort to stay alive.

Additionally, since the Ring is a female symbol, the possession—not the use—of it makes Frodo a type of the perfect hermaphrodite, the perfect androgynous Adam, or simply a child. Norman Brown says that for the unconscious or for the child,

> the sexual differentiation of the adult libido, as presupposed in genital organization and the human family—masculine aggressiveness and feminine passivity—is a loss of sexual completeness; hence the fact of sexual differentiation is regarded with horror. In each sex, says Freud, it is the attitude belonging to the opposite sex which succumbs to repression. In each sex the unconscious does not accept the repression but wants to recover the *bisexuality of childhood*. (italics mine)

Frodo's conscious assumption of the Ring is a symbolic assumption of sexuality, a symbolic coitus and acceptance of death. Gollum rushes forward and bites off the finger of the invisible and therefore symbolically dead Frodo. This symbolic castration returns Frodo to life temporarily. But as castration is not unconsciousness of sexual role (the child's state) but loss of sexuality, the act represents a death of the body. On his return to the Shire, Frodo's conduct is marked by passivity as compared to the masculine aggressiveness of Sam, Merry, and Pippin. He becomes a retired, Messianic figure; in a short time, he is almost forgotten by the hobbits whom he leaves for the Grey Havens.

One should notice that this decline in aggressiveness and this change in Frodo's protagonist role are compensated for by an increased focus on the developing strength of Sam. Same becomes the vital, the interesting hero in the latter pages of the novel. He fights the orcs at Cirith Ungol and becomes increasingly protective toward the rapidly weakening Frodo, who in Mordor loses his zest for life.

This life strength of Sam's comes from his gardening, his relation to the soil. He is the good country person *par excellence*. Only two characters wear the Ring without ill effects: Tom Bombadil and Sam, who becomes Samwise. As the more primitive, the more vital, and the more mysterious, Tom Bombadil has the greater strength. When he puts on the Ring, he does not vanish. Tom can laugh and then return the Ring to Frodo without hesitation. Because Sam is weaker that Tom, Sam vanishes when he wears it. But his vitality and his love for Frodo are so strong that he can return the Ring easily to Frodo.

One many notice that the last volume closes with Sam happily married, a fulfilled adult, the father of his first child. It is he to whom Galadriel entrusts the magic dust which makes the seedlings sprout into saplings in one season, thus replacing the Shire trees destroyed by the Enemy's minions. Since Sam is the agent for this reforestation, he becomes closely akin to Tom Bombadil, who has been called "a kind of archetypal 'vegetation god.'"

The marked absence of women in the novel calls attention to its fertility theme, an important part of the continuing struggle of life against death. It might be argued that women are naturally excluded from a battle story. But here the story is more that of a journey than that of a battle or wars. The women are missed. The Ents tell of the disappearance of the Entwives long ago in explaining why there are no young Ents; the dwarfs have few women and fewer children. In Gondor, too, there are not enough young people.

In considering the women who are present, we need not be as unchivalrous as Edmund Wilson, who says that "the fair ladies would not stir a heartbeat; the horrors would not hurt a fly." Though the ladies are scarce, they do capture hearts. Though a dwarf and an enemy, Gimli becomes enraptured of the elven queen Galadriel, so much so that he offers to fight Faramir. The hobbits—Frodo, Merry, Pippin, and Sam—are charmed by Goldberry, Tom Bombadil's consort. There is the inset story of Tinúviel, the elf queen, and her tragic love for Beren, a mortal man. This story of Elrond's ancestors foreshadows the love of Elrond's daughter Arwen for Aragorn. There is Éowyn's unrequited love for Aragorn and her happy marriage with Faramir. There is nurse Ioreth, who is the garrulous domestic. Although her type characterization has charm, it is underdeveloped.

What the trilogy lacks is a mother with children. The women, even if married, are not shown as mothers. They have charm but not earthiness. Or they are cold, though they may not be as cold as the Lady Éowyn. She becomes a Britomartis figure. Disguised as a young man, she rides to war alongside her uncle Théoden, without his knowledge or consent. After the defeat of Mordor, she abandons significantly her desire to be a soldier or a queen; she elects instead to be "'a healer, and love all things that grow and are not barren'."

Not until the end of the book do women as child-bearers appear. Then their role is prominent. When Sauron is defeated, the Ring destroyed, and the lands cleansed, there comes a succession of marriages: Faramir marries Éowyn; Aragorn marries Arwen; Sam marries Rose Cotton. The marriage of Aragorn and Arwen has been foreshadowed. That of Sam and Rose is more of a surprise. Like the end of a Shakespearean comedy, the trilogy concludes with a series of engagements and marriages.

One famous female—Shelob—has been passed over. This horror, this travesty of love and generation, refutes Edmund Wilson's pronouncement that the horrors would not hurt a fly. True, if her appearance and function are judged by standards of realism, the giant spider is a flaw. She reminds us of the insect villains of too many poor science fiction movies. But in the story, Shelob is symbolically appropriate.

She is the feminine counterpart to Sauron. As he represents Death, the opposite of Life, she represents destruction and physical corruption, the opposites of generation and birth. This mistress of Sauron greets the visitors to Mordor with death. Nor does she spare even her own brood, she "who only desired death for all others, mind and body, and for herself a glut of life, alone, swollen till the mountains could no longer hold her up and the darkness could not contain her."

When one considers the structure of the trilogy in which these characters play their parts, the struggle of life against death is very important. To a reader of Jessie L. Weston's *From Ritual to Romance*, Tolkien's use of the Wasted-Land-and-the-Wounded-King theme is obvious. As Tolkien uses these traditional elements in the fertility theme, Gandalf comes to

Théoden's court, rouses the old king from illness, drives out Wormtongue, and thus restores the leader to his people and the land to its former vigor. (There is a parallel to Beowulf and Hrothgar too in all of this.) Traditional elements appear also in Aragorn's restoration of the kingdom of Gondor: the reforging of the broken sword, the return of the kingdom to its rightful owner, and the consequent revitalization of the city and its inhabitants.

Older than these motifs is the seasonal significance of the time span of the novel. The Quest begins in winter, a traditionally dead period. Frodo and his friends leave the Shire on September 22, for Rivendell; they depart from Rivendell on the last of December. The Quest is achieved in the spring, March 25, to be exact. And at the end of a year, Frodo and Sam are home again in the Shire. The traditional associations of the seasons underscore the theme of a change from death to life.

The change in landscape is symbolic. As Miss Spacks observes,

> The progress toward the heart of evil, toward the Crack of Doom into which, in the trilogy's central fable, the Ring-bearer must throw his Ring of Power, is a progress from natural fertility to the desolation of nature.

To this observation, one need add only two comments. First, the desolation of nature at Isengard and at Mordor is due to the technological devices of the Enemy. Second, the journey does not stop at the Crack of Doom; Frodo and Sam return to the Shire and restore the land to its former fertility. So the complete pattern circles from natural fertility in the Shire to technological desolation of nature at Mordor and afterwards ends at the Shire and fertility again. Or as Bilbo might say, "'there and back again.'"

Tolkien regards advanced tools and mechanics with suspicion. He praises the hobbit and dwarfs for using only simple hand tools and such necessary, simple machinery as water mills. Fangorn characterizes Saruman as having "'a mind of metal and wheels'" and possessing no concern "'for growing things, except as far as they serve him for the moment'." The land of Mordor itself is a place of "mines and forges." On the other hand, the Elves have as their concerns, not "strength or domination or hoarded wealth, but understanding, making, and healing, to preserve all things unstained."

The numerous tunnels, the trees, and the bodies of water—especially the Sea—are important to the fertility theme, although Mark Roberts doubts that the numerous tunnels are so much Freudian symbols as they are ruts marking the author's lack of inventiveness. Some are associated with death and corruption, such as the lair of Shelob, the Paths of the Dead, and the tunnels of Moria. But in the Shire and at Helm's Deep, tunnels are linked with health, happiness, and safety. While none are insignificant, context determines whether they are associated with death or with life. Although trees seem ambiguous at first, they stand for life. The malevolent trees in the Old Forest and in Fangorn are more than offset by the good influences of Tom Bombadil and the Ents. Trees, as a general symbol of naturalness and fertility, are more than commonly important to the hobbits returning to the Shire. The elves are almost druidic in their worship of and empathy with trees. Legolas is drawn to them as strongly as Gimli is to caves. And still better, elves understand the language of the trees. In Lothlórien the elves make their homes in giant trees and venerate especially the *mallorn* tree. In Gondor one of the primary symbols of the life of Minas Tirith is the White Tree in the courtyard. Its dead trunk and branches betoken the dying of the city. Likewise the discovery of a scion of this tree symbolizes the rebirth of Minas Tirith under the leadership of Aragorn.

Finally there are the Ents—especially Fangorn or Tree-beard—and their tree herds. The life history of these living trees demonstrates the literal and symbolical import of their preservation. For as the forests have disappeared by being pushed back, burned, or cut down, the land and its people have suffered. The return of the forests to Isengard and to the Shire signals the return of life to the dead and dying lands.

In addition to symbols, we find patterns of contrast in character, incident, and place which define the theme of life against death. At the beginning of the journey, Frodo and the three hobbits meet Tom Bombadil and his consort Goldberry. At the end of the journey, Frodo and Sam encounter Gollum and his mistress-ruler Shelob. Besides the parallels and contrasts of character—Tom Bombadil (life) and Gollum (death), Goldberry (preserver) and Shelob (destroyer)—there are parallel actions. At the beginning of the story, Tom rescues the lost Frodo and company from the Old Forest and then saves them from the Barrow-wights. Later Gollum rescues the lost Frodo and his companion Sam in the wilderness of Emyn Muil and guides them through the treacherous Valley of the Dead. As one guide leads them to safety and life, the other one leads them to treachery and death. While Tom Bombadil cannot be moved by the Ring, Gollum can never be free of it.

The contrasts of Minas Tirith and Minas Morgul are equally clear. The Tower of the Sun, which is held by the Men of Gondor, rises up on the mountain. The Tower of the Moon, which is held by the Enemy, lies in the valley. Both are white-walled cities, but one has the white color of life (though it is dying) and the other has the white pallor of death. The decay of the Babylon-like, seven-tiered city of Minas Tirith is clear to Pippin:

> Pippin gazed in growing wonder at the great stone city, vaster and more splendid than anything that he had dreamed of; greater and stronger than Isengard, and far more beautiful. Yet

it was in truth falling year by year into decay; and already it lacked half the men that could have dwelt at ease there. In every street they passed some great house or court over whose doors and arched gates were carved many fair letters of strange and ancient shapes: names Pippin guessed of great men and kindreds that had once dwelt there; and yet now they were silent, and no footstep rang on their wide pavements, nor voice was heard in their halls, nor any face looked out from door or empty window.

To Sam, Frodo, and Gollum, Minas Morgul (Ithil) appears even worse:

Paler indeed than the moon ailing in some slow eclipse was the light of it now, wavering and blowing like a noisome exhalation of decay, a corpse-light, a light that illuminated nothing. In the walls and tower windows showed, like countless black holes looking inward into emptiness; but the top-most course of the tower revolved slowly, first one way and then another, a huge ghostly head leering into the night.

Unlike the eager travellers to Minas Tirith, Frodo and Sam pass this dead city with fear and reluctance. The river, the flowers, and even the statuary there are corruptions of life, bitter opposites to the fruitful land of Gondor and the healthful Anduin River:

Wide flats lay on either bank, shadowy meads filled with pale white flowers. Luminous these were too, beautiful and yet horrible of shape, like the demented forms in an uneasy dream; and they gave forth a faint sickening charnel-smell; an odour of rottenness filled the air. From mead to mead the bridge sprang. Figures stood there at its head, carven with cunning in forms human and bestial, but all corrupt and loathsome. The water flowing beneath was silent, and it steamed, but the vapour that rose from it, curling and twisting about the bridge, was deadly cold.

The implication left is that as Minas Morgul is, so Minas Tirith will be if the war goes against Gondor.

The decay theme of the trilogy is carried out in the contrasts of Edoras and Minas Tirith too. Of the cities, that of Rohan is the more healthful, the brighter, the stronger in spirit, the more natural. Legolas is first to see

Edoras set on a green hill in a valley and close by a white stream. From afar, the elf sees the Meduseld, the hall of Théoden, shine like gold. This land is spring-like, grassy, well-watered, and planted with budding willows and ever-blooming white flowers. The gleam of the armor of the men, their bright golden hair, and their formal yet ceremonious courtesy are in contrast to the dark armor and the coldness of spirit found at Gondor.

The interior of the Meduseld is much brighter and livelier than that of the Hall of Minas Tirith:

> The hall was long and wide and filled with shadows and half lights; mighty pillars upheld its lofty roof. But here and there bright sunbeams fell in glimmering shafts from the eastern windows, high under the deep eaves. Through the louver in the roof, above the thin wisps of issuing smoke, the sky showed pale and blue. As their eyes changed, the travellers perceived that the floor was paved with stones of many hues; branching runes and strange devices intertwined beneath their feet. They saw now that the pillars were richly carved, gleaming dully with gold and half-seen colours. Many woven cloths were hung upon the walls, and over their wide spaces marched figures of ancient legend, some dim with years, some darkling in the shade. But upon one form the sunlight fell: a young man upon a white horse. He was blowing a great horn, and his yellow hair was flying in the wind. The horse's head was lifted, and its nostrils were wide and red as it neighed, smelling battle afar. Foaming water, green and white, rushed and curled about its knees.

Théoden, their leader, retains some of the vigor of this young heroic man. Though white-haired, the Lord of Rohan leads his men against Sauron's forces and laughs to scorn the wiles of Saruman at Isengard. Even Aragorn recognizes the unfallen state of these Men in contrast to the lesser vigor of those of Gondor.

In Gondor, the Hall of Minas Tirith is much darker, less lively, less human, more like a tomb; its Steward Denethor, unlike Théoden, scorns help, despairs of victory, and commits suicide. Here is the Hall as Pippin sees it:

> It was lit by deep windows in the wide aisles at either side, beyond the rows of tall pillars that upheld the roof. Monoliths of black marble, they rose to great capitals carved in many

strange figures of beasts and leaves; and far above in shadow
the wide vaulting gleamed with dull gold, inset with flowing
traceries of many colours. No hangings nor storied webs, nor
any things of woven stuff or of wood, were to be seen in that
long solemn hall; but between the pillars there stood a silent
company of tall images graven in cold stone.

The two halls mirror the different natures of their leaders and peoples.

This contrast of the quick and the dead is seen most simply in the cities
of Caras Galadon and its enemy Dol Guldur. From a platform in the ancient
city of Cerin Amroth, Frodo sees the green city of the Elves and the dark
tower (Dol Guldur) of the Enemy in Southern Mirkwood, the evil forest.
Haldir tells him:

'In this high place you may see the two powers that are
opposed one to another; and ever they strive now in thought,
but whereas the light perceives the very heart of the darkness,
its own secret has not been discovered. Not yet.'

Caras Galadon, which from a distance appears "a hill of many mighty
trees, or a city of green towers," reveals itself to be a city built in great
branches of the forest, a city gleaming with green, gold, and silver lamps.
This is the good place for Frodo, Gandalf, Legolas, Aragorn, Sam, and even
Gimli the dwarf. But this natural paradise set in a tree is fated to perish and
its Elves must depart to the West when the battle against Sauron is over.

Perhaps one more contrasting pair in the life and death theme may be
added. In the central incident of the journey through the tunnels of Moria,
whose name carries important suggestions, we find two contrasting lakes.
The one before the entrance is dark, loathsome, and artificial, a product of
the evil within; and in it lurks an octopus-like monster. Only two ancient
holly trees remain there as evidence of benevolent influence and symbols of
the former friendship between the Elves and the Dwarfs. On the other side
of Moria lies the beautiful, natural, life-giving lake of Mirrormere, which is
worshipped by the dwarf Gimli as he looks into its depths with Frodo:

At first they could see nothing. Then slowly they saw the
forms of the encircling mountains mirrored in a profound blue,
and the peaks were like plumes of white flame above them;
beyond there was a space of sky. There like jewels sunk in the
deep shone glinting stars, though sunlight was in the sky above.
Of their own stooping forms no shadow could be seen.

By looking deeply into *The Lord of the Rings*, we see our world and something beyond. The hero, the other characters, and the structure of the trilogy appeal to us not rationally but emotionally. Its characters are caught up in the decay theme of the novel, the eternal struggle of life against death, just as we are. We recognize that the hobbits are emblematic of naturalness, of childhood, and of a life which will yield to the Age of Men with its technology, its rational adulthood, and death. This recognition strikes a sympathetic chord in the human heart. The reiteration of the decay theme and the recognition of the temporary triumph of the forces of life over the forces of death as the Third Age ends—both of these give the book a bitter-sweet tone. This truth of vision makes the book appealing to readers who acknowledge that of them also, at the last, not a shadow of their stooping forms will be seen.

BURTON RAFFEL

The Lord of the Rings *as Literature*

My position is this: *The Lord of the Rings* is a magnificent performance, full of charm, excitement, and affection, but it is not—at least as I am here using the term—literature. Tolkien's three volumes tell an entrancing "good and evil story" and tell it with power and wisdom; he has succeeded in constructing a self-contained world of extraordinary reality—and grace. "I have been a lover of fairy-stories since I learned to read," Tolkien has noted, and by his own definition "*Faërie* contains many things besides elves and fays, and besides dwarfs, witches trolls, giants, or dragons: it holds the seas, the sun, the moon, the sky; and the earth, and all things that are in it: tree and bird, water and stone, wine and bread, and ourselves, mortal men, when we are enchanted. . . . [And] if fairy-story as a kind is worth reading at all it is worthy to be written for and read by adults." Fair enough. But not only that: "The peculiar quality of the 'joy' in successful Fantasy can . . . be explained as a sudden glimpse of the underlying reality or truth. . . . [This is] indeed narrative art, story-making in its primary and most potent mode." Yet I contend that making stories, even wonderful stories, is not the same thing as making literature.

Let me divide what I mean by literature into three parts; without defining the whole under which they are subsumed: style, the way in which language is used, characterization, the way in which human (or human-like)

From *Tolkien and the Critics: Essays on J. R. R. Tolkien's* The Lord of the Rings, edited by Neil D. Isaacs and Rose A. Zimbardo. © 1968 by University of Notre Dame Press.

traits are portrayed, and incident, the way in which events are organized and presented. Not all literature can be readily discussed under each of these three headings; *The Lord of the Rings*, however, not only requires examination under all three headings, but the first heading, style, needs to be subdivided to account for both the prose and the poetry. It is I think obvious from Tolkien's remarks in *Tree and Leaf* that the third heading is most important to him. In addition a fourth heading, morality, although not strictly a part of literature, can be briefly examined and will afford some additional insights.

I. STYLE

A. PROSE

It would be foolish to say that Tolkien does not write well. He does, he writes admirably, whether his prose be discursive, scholarly, or imaginative. His deservedly famous essay "*Beowulf:* The Monsters and the Critics" broke upon the philological walls and released the poetry long hidden behind them. "For it is of their nature that the jabberwocks of historical and antiquarian research burble in the tulgy wood of conjecture, flitting from one tum-tum tree to another. Noble animals, whose burbling is on occasion good to hear; but though their eyes of flame may sometimes prove searchlights, their range is short." The *Proceedings of the British Academy* cannot often have been graced with such supple prose, nor could Tolkien have virtually forced literary awareness on *Beowulf* scholars had he not been so abundantly possessed of it himself.

But prose is not autotelic, and if Tolkien writes admirably one still must ask, to what purpose? That is, his prose may do admirably just what he wants it to do, and what he wants it to do may be—and in fact is—very much worth doing, but if his objectives are limited and basically exclude what I here term literature, then his prose must be limited similarly. I think it is. I repeat: it does not denigrate Tolkien or his superb book to assert and to try to prove this. I would hope that Tolkien himself would prefer not to be praised for what he has neither tried to do nor succeeded in doing. *The Lord of the Rings* is not only not *The Iliad* or *The Odyssey*, neither is it *Beowulf* or *Paradise Lost*, or *The Great Gatsby*.

Consider simple description. For most purposes Tolkien's prose is brilliantly adequate, straightforward, just starched enough to have body, resilient enough to catch the echoes of speech, not a supercharged instrument, nor one with great range, but very competent. "On this occasion the presents were unusually good. The hobbit-children were so excited that for a while they almost forgot about eating. There were toys the like of which they had never seen before, all beautiful and some obviously magical. Many of them had indeed been ordered a year before, and had come all the way from the Mountain and from Dale, and were of real dwarf-make." There are traces of coyness in the references to "Mountain and Dale" as specific places; there are traces of sentimentality in the references to the hobbit-children. But this is good clean writing; in the narrative it fits neatly into place. So too with most reported conversation: "'Oh, they're both cracked,' said Ted. 'Leastways old Bilbo *was* cracked, and Frodo's cracking. If that's where you get your news from, you'll never want for moonshine. Well, friends, I'm off home. Your good health!' He drained his mug and went out noisily."

But other sorts of description strain Tolkien's powers. When Bilbo disappears, "he jumped over a low place in the hedge at the bottom, and took to the meadows, passing into the night like a rustle of wind in the grass." Bilbo is to disappear quickly, the language is apt. But is it anything more than that? There is, first of all, virtually no sense impression of the hedge; it is generalized, as is the "low place" through which Bilbo jumps. But more important, to have Bilbo "passing into the night like a rustle of wind in the grass" is to write something perilously close to stereotyped prose. In context this is not a cliché, nor is it notable for anything more than the bare transmission of information: Bilbo left, fast, quietly. I would argue that the language of literature must do more than this, must transmit information as well as sense impressions of some sort, and to effect this the language must be both more deeply felt and more deeply worked.

A larger sample will perhaps make my point more clearly:

> Next morning after a late breakfast, the wizard was sitting with Frodo by the open window of the study. A bright fire was on the hearth, but the sun was warm, and the wind was in the South. Everything looked fresh, and the new green of Spring was shimmering in the fields and on the tips of the trees' fingers.

Can one *feel* that fire? It is "bright"; we know that and know all we are meant to know. "Everything looked fresh": we know exactly what that means, and it is not much. "The new green of Spring" is surely *not* fresh; to have it "shimmering in the fields" is to rely on the essentially stale diction of the nineteenth century; "the tips of the trees' fingers" is outright cliché. And yet the paragraph is in context more than adequate. What we are to know is that the wizard (Gandalf) and Frodo were sitting peacefully at talk, having breakfasted, and that the world too was (or seemed to be) at peace. Except for the final barefaced cliché there is no real attempt to explore sensory realities; only narrative realities matter to Tolkien, and so adept is he that nothing more matters to us.

Tolkien's nature descriptions are frequently somewhat overwrought. (This is, as I shall show, especially true of the poetry.) It is as though Tolkien in person, not Tolkien as author, feels both more than he can express and things which are irrelevant to his tale. "In the morning Frodo woke refreshed. He was lying in a bower made by a living tree with branches laced and drooping to the ground; his bed was of fern and grass, deep and soft and strangely fragrant. The sun was shining through the fluttering leaves, which were still green upon the tree. He jumped up and went out." Frodo has been with elves the night before; the elves are wood people; when Frodo wakes he quite properly wakes "refreshed"—the word is totally generalized, a state, an idea, rather than a specifically felt and explored sensory reality—and he quite properly wakes in bright woody greenness. This is however two-dimensional surface description: whatever Tolkien may have imagined he was conveying by "fluttering leaves," for example, it seems plain that he in fact conveys nothing more than that the leaves were in motion. There is no further depth to the words.

> Christmas passed, the wet, drenched, cold days of January recurred monotonously, with now and then a brilliance of blue flashing in, when Brangwen went out into a morning like crystal, when every sound rang again, and the birds were many and sudden and brusque in the hedges. Then an elation came over him in spite of everything, whether his wife were strange or sad, or whether he craved for her to be with him, it did not matter, the air rang with clear noises, the sky was like crystal, like a bell, and the earth was hard. Then he worked and was happy, his eyes shining, his cheeks flushed. And the zest of life was strong in him

This passage, which is not by Tolkien, is description of a very different order. It is not that the scene is more visual: Tolkien is capable of great accuracy and detail. Rather, this is much more fully felt: D. H. Lawrence has a story to tell, but he is interested in more than the story and the stark facts of good and evil. This deals with matter just as primeval as that Tolkien writes of, but Lawrence sees complexities, complications, subtleties, which Tolkien does not admit. It would destroy *The Lord of the Rings* if Tolkien wrote as D. H. Lawrence did, and vice versa. But Lawrence was writing literature, his style suited his aim. Tolkien is working in a separate genre.

When Gandalf tells Frodo that the Enemy, universally feared and hated, knows that the Ring has survived, Tolkien breaks into the text with a space—and there follows this paragraph:

> A heavy silence fell in the room. Frodo could hear his heart beating. Even outside everything seemed still. No sound of Sam's shears could now be heard.

It is just right, in context. The ominous quality is what we are to feel, and we feel it. Frodo has the Ring, the Enemy is after it, knows it is somewhere but not exactly where—oh Lord, oh Lord. We make sure the room is not too dark and go on reading, entranced. But out of context it is easy to see how distinct from literature this language is. "A *heavy* silence" is a silence in capital letters; if it "falls" we do not notice, because falling is what heavy silences regularly and invariably do. We expect the word, it comes, and we read rapidly on. "Frodo could hear his heart beating": to be sure, the little hobbit is frightened, yes, what else, quick, quick, tell us more. The narrative drives ahead—but all the same, to have the frightened hero "hear his heart beating" is not, as language, very communicative.

Here is Tolkien's account of the hobbits' arrival at the Prancing Pony Inn, in Bree, proprietor Barliman Butterbur:

> Off he went at last, and left them feeling rather breathless. He seemed capable of an endless stream of talk, however busy he might be. They found themselves in a small and cosy room. There was a bit of bright fire burning on the hearth, and in front of it were some low and comfortable chairs. There was a round table, already spread with a white cloth, and on it was a large hand-bell. But Nob, the hobbit servant, came bustling in long before they thought of ringing. He brought candles and a tray full of plates.

Disregarding aspects of characterization, the basic impression is that of a rural Old English inn. The operant words are *small and cosy, bit of bright fire, low and comfortable, white cloth, bustling*. The picture is clearly painted; one cannot mistake either the setting itself or the things about it of which Tolkien approves. And in the narrative these are the notes Tolkien needs to sound: the party of hobbits has just come to Bree, after a series of harrowing adventures and, in particular, after leaving the sanctuary provided by Tom Bombadil. They wanted "only to find a fire, and a door between them and the night" and what they found was the Prancing Pony Inn. But to tell us, for example, that a room is "small and cosy," is to tell us only that the feeling Tolkien wants us to have about the room is one of comfortableness and modest size. "Low and comfortable chairs" tells us, again, what we are to feel about the chairs, not very much of the chairs themselves.

> She replaced the disreputable furniture of the house by new shiny Grand Rapids chairs and tables. There was a varnished bookcase, forever locked, stored with stiff sets of unread books—*The Harvard Classics*, and a cheap encyclopaedia.

Even to say that the furniture is "new shiny" is to describe it in a way very unlike Tolkien's. The information we are given is slanted, to be sure; Thomas Wolfe has a point to make, and he bangs it home relentlessly. But he also allows the reader to experience the chairs and tables for himself. We can see the "varnished bookcase," the rows of "unread books" in "stiff sets": "Grand Rapids" furniture is mass-produced, factory-made furniture—but what is a "low and comfortable" chair? Wolfe is not I think as durable a writer as Tolkien; I would far rather read *The Lord of the Rings* than *Look Homeward Angel*, and nothing could persuade me to reread the others of Wolfe's repetitious, sprawling, adolescent novels. But for all that Wolfe's style belongs to literature and Tolkien's does not. When Tolkien tells us about "small and cosy" rooms or "low and comfortable chairs" he is writing as a narrative moralist. The social and esthetic virtues of the room and the chairs are basic to his tale, but neither have independent existence, neither are experienced for us or by us. They are no more than Faërie props.

Tolkien has argued, in a lecture written about 1938, that "true literature . . . works from mind to mind," rather than from object to mind. The specific contrast he intends is that of the writer, on the one hand, the illustrator and the man of the theater on the other; the comparison shows a good deal about his own conception of what language is intended to do:

> Should the story say 'he ate bread,' the dramatic producer or painter can only show 'a piece of bread' according to his taste or fancy, but the hearer of the story will think of bread in general and picture it in some form of his own. If a story says, 'he climbed a hill and saw a river in the valley below,' the illustrator may catch, or nearly catch, his own vision of such a scene; but every hearer of the words will have his own picture, and it will be made out of all the hills and rivers and dales he has ever seen, but especially out of The Hill, The River, The Valley which were for him the first embodiment of the word.

"He climbed a hill and saw a river in the valley below" does not, I suggest, evoke any kind of scene at all. It is a cog in some narrative machine: there was some reason for this person to climb a hill, there was some reason for him to see a river, and some consequences perhaps flowed therefrom. What were they, these reasons and these possible consequences? Read on and discover. None of this has anything to do with what words as words can communicate; the question of style is simply not at issue.

A piece of writing which is part of literature, but which is bad literature and bad style, may show the distinction more clearly:

> He watched a tomcat slink along the fence ledge; he stared at the spot he had newly boarded so that his old man wouldn't yelp about loose boards; he looked about at the patches in the grass that Martin and his gang had worn down playing their cowboy and Indian games. There was something about the things he watched that seemed to enter Studs as sun entered a field of grass; and as he watched, he felt that the things he saw were part of himself, and he felt as good as if he were warm sunlight; he was all glad to be living, and to be Studs Lonigan.

This has not got Tolkien's stately, nicely old-fashioned cadences; it does not have the extraordinary, detailed luminescence of D. H. Lawrence; it does not have even the whipped-up intensity of Thomas Wolfe. But there is no need to train an elephant gun on the 1930's prose of James T. Farrell: it is bad prose, and Tolkien's is relatively good prose—and once again it needs to be said that Farrell is trying (in good part unsuccessfully) to do something quite beyond Tolkien's purpose. The fence is not a prop, neither are Studs' father and younger brother Martin. The fence is decaying, as the discarded furniture in the Thomas Wolfe paragraph was "disreputable," because these are particular objects in particular relationships with the characters in Farrell's and Wolfe's books. But for Tolkien a hill is the generality of hill-ness, a chair is "low and comfortable"—that is, the generality of comfortableness. They are, in his terms, "at once more universal and more poignantly particular." Indeed, if we knew about them what literature would be apt to tell us, we might no longer be interested.

> . . . it looked like a dark black bundle left behind. But as they looked it seemed to move and sway this way and that, as if searching the ground. It then crawled, or went crouching, back into the gloom. . . .

"Crawled, or went crouching": the uncertainty, the ambiguity, are what Tolkien's style aims to create. "The realm of fairy-story is wide and deep and high . . . but its very richness and strangeness tie the tongue of a traveler who would report them. And while he is there it is dangerous for him to ask too many questions, lest the gates should be shut and the keys be lost.

B. POETRY

I do not want to discuss the poetry of *The Lord of the Rings* at any length. A very few examples will suffice.

> Hey! Come merry dol! derry dol! My darling!
> Light goes the weather-wind and the feathered starling.
> Down along under Hill, shining in the sunlight,
> Waiting on the doorstep for the cold starlight,
> There my pretty lady is, River-woman's daughter,
> Slender as the willow-wand, clearer than the water.
> Old Tom Bombadil water-lilies bringing
> Comes hopping home again. Can you hear him singing?
> Hey! Come merry dol! derry dol! And merry-o,
> Goldberry, Goldberry, merry yellow berry-o!
> Poor old Willow-man, you tuck your roots away!
> Tom's in a hurry now. Evening will follow day.
> Tom's going home again water-lilies bringing.
> Hey! Come derry dol! Can you hear me singing?

Tolkien notes that the hobbit listeners to this song, Frodo and Sam, "stood as if enchanted." My two oldest sons, when I read them the trilogy aloud, were equally fascinated; they considered Tolkien a fine poet, as do, apparently, other serious observers. I find almost all of Tolkien's verse embarrassingly bad. The "kind of balladry" in the Tom Bombadil song I have reproduced is a tissue of ill-digested borrowings from Shakespeare's plays, Longfellow, Browning, and I-know-not-what-else. The very first line, intended to be hearty, is to my ear thumpingly dull. The starling is "feathered," in line two for prosodic reasons: it might be more interesting if a starling were not feathered. "Shining in the sunlight," "the cold starlight," "slender as the willow-wand": this is all stale and virtually meaningless. Tom Bombadil is an earth-figure: his song typifies what I have called the overwrought quality of Tolkien's nature verse.

Bilbo sings an elven song. I cannot quote it at full length, but the long fifth stanza will do it justice:

The winds of wrath came driving him,
and blindly in the foam he fled
from west to east and errandless,
unheralded he homeward sped.
There flying Elwing came to him,
and flame was in the darkness lit;
more bright than light of diamond
the fire upon her carcanet.
The Silmaril she bound on him
and crowned him with the living light,
and dauntless then with burning brow
he turned his prow; and in the night
from otherworld beyond the Sea
there strong and free a storm arose,
a wind of power in Tarmenel;
by paths that seldom mortal goes
his boat it bore with biting breath
as might of death across the grey
and long-forsaken seas distressed:
from east to west he passed away.

"The winds of wrath," "the living light," "and dauntless then": one begins to wonder if Tolkien is not pretty clearly more poetaster than poet?

The poetry is at its best in relatively simple forms like that of Bilbo's "farewell":

The Road goes ever on and on
    Down from the door where it began.
Now far ahead the Road has gone,
    And I must follow, if I can,
Pursuing it with eager feet,
    Until it joins some larger way
Where many paths and errands meet.
    And whither then? I cannot say.

This has at least the virtues of directness. The general use of enjambement, followed by the striking caesura of the final line, varies the rhythm pleasantly. It is bland, inoffensive verse, and it fits the story, it communicates something about Bilbo. But is it poetry? Even the introductory poem to the trilogy succeeds, as it definitely does succeed, in good part by extrapoetic means:

> Three Rings for the Elven-kings under the sky,
>   Seven for the Dwarf-lords in their halls of stone,
> Nine for mortal men doomed to die,
>   One for the Dark Lord on his dark throne
> In the Land of Mordor where the Shadows lie.
>   One Ring to rule them all, One Ring to find them,
>   One Ring to bring them all and in the darkness bind them
> In the Land of Mordor where the Shadows lie.

This is far more skillful than most of the poetry. It has unusual restraint, for Tolkien: words are used as magical incantations, and the magic is not marred by inversions, frantic adjectives, and the like. The rhyming and the repetitions are deft: this is, in my view, the one unforgettable verse in the trilogy. But for all that, the poem is a charm which works only within the tale. Not, that is, that only those who know the tale can understand the poem: rather, that without the magical intensity of the tale the poem is slight, trivial. It lacks—and is meant to lack—poetic existence in its own right.

I concede the trilogy's poetry almost no independent literary merit. Why then did Tolkien include it, and what purpose does it serve? It does serve a purpose: the song within a tale is a recognized convention, breaking into a narrative where a break is needed, providing lyric (or comic) relief, expounding on a character's feelings more succinctly (or at least differently) than prose might do. In context, too, the poetry is less conspicuous than naked on the critical page. It is interesting, often, even when it is bad—and the narrative is so powerful that one easily condones its badness. But why did Tolkien include it, in spite of its badness? The question is perhaps best answered with another question: if he knew how bad the poetry was, would he have published it as a separate volume, *The Adventures of Tom Bombadil?* Clearly not. There is relatively little poetry in *The Lord of the Rings*: it does not get in the way, and when it does it can be skipped with no loss to the tale. I think it should also be kept in mind that there is much more, and much better (because less pretentious) poetry in Tolkien's earlier tale, *The Hobbit.* Since Tolkien had gotten into the habit of poeticizing, and indeed having carried over many of the same characters who indulged in verse-making, it surely would have been difficult for him to be objective about the later and much less good poetry. But isn't it time—like the emperor in the famous fairy-story about the nonexistent new clothes—that he was told?

II. CHARACTERIZATION

What we are entitled to ask of characterization is that it portray for us, meaningfully, significant aspects of human reality. The four or five chief characterizations in *The Lord of the Rings* are the hobbits Bilbo, Frodo, and Sam, the wizard Gandalf, and Aragorn. It will surely put both my approach and *The Lord of the Rings* to the severest test to consider these major characterizations rather than any of the numerous lesser ones.

Bilbo, who first encounters the Ring, is abundantly characterized in *The Hobbit*, of which he and Gandalf are the two principal figures. It is a cheerful, amiable characterization: Bilbo is full of vitality, courageous, generous, honest—in short, a kind of small-sized exemplar for the small-sized readership for whom Tolkien intended the book. Bilbo has moments of laziness, moments of fear, but in a crisis regularly rises to the occasion, whether with mercy (as with Gollum), truthfulness (as with Thorin), or varieties of imaginative resourcefulness (decoying the huge spiders, riddling with Gollum, bringing the Arkenstone to Bard, and the like). Bilbo as child-exemplar ages in *The Lord of the Rings*: the trilogy is in all respects a more mature tale. He is still full of fun and poetry, but he dozes more—and under the Ring's long-continued influence he whines and snivels a bit, too, rather like Gollum, but in a milder way. It takes Gandalf's insistence to make him give up the Ring; however, true to his virtuous origins, Bilbo is, as Gandalf explains, the first in the Ring's history to surrender it voluntarily. Nor is Bilbo *the* hobbit in *The Lord of the Rings*. Frodo has taken that position; Bilbo is slightly off to the side, a little like the old man dozing by the chimney corner. He is still amiable, courageous, generous: he volunteers to become the Ring-bearer again; without being asked he gives Frodo Sting, his elven sword, and the fabulous *mithril* shirt. When Bilbo offers to take up the Quest, Boromir, knowing nothing of hobbits, is about to laugh, "but the laughter died on his lips when he saw that all the others regarded the old hobbit with grave respect." For as Gandalf says frequently, "Hobbits really are amazing creatures, as I have said before. You can learn all that there is to know about their ways in a month, and yet after a hundred years they can still surprise you at a pinch.'"

What "significant aspects of human reality" (the phraseology is horribly academic and would surely offend Tolkien) are portrayed for us by the hobbit Bilbo? We are made to feel that small things can be very good things; that generosity is heartwarming in both the giving and the receiving, and is furthermore not very difficult to accomplish if only the heart is willing; that one can be courageous even if afraid, bold even if uncertain, decent even if provoked. These are surely significant aspects of human reality; to be made to feel these things is salutary. But how "meaningfully"are we offered these lessons? The morality is fine: how subtle is it, how aware of the true complexities of existence? There is no inherent virtue in being small, especially in a world where most things are larger. There is no universal joy in gift-giving and receiving, as there is no universal sense of honor in men: I think of the scene in Nathaniel West's *A Cool Million*, where the naive hero defends a young lady from a bully, beats the bully fair and square, holds out his hand to the bully afterwards, and is promptly hauled into oblivion (the young lady, who faints at this sight, is promptly raped by the bully). West did not intend anything but an exaggeration of traits usually somewhat less rank; Tolkien does, I think, intend his portrayal as Truth.

It is almost a religious teaching, rather than a literary one: it should not surprise us that Tolkien has said that "The Gospels contain a fairy-story, or a story of a larger kind which embraces all the essence of fairy-storie. . . . There is no tale ever told that men would rather find was true. . . . To reject it leads either to sadness or to wrath." This too is Noble, this is Good, this is plainly one way to happiness. It would be good, too, if it were in fact Truth which *The Lord of the Rings* offers us—and there is the difficulty. This is Faërie, not reality, and in response to the question, "Is it true?" Tolkien has proferred the answer, "If you have built your little world well, yes: it is true in that world." It is, I am afraid, not a sufficient answer, for "in that world" the artist controls everything. If Bilbo is to be rewarded for his virtue, Tolkien is the executive force which sees to it that he is rewarded. Outside that "little world," however, nothing better illustrates Tolkien's own awareness of human impotence than the introductory note to *Tree and Leaf*. After explaining that the story, "Leaf by Niggle," was influenced by "a great-limbed poplar tree that I could see even lying in bed," he adds: "It was suddenly lopped and mutilated by its owner, I do not know why. It is cut down now, a less barbarous punishment for any crimes it may have been accused of, such as being large and alive. I do not think it had any friends, or any mourners, except myself and a pair of owls." It is a very short step to Tolkien's convictions about the Escape function of Faërie:

> I have claimed that Escape is one of the main functions of fairy-stories, and since I do not disapprove of them, it is plain that I do not accept the tone of scorn or pity with which 'Escape' is now so often used. . . . Why should a man be scorned, if, finding himself in prison, he tries to get out and go home? Or if, when he cannot do so, he thinks and talks about other topics than jailers and prison-walls? . . . The critics have chosen the wrong word, and, what is more, they are confusing, not always by sincere error, the Escape of the Prisoner with the Flight of the Deserter.

Tolkien adds:

> I do not think that the reader or the maker of fairy-stories need even be ashamed of the 'escape' of archaism: of preferring not

dragons, but horses, castles, sailing-ships, bows and arrows; not
only elves, but knights and kings and priests. For it is after all
possible for a rational man, after reflection (quite unconnected
with fairy-story or romance), to arrive at the condemnation . . .
of progressive things like factories, or the machineguns and
bombs that appear to be their most natural and inevitable, dare
we say 'inexorable', products. . . . The maddest castle that ever
came out of a giant's bag in a wild Gaelic story is not only very
much less ugly than a robot-factory, it is also (to use a very
modern phrase) 'in a very real sense' a great deal more real. . . .
It is indeed an age of 'improved means to deteriorated ends.'

Let me be clear: I am not concerned, here, with Tolkien's social views. As
T. S. Eliot said of another writer of epic narrative, "You cannot afford to
ignore Dante's philosophical and theological beliefs, or to skip the passages
which express them most clearly; but . . . on the other hand you are not called
upon to believe them yourself." I am however concerned with what Tolkien
is able, by means of characterization, to tell us, "meaningfully," about our
own existences. He props up Faith: I think that is a fair summary of the
maximum effect which can legitimately be claimed for him in this line. And
this is not, I think, an achievement for which one need go, or for which one
usually does go, to literary characterization.

It would be dull stuff to march doggedly through the four other characterizations I have named, making the same (or similar) points. Summary
discussion will do. Sam is, I maintain, pure stock character—loveable, useful
ficelle (in Henry James' terms), but as a characterization virtually meaningless. Sam grows a bit, in the course of the trilogy; he learns to compose verse,
he sobers and matures, and these are tributes to Tolkien's organizing genius.
It was not only the tale which "grew in the telling."

We are made suspicious of Aragorn, at first meeting. He is "a strange-
looking weather-beaten man, sitting in the shadows near the wall . . .
listening intently to the hobbit-talk. . . . The gleam of his eyes could be seen
as he watched the hobbits." But as Frodo and the others quickly discover,
Aragorn is all gold and a yard wide. He is brave, loyal, honest, faithful—
everything in Faërie one would expect of a king (which is what he becomes,
at the end). Gandalf too is everything one might expect of a wizard, and for
much of the way he is rather more than that. Gandalf is mercurial, in the
sense that he adjusts to his setting, to his environment, human, hobbit, elf,
or wizard, not becoming all things to all persons, but not presuming, either,
on the knowledge or capacities of anyone. He is flexible, and he is also
limited: this is not a wizard who can do anything he likes, but a "real" wizard,
who makes mistakes, who exceeds his own capacity—and who, as far as we

know, dies in the tunnels of Moria, pulled to his death by a Balrog, "a great shadow, in the middle of which was a dark form, of man-shape maybe, yet greater; and a power and terror seemed to be in it and to go before it." At the end of the first volume of the trilogy, Gandalf is a heroic memory, a beloved memory. Less than two hundred pages later, in the second volume, he has returned, "passed through fire and deep water," resurrected after his—one is tempted to say, after His Passion, though "Sacrifice" will do. And Aragorn says to him "'You are our captain and our banner. The Dark Lord has nine: But we have One, mightier than they: the White Rider. He has passed through the fire and the abyss, and they shall fear him. We will go where he leads.'" The biblical tone is no accident. Not that Gandalf is to be taken as a Christ-figure pure and simple: "'I am Gandalf, Gandalf the White, but Black [the Enemy] is mightier still.'" It is an impressive transformation, and for the forces of Good a necessary resurrection. One is delighted to have Gandalf back, even if he has mutated from Grey to White and has become distinctly otherworldly. But one is also disappointed: the limited wizard, the less than omnipotent wizard, the "real" wizard, has become a figure of impressive magic. As a characterization Gandalf is necessarily less meaningful from that point on: he is a force more than he is a personage.

I have saved Frodo, the Ring-bearer, for last. He is the hardest case to deal with. Frodo has something of Bilbo in him, and something of Sam, and something almost like Aragorn—but something more, too, which is very much himself. It is in Frodo, and in Frodo only, that I think Tolkien achieves something of what one can call the characterization of literature. It is not the keen sharp portrayal of, say, Jay Gatsby, "with his hands plunged like weights in his coat pockets, . . . standing in a puddle of water glaring tragically into my eyes," stepping outside so he can step inside and meet, again, Daisy Buchanan, for whom he has waited and schemed. It is not simple that Tolkien has not Fitzgerald's style, that he cannot do with a single sentence what Fitzgerald can. The slow subtlety of Gatsby's portrayal is I think considerably more meaningful than the portrait of Frodo. "'Why, my God! They used to go there [Gatsby's mansion] by the hundreds','" a casual, once-drunken guest has just been saying, at Gatsby's lonely funeral. "He took off his glasses and wiped them again [it is raining hard], outside and in. 'The poor son-of-a-bitch', he said." This is a sparse epitaph beyond Tolkien's stylistic powers. When Sam, Merry, and Pippin see Frodo and the others off on their journey out of life, the testimonial is more elaborate but much less eloquent: "At last the three companions turned away, and never again looking back they rode slowly homewards; and then spoke no word to one another until they came back to the Shire, but each had great comfort in his friends on the long grey road." Fitzgerald has shown us, through Gatsby, something we did not know, or knew only vaguely or partially: the pathos of Gatsby's love for Daisy, and the bitterness of "society's" use of him. Tolkien has demonstrated to us, again, that Friendship is a Good Thing.

But Frodo throughout is something more than this. He grows in stature much more impressively than his servant and friend, Sam: open, jolly, in many ways like Bilbo at the start, Frodo also has a reflective, almost a worldly-wise side. His long series of incredible experiences, his hardships, pain, the friends he meets, loses, the enemies he must confront—all temper his openness, all deepen and broaden his reflectiveness. His mission succeeds, but though it has not been too much for him in any literal sense it proves, afterwards, too much to have lived through. "Saruman [a fallen wizard] . . . stared at Frodo. There was a strange look in his eyes of mingled wonder and respect and hatred. 'You have grown, Halfling,' he said. 'Yes, you have grown very much.'" But as Frodo soon after tells Sam, who finds him "very pale and his eyes [seeming] to see things far away, . . . 'I am wounded, . . . wounded; it will never really heal.'" And when Frodo decides it is time to take the final journey he again tells Sam: "'I have been too deeply hurt, Sam. I tried to save the Shire, and it has been saved, but not for me. It must often be so, Sam, when things are in danger: some one has to give them up, lose them, so that others may keep them.'" The message is true but not remarkable; what gives it power is that we have by this point seen Frodo living it, seen him pass from unknowing hobbit to something larger and wiser and sadder. The strength of Tolkien's faith supports this renunciation: there do have to be heroes, and if Frodo has not been one, no one ever has. Nor are heroes a notably happy breed. Frodo goes, life goes on; Sam weeps, but he goes back to the Shire—and the trilogy ends, in perhaps the highest tribute to the just-departed Frodo that one could imagine, with Sam returning home, sitting down with his new daughter in his lap, and drawing "a deep breath. 'Well, I'm back', he said."

III. INCIDENT

Little needs to be discussed, I think, under this heading. *The Lord of the Rings* is a genuine epic, with all the vast sweep and complex dovetailing necessary to sustain a large and powerful tale. Narrative art is, as I said at the start, Tolkien's primary concern; it is also and quite obviously his forte. The trilogy almost never flags. Tolkien's inventiveness carries off variation after variation; his story-telling virtuosity is wonderful, and I do not want to deny this talent its worth.

All the same, there is a certain amount of what comes close to the trickery, the mechanical plot manipulation of the lesser tale-teller. After the first appearance of the Black Riders (we are still in the Shire), Frodo is being taken to the ferry by Farmer Maggot.

> *Clop-clop, clop-clop.* The rider was nearly on them.
>
> 'Hallo there!' called Farmer Maggot. The advancing hoofs stopped short. They thought they could dimly guess a dark cloaked shape in the mist, a yard or two ahead.
>
> 'Now then!' said the farmer, throwing the reins to Sam and striding forward. 'Don't you come a step nearer! What do you want and where are you going?'
>
> 'I want Mr. Baggins. Have you seen him?' said a muffled voice—but the voice was the voice of Merry Brandybuck. A dark lantern was uncovered, and its light fell on the astonished face of the farmer.
>
> 'Mr. Merry!' he cried.
>
> 'Yes, of course! Who did you think it was?' said Merry coming forward. As he came out of the mist and their fears subsided, he seemed suddenly to diminish to ordinary hobbit size. He was riding a pony, and a scarf was swathed around his neck and over his chin to keep out the fog.

It cannot reasonably be argued, I think, that this is tongue-in-cheek. Tolkien has a sense of humor, but not about Black Riders and the Quest.

There are other, essentially similar manipulative incidents. I have mentioned the resurrection of Gandalf; there is throughout something of a propensity for last-minute, *deus ex machina* rescues, for what can be called "O. Henry" endings. This is part of the delight which we take in the story, and surely part of the delight Tolkien takes in it—discovering for us, and for himself, how Good is to prevail over Evil. These ironical confrontations of Evil with sudden-appearing Good rest on Faith; they do not harm the narrative per se but certainly they lessen the stature of the trilogy.

IV. MORALITY

Tolkien's foreward to the trilogy declares, flatly:

> As for any inner meaning or 'message', it has in the intention of the author none. It is neither allegorical nor topical. . . . I cordially dislike allegory in all its manifestations, and always have done so since I grew old and wary enough to detect its presence. I much prefer history, true or feigned.

C. S. Lewis has said something very similar: "Some published fantasies of my own have had foisted on them (often by the kindliest critics) so many admirable allegorical meanings that I never dreamed of as to throw me into doubt whether it is possible for the wit of man to devise anything in which the wit of some other man cannot find, and plausibly find, an allegory." If it is hard to quarrel with an author on a subject as to which he has so peculiarly excellent a source of information, it is perhaps harder to ignore the contrary evidence of the stories themselves.

Consider, first, a tale called "Leaf by Niggle." Written in 1938-1939, "when *The Lord of the Rings* was beginning to unroll itself," it is from beginning to end an allegory of salvation. "There was once a little man called Niggle," the tale begins, "who had a long journey to make." The "long journey" is physical death—this is distinctly Christian allegory, in which life after death, and redemption through purgatory, play a large role—and Niggle is a failed artist. He, and also his neighbor (called Parish!), meet with success (i.e., redemption), finally, by dint of concern for others rather than with themselves. It is all very sentimental, with a style to match: questioned, in purgatory, by a pair of Judging Voices, all Niggle can talk about is his poor neighbor, at rather nauseating length. When shortly thereafter he and his neighbor meet, in the afterlife, "They did not speak, just nodded as they used to do, passing in the land; but now they walked about together, arm in arm." When Parish decides to wait for his wife, Niggle declares, as he moves to higher ground, "'Things might have been different, but they could not have been better. . . . Good-bye!' He shook Parish's hand warmly: a good, firm, honest hand it seemed. He turned and looked back for a moment. The blossom on the Great Tree was shining like flame. All the birds were flying in the air and singing. Then he smiled, and nodded to Parish, and went off. . . . " The story is slight, uninteresting even as narrative: in spite of his concern with small things and small people, Tolkien is distinctly not a miniaturist. He requires the vast machinery of plot complexity, a challenge to which he rises with apparent ease. But as an indication of Tolkien's frame of mind, "Leaf by Niggle" is fascinating. It underlies the basically moral purpose of his work, and emphasizes, too, some of the things of which his morality approves: kindness, friendship, artistic devotion and single-mindedness, trees and birds and mountains. A train finds its way into the story, but it is "a very pleasant little local train," it has a "little engine [which] puffed along," and when the train arrives at its destination "There was not station, and no signboard, only a flight of steps up the green embankment."

Taking allegory in its very loosest sense, I think *The Lord of the Rings* is indisputably allegorical. I do not mean that Frodo, or even Gandalf (as we first meet him), is a symbolic representation of Good—though surely the Nazgûl, not to mention the Lord of Mordor, are symbols of Evil. Nor do I mean that Frodo's journey is a neat representation of, say the kind of journey undertaken by Niggle. Rather, so much Faith underlies the trilogy, so much strong feeling about the world (the so-called real world, as Tolkien might say), that representational elements are unavoidable: this is, again, a "good and evil story." When Frodo has reached Rivendell, for example, and Gandalf is telling him about "the Dark Lord in Mordor," Gandalf exclaims: "'Not all his servants and chattels are wraiths! There are orcs and trolls, there are wargs and werewolves; and there have been and still are many Men, warriors and kings, that walk alive under the Sun, and yet are under his sway. And their number is growing daily.'" It can be argued that the reference to men is essential, since they too are part of Middle-earth. It must however be clear that Men are singled out by Gandalf-Tolkien, receiving very special and detailed attention beyond the needs of the story proper. One does not need to claim any precise allegory, or even any particular topical reference, to see what C. S. Lewis has called the trilogy's relevance "to the actual human situation." In loose terms this is allegorical enough.

Tolkien's strong Christian beliefs underly the ultimate frailty of *all* the personages in *The Lord of the Rings,* not excluding the greatest of them, Sauron, the Dark Lord, the Enemy. Man needs God (or whatever the unnamed Force ought to be termed), and God needs Man's goodness to carry out His will. It is Gandalf once more who phrases it; again he is speaking to Frodo, rather earlier in the story, and discussing Bilbo's finding of the Ring:

> 'Behind that there was something else at work, beyond any design of the Ring-maker. I can put it no plainer than by saying that Bilbo was *meant* to find the Ring, and *not* by its maker [its maker is Sauron, the Enemy]. In which case you also were *meant* to have it. And that may be an encouraging thought.'

Tolkien never becomes more specific than this; he hardly needs to. When Frodo tries to make matters clearer, demanding "why was I chosen?", Gandalf replies:

> 'Such questions cannot be answered. . . . You may be sure that it was not for any merit that others do not possess: not for power or wisdom, at any rate. But you have been chosen, and you must therefore use such strength and heart and wits as you have.'

And Gandalf assures Frodo, "'It may be your task to find the Cracks of Doom; but that quest may be for others: I do not know. At any rate your are not ready for that long road yet.'" Frodo's Quest is, in these terms, the education of the soul, the striving for salvation. There is no need to push the representational element, or to force it into a consistently Christian-like mould. It is there, it conditions Tolkien's whole approach to the "good and evil" of his long tale, and its importance in any literary estimate of the trilogy seems unmistakable.

My position, from the start, has been that *The Lord of the Rings* is magnificent but that it is not literature. I have taken a deliberately narrow view of literature, and pursued my analysis in rather narrow fashion. And I have omitted, also deliberately, what is of course the primary requirement of any literary work: imagination. That Tolkien has it, and that *The Lord of the Rings* abundantly displays it, is so obvious as to need no discussion. In broader terms than I have here employed, accordingly, there is small doubt that the trilogy is literature and very fine literature. I have meant this paper as a corrective, as a curb on some of the irresponsible adulation currently being extended to Tolkien. He deserves high praise, even adulation, but there is little sense in praising Milton as a writer on domestic science, Wordsworth as a botanist, or T. S. Eliot as a teacher of Sanskrit.

RANDEL HELMS

Frodo Anti-Faust: The Lord of the Rings *as Contemporary Mythology*

> The two great external facts of our time are the explosion of populations and the explosions of the new energies. The two great internal facts of our time are the re-creation of the devil (or pure behavior) in a place of authority and the development of techniques for finding destructive troubles in the psyche of individuals.
>
> — R. P. Blackmur

> By dipping them in myth we see them more clearly.
>
> — C. S. Lewis

Why do certain contemporary readers seem to require so absolutely what Tolkien has to give to the extent that regularly, on completion of the third volume of *The Lord of the Rings*, they begin again on the first? Perhaps the outlines of an answer emerge from a remark by Stanley Hyman in *The Tangled Bank*, his study of the four chief myth-breakers of our time, Darwin, Marx, Frazer, and Freud. Hyman compares T. K. Cheynes's monumental *Encyclopedia Biblica* of 1903 with the *Oxford Dictionary of the Christian Church*, published in 1957. The first, he says, with its triumphantly reasonable conclusions about the human origins and wayward evolution of the biblical text, seems not so much the beginning of something completed in our own time as a "splendid monument to the nineteenth century's frustrated hopes for the rational intelligence." The second, on the other hand, once again securely neoorthodox after a half century of painful struggle, seems as some-

---

From *Tolkien's World* by Randel Helms. © 1974 by Randel Helms.

thing from a "thousand years earlier," a sign that "all that a century of labor had painfully uncovered is once more buried under the sea of faith." Indeed it ought to be clear by now that our century has been not so much an age of demythologizing as of remythologizing, a time of agonized and sometimes frenzied search for new mythologies, new explanations for an increasingly incomprehensible world.

Hyman has put his finger on a real epistemological sore spot. We know, we modern rationalists, that myth contains no real "knowledge" (at least as we now define the term), yet when we deflate and discard myth, we find gaping windy holes in our defenses against the cold terrors of pain and death. The problem is already an old one. The nineteenth century, and much of our own, troubled and put on the defensive by the myth-destructive forces unleashed by such thinkers as Darwin and Freud, began to lose faith in any kind of mythologizing. The greatest capitulation (or victory) came when religious thinkers began to assert that religion and myth were things apart, that myth-making was not, essentially, a sacral activity. William Blake was probably the first great English thinker to foresee the disastrous consequences of such an idea for the literary imagination and the soul's health and set about, perhaps even before he was needed, attacking it with the profound force of such polemics as "What is a Church & what is a Theatre, Are they two and not one?" and "Jesus & his Apostles & Disciples were all Artists." Indeed perhaps one of the reasons the English-reading world started needing Blake (more than fifty years after his death) was that he spoke to this very issue, asserting the sacral functions of the artistic, mythopoeic imagination and giving answers that people like Yeats needed desperately.

At any rate it seems to me that Tolkien speaks to this issue for the second half of our century, reasserting the supreme importance of the myth-making imagination and providing, in the process, a set of myths that express, more fully than the works of any other contemporary writer I know, a complex of otherwise inexpressible emotions riving the breasts of a whole generation of readers. The feelings I speak of are the emotional correlatives of the cultural "facts" so aptly described by R. P. Blackmur at the head of this chapter; the myths preside over our response to *The Lord of the Rings*.

The need to be, if only for brief moments, in a world of coherence, where all is relevant and has meaning, is a profoundly human need and one that was for most of our culture's history satisfied by religious myths. During that time a cosmos was given shape, significance, and destiny by its Christian foundations. That wold, for many, no longer exists, but when it did art spoke with a greater resonance, being couched in stories and symbols rich in context and interrelationship. It is of course now a commonplace of criticism that the modern artist must create his own cosmos of mythical significances before he can set his creatures afoot in it, must devise a symbolism before its resonances may sound. Tolkien, for our time, has created such a world with his Middle-earth, and the actions transpiring in that world have symbolic relevance to some of the profoundest issues of our age, specifically, we might say, to those cultural facts named by Blackmur

The most striking of Blackmur's facts is what he calls the "explosions of the new energies," a fact of such consequence for the postwar imagination that immense emotional energies must be expended continuously by our psyches just to keep us from going insane in the face of it. Like it or not, we all subliminally contemplate the Bomb, waking and dreaming, and are all in need of useful ways to pattern and express the destructive emotions evoked by this fact. Now Tolkien, like Blake, knew well that the literary imagination is perhaps our richest source of mythological expressions of internal states. Literature gives us ways of looking at our situation that are unavailable elsewhere: ways of taking it apart and reassembling it to make sense and ways of coming to terms with it emotionally. In *The Lord of the Rings*, Tolkien has symbolically expressed our situation in a strikingly profound and useful set of myths that can evoke and pattern a healing emotional response to literary situations deeply symbolic of our own. We must carefully note that the *Rings* patterns a response to its *own* situation, not directly to ours. Literature gives no direct moral answers, it only exercises and enriches the wisdom of spirit that must ponder and respond to its own dilemmas. Tolkien himself has seen the possibilities for finding simple-minded allegory in his work and has repeatedly insisted that the Ring is not the atom bomb and the War of the Rings is not World War II. We need not doubt his sincerity; a powerful symbol is not the allegorical equivalent of a single technological item. The Ring does not equal the Bomb, but is rather a symbol for the entire complex fact that twentieth-century man has, like Frodo, suddenly found himself, without wanting it, without even guessing it would find a way into his pocket, in possession of a power over nature so immense even the desire to use it will inevitably corrupt his soul. And again, like Frodo, he would really rather throw the whole thing into the sea and forget it, but knows he cannot. Here we arrive at a perception of one of Tolkien's supremely valuable contributions to the imaginative health of us all—what I have called the anti-Faustian myth.

From the end of the Middle Ages to the first nuclear explosion (to be overly precise) our deepest spiritual urges have been Faustian, directing our emotional and intellectual energies in an endless quest for knowledge of and power over nature, over our world. Now we have become like Sauron; we *can* control nature, but we find in the process that every controlling touch spoils and corrupts. Like Sauron, we can darken the sky, blast the vegetation, pervert and control even the minds of men; and again like Sauron, we remain the prisoners of our own assumptions, seeing no alternative to ever expanding our corrupting control. It is gradually becoming apparent, however, that a different course is necessary if humankind is to survive, and some of the finer spirits among us are suggesting that course, Tolkien not least among them: simplify, put away the desire to control and thereby pervert nature, resubmit to the pattern of nature's rhythms. Those who so argue place themselves in Frodo's position, or, to put it another way, the hobbits are Tolkien's symbols for this anti-Faustian urge. Frodo has the Ring, the symbol of all corrupting power, and his every desire is to *get rid of it*. Even at the risk of letting it fall again into the blackened hand of Sauron, he must try to destroy this source and symbol of the Faustian will to power and knowledge so that he may return in peace to Tolkien's Great Good Place, the Shire, the quiet little land ruled only by the swing of the seasons.

Blackmur's internal cultural facts also receive mythic treatment in *The Lord of the Rings*. Tolkien is indeed a keen analyst of the modern psyche and its need for realignment with the natural world; he was one of the first to grasp that everything depends on whether we can adjust our ego-ideals away from the Faustian and toward whatever it is Frodo represents—Frodo anti-Faust but by no means Frodo anti-hero. Frodo is hero, but surely that word must undergo some radical changes in meaning to be applicable to a three-foot-high bundle of timidity with furry feet. This indeed is another of Tolkiens gifts to us in *The Lord of the Rings*—a profound criticism and revaluation of the meaning of heroic behavior. He did not, however, summon the insight overnight but rather developed it over a period of years as his own vision of his world and its meanings grew. Perhaps the clearest picture of Tolkien's deepening notions about the nature of heroic behavior can be found in a comparison of his lecture on *Beowulf* before the British Academy in 1936 with his brief essay on *The Battle of Maldon* published in *Essays and Studies* for 1953, dates important in the history of Tolkien's world, as the first is the year *The Lord of the Rings* was begun, and the second is the year before its initial two volumes were published. The two works present strikingly different attitudes toward heroism, and as is usual with Tolkien, his critical thinking is a function of his creative interests at the time. As chapter I has shown, the *Beowulf* lecture was to a considerable extent the outgrowth of Tolkien's creative struggles with *The Hobbit* and its mythological depiction of radical evil in a literary universe. He argued that in the heroic literature of northern Europe, and in *Beowulf* pre-eminently, the mythical sense of radical evil expresses itself in the form of monsters like Grendel and the Worm. The glory of that literature, he declared, is that it recognizes and does not shirk the question of radical evil, potent beyond man's measure to conquer, nor does it flinch in the face of inevitable defeat, but—and this is its greatness—poises a hero in foredoomed but magnificent conflict, seeking the only death with meaning in a pre-Christian world—bravely fighting the unconquerable. Tolkien was perhaps the first critic of *Beowulf* to express forthrightly the metaphysical stance darkly stated in the mythology of the poem—a despair that yet cast a cold eye on death, giving it the dignity of Beowulf's own defeat.

Finding historical parallels to moments of critical insight is dangerous but always fascinating; in this case, it was but four years after Tolkien expressed the spirit of Beowulf's heroism that it reappeared in the eye and voice of Winston Churchill, and thence the nation, during the Battle of Britain. The parallel need be taken as no more than a curiosity, yet surely one of the central tasks of criticism is to find, and when necessary rediscover, in the literature of a nation, the spirit and will of whatever kind of heroic endeavor it may need. This fruitful collaboration between literature and criticism can be doubly rich if the heroic author is critic as well, for what the writer needs in order to create is likewise what the critic (as representative, intellect, as it were, of his society) needs in order to see clearly. In 1936 Tolkien needed a clear grasp of the mythological revelation of the workings of radical evil and of the heroic necessities evil creates. Writing *The Hobbit* gave him that clear grasp, and, as a gift almost, a critical footnote to creative discovery, it taught him also how to read *Beowulf* in a way precisely relevant to England's need at the time for insight into heroic behavior. Then, feeding on what he had learned from writing *The Hobbit* and from reading *Beowulf* through the lenses of Middle-earth, Tolkien gave us *The Lord of the Rings*; and behold, another gift: he had learned yet another new insight into *Beowulf* and a new way to read *The Battle of Maldon*, finding once again a critique and evaluation of heroic behavior deeply relevant to the changed needs of his society. For what England needed in 1940 was much different from what she, and the world, needed in 1953. Too neatly put, the reason for the difference was the war and all its aftermath, specifically the need for what I have defined as an anti-Faustian myth. It would be too much to say that Tolkien changed his view of heroic behavior because of World War II; indeed he has made plain that the First War affected him far more deeply than the Second. His mind and views changed during his sojourn in Middle-earth, facing Sauron with Frodo and Sam, not facing Hitler with his countrymen. But the internal experience of the best writers is the internal history of their age, and no less is true of Tolkien. He saw in 1953 that part of Beowulf's heroism was pointless bravado, excess "chivalry": Beowulf in facing Grendel without a sword, and the Worm with only a sword, was doing little more than show off. Tolkien's perception in 1953 is that "this 'northern heroic spirit' [which in

1936 he had tried to make the British Academy understand was indissolubly tied to a living mythology] is never quite pure; it is of gold and an alloy. Unalloyed it would direct a man to endure even death unflinching, when necessary: that is when death may help the achievement of some object of will, or when life can only be purchased by denial of what one stands for. But since such conduct is held admirable, the alloy of personal good name was never wholly absent." So Beowulf seems not so admirable in 1953 as he did in 1936. Even in his fight with Grendel, Beowulf "does more than he need, eschewing weapons in order to make his struggle . . . a 'sporting' fight: which will enhance his personal glory, though it will put him in unnecessary peril, and weaken his chances of ridding the Danes of an intolerable affliction" (*Essays and Studies*). His action is saved from being altogether reprehensible by the twin facts that he wins (victory covers a multitude of sins) and that he acts as an independent agent, with "no responsibilities downwards" for the lives of others. He has not this excuse, however, when he battles the Worm; as king of the Geats "he does not rid himself of his chivalry, the excess persists, even when he is an old king upon whom all the hopes of a people rest." Beowulf's responsibility is clear; he must seek not his own glory but the welfare of his people, and in this he fails: "He will not deign to lead a force against the dragon, as wisdom might direct even a hero to do; for, as he explains in a long 'vaunt', his many victories have relieved him of fear." But apparently they have not taught him the duties of a king:

> He is saved from defeat, and the essential object, destruction of the dragon, only achieved by the loyalty of a subordinate. Beowulf's chivalry would otherwise have ended in his own useless death, with the dragon still at large. As it is, a subordinate is placed in greater peril than he need have been, and though he does not pay the penalty of his master's *mod* [pride] with his own life, the people lose their king disastrously.

Tolkien's new insight into *Beowulf*, altogether different from what he needed to see (and had been taught to see by *The Hobbit*) in 1936, is coupled with enriched insight into another heroic poem, *The Battle of Maldon*. He settles upon, and retranslates, two lines in the poem the significance of which suddenly looms up, in our own time and in the light of Frodo's and Sam's experiences in Mordor, in a way it could not have done in 1936: *oa se eorl ongan for his ofermode alyfan landes to fela lapere oeode* ("then the earl in his overmastering pride actually yielded ground to the enemy, as he should not have done"). Tolkien finds, in 1953, that the more standard translation of W. P. Ker does not fully express the poem's intended criticism of Beorhtnoth's prideful excess, his "sporting" act of letting the Vikings freely cross the causeway to better fighting position: "then the earl of his overboldness granted ground too much to the hateful people." Unlike Ker, Tolkien sees severe criticism of the earl in the line, for his making a "'sporting fight' on level terms" with the enemy took place at "other people's expense. In his situation he was not a subordinate, but the authority to be obeyed on the spot; and he was responsible for all the men under him, not to throw away their lives except with one object, the defense of the realm from an implacable foe." The true heroism in this situation was not the *ofermod* ("overmastering pride") of Beorhtnoth but the endurance of his men, forced by his prideful act to exhibit their loyalty to the death. For, as Tolkien concluded in 1953, it "is the heroism of obedience and love not of pride or willfulness that is the most heroic and most moving; from Wiglaf under his kinsman's shield, to Beorhtwold at Maldon, down to Balaclava," and, Tolkien might as well have added, down to Sam at Orodruin. If we look closely here, we shall once again find Tolkien's professional scholarship following upon, even standing as implicit commentary upon his own creative work of the time. Moreover, the scholarly revaluation and critique of the heroic poem is printed only a few months before the work for which it is a covert preparation—*The Lord of the Rings*. The little essay on *The Battle of Maldon* is the critical fruit of Middle-earthly discovery and the preparation of an audience for the new mode of heroism he has formulated through Frodo and Sam, even as the *Beowulf* essay was preparation for *The Hobbit*. And again, this new mode of heroism (renunciation of power for the sake of all men) is precisely relevant to the changed needs of the world to which *The Lord of the Rings* addresses itself, for the world had the Bomb in 1953, as it did not in 1940: it no longer needed the bravado and recklessness of a Beowulf or the *ofermod* of a Beorhtnoth, but as never before required restraint, national as well as personal selflessness, and a concern for the good of all rather than merely of the national group. It required, in other words, precisely the human equivalent of the self-effacing hobbit heroism of Frodo and Sam, death to the contemporary equivalents of Boromir, and, most of all, an end to the desires of Sauron.

Mention of Tolkien's spirit of malice, Sauron, brings us to another of Blackmur's internal cultural facts, the re-creation of the devil in our own age. Tolkien's personification of the urge toward power is in fact a Middle-earthly version of Satan; even his name smacks of serpent-ness, probably coming from the Greek *sauros*, "lizard." We know already of Tolkien's strong feelings about the imaginative value and literary propriety of mythological representations of radical evil; for him, myth is one of our most perfect and least valued ways of fully perceiving the real, and in this, of course, he has the tradition of Western culture behind him. The myth of a personal Satan

provided for centuries a satisfactory resting place for our notions of evil
and its workings and an at least sometimes healthy source of enriching
imaginative activity (*Paradise Lost*, for example). The gradual death of that
myth, along with many others, has left a large hole in our imaginative grasp
of reality; we lack working imaginative constructs to do justice to our real
sense that there is radical or at least inexplicable evil in our experience. It
seems not unreasonable that imaginative poverty in this regard would
result in the inability to see the world clearly. An inadequate imaginative
apprehension of evil, worse yet, could result in the inability to understand
our experience and in the casual acceptance of barely perceived evil. The
gassing of Jews can easily be screened behind abstractions like "the final
solution," the burning of Vietnamese villages explained away with empty
jargon like "pacification" if the imagination is too weak to conjure a living
sympathy for what is actually happening.

I think a sizable part of our culture has long since felt the pang of imaginative hunger; there is little doubt that much of the history of our century
has been the symptom (or cause) of numberless desperate attempts to create
or revive mythological systems to explain what has gone wrong. If I read the
present climate correctly, part of the reason Tolkien's vision is so necessary
to so many is that it provides a richly satisfying experience of a fully worked
out mythological perception of radical evil. Tolkien's particular myth parallels his Christianity, positing a malevolent and corrupting outside influence,
spiritual and probably eternal, against which man is doomed to fight, but
which he has no hope of conquering on his own—Sauron the Great, Lord of
the Rings. Sauron's career is modeled after those of the biblical and Miltonic
Satan. In Appendix A of *The Return of the King*, Tolkien gives a brief sketch
of Sauron's history, and it is clear that he finds the Satan myth an altogether
satisfying center for his own exploration of radical evil. Originally Sauron
was a fair creature to look upon and had been given supremacy in Middle-
earth. The original men, the Númenoreans, had been placed, like Adam,
under a single prohibition, not to set foot upon the Undying Lands to the
west; the command was called the Ban of the Valar. Toward the end of the
Second Age, Sauron bewitched the king of Númenor and most of his
subjects, telling them that "everlasting life would be his who possessed the
Undying Lands, and that the Ban was imposed only to prevent the Kings of
Men from surpassing the Valar." Deceived, the Númenoreans committed
Middle-earth's Original Sin, their kingdom was destroyed, and Sauron fell
with them. The "bodily form in which he long had walked perished; but he
fled back to Middle-earth, a spirit of hatred borne upon a dark wind. He was
unable ever again to assume a form that seemed fair to men, but became
black and hideous." Sauron's story aligns, point by point, with Satan's.

Sauron's imps, the Orcs, are likewise expressions of one of Blackmur's cultural facts, the discovery of techniques for finding destructive troubles in men's psyches. Tolkien is, of course, no psychoanalyst, but his Orcs are the products of a keenly perceptive imaginative grasp of the side of the human mind that has traditionally been associated with energy and evil; they are, in Freudian terminology, id projections, and perhaps the best way to see what Tolkien is doing with these hideous creatures is with the careful application of the kind of analysis Blackmur mentions. To say what the Orcs are, where they come from, and what they are related to is to reveal a fascinating aspect of Tolkien's mythological imagination.

Tolkien the philologist probably took his word "Orc" from *Orcus*, the Italic god of death and the underworld and the original of the French word *ogre*. And by a remarkable coincidence, if it is one, Tolkien's name for the foulest imaginable picture of humanity is the same as William Blake's name for the fairest picture, his revolutionary figure Orc. Where Blake got his word is still in debate. S. Foster Damon suggests that the word is an anagram of the Latin *cor*, "heart"; the *Oxford English Dictionary* tells us that as early as 1611 "orc," from the Latin *orca*, "whale," denoted in English a devouring land or sea monster, and Harold Bloom has suggested that Blake knew enough Latin to derive "Orc" from the same *Orcus* Tolkien quite independently drew upon. I am not so much interested in the names, however, as in what a comparison of Blake's and Tolkien's attitudes toward and literary uses of their creatures can tell us about the vision of life in Tolkien's mythic argument.

Both Orcs are symbols or representatives of a disruptive power inimical to established order, whose function is to rebel against the overthrow the status quo. But from this point, the parallel between the two Orcs becomes a polarity, for whereas in the radical Blakean vision the status quo is destructive and sterile, in Tolkien the status quo of the Shire is the thing most desirable. In Blake, Orc appears as a symbolic picture of the return of the repressed to the level of consciousness by the vehicle of political revolution; he is the inevitable result of sexual repression, which Blake, unlike Freud, regarded as inimical rather than necessary to civilized life. Though disagreeing with Freud about the necessity of repression, Blake anticipated by more than a hundred years the psychoanalytic insight that the energies of the id, when denied outlet in one form, will find an exit in another form, often with terrible psychic or physical violence. In the terms of Blake's myth, when the psychological category he calls Luvah (probably derived from the word "love" and loosely identifiable with the id) is repressed (in the myth, chained down by the father-figure Urthona—"Earth-owner?"), it will break forth with terrible force as Orc, the "vehicular form" of Luvah or the aspect of Luvah perceivable in the world of time and space, as political revolution.

In Blake's myth, the sexual nature of this terrible force is glorified and given powerful mythic statement in the Preludium to *America: A Prophecy*. Here, the American Revolution, or rather the mythic figure of revolution itself, appears as a saving explosion of long-repressed libidinal energy. "Red Orc" has been chained in an underworld (a "dark abode") by his repressive father Urthona for fourteen years, or until he has reached sexual maturity, at which point the chains of repression can hold him no longer:

> *Silent as despairing love, and strong as jealousy,*
> *The hairy shoulders rend the links; free are the wrists of fire.*

Once released from the iron links of repression, Orc's first act is sexual: he copulates with his sister and keeper, the "shadowy Daughter of Urthona":

> *Round the terrific loins he seiz'd the panting, struggling womb:*
> *It joy'd: she put aside her clouds & smil'd her first-born smile.*
> (*America*, Plate 2)

In Blake, then, political revolution revitalizes, indeed impregnates; political violence is overtly sexualized.

The Lord of the Rings can likewise be seen as a political fantasy expressed in covert sexual symbols. Its basic subject is the end of one world order—the Third Age of Middle-earth—and the competition between the two world orders seeking to replace it; the Fourth Age will be either that of Sauron and the Orcs or that of man. As it turns out, Sauron loses, whereas in Blake, Orc wins. This is very instructive and tells us much about the contrast between the two authors. For though the perspectives and sympathies toward the two Orcs are radically different, their underworlds and their figures are presented in the same kind of infernal and sexual imagery. Just as Orc's "dark adobe" is in "regions of dark death" and "black clouds," deep in "caverns" of the earth (*America*, Plate 1) so is Mordor a hell of ashes and smoke. As Frodo and Sam stand ready to enter Sauron's infernal land, they see Mount Doom,

> its feet founded in ashen ruin, its huge cone rising to a great height, where its reeking head was swathed in cloud. Its fires were now dimmed, and it stood in smouldering slumber, as threatening and dangerous as a sleeping beast. Behind it there hung a vast shadow . . .
>
> Frodo and Sam gazed out in mingled loathing and wonder on this hateful land. Between them and the smoking mountain . . . all seemed ruinous and dead, a desert burned and choked.

And just as Orc's nature is purely libidinous, as is clear from his first act of freedom, so the Orcs are rabbit-like in their breeding and swarming. Sauron has spawned literally millions of them in his desire for armies, and Saruman has even gone so far as to crossbreed men and Orcs to form the hideous Uruk-hai. Again, the two creatures are almost preternaturally alike in the symbolic character of their appearance, though their actual physical like-nesses are worlds apart. Just as Orc's most interesting (and only noted) secondary sexual characteristic, his body hair, has been located with symbolic propriety in his place of greatest strength—his "hairy shoulders" that "rend the links" of sexual repression—so Tolkien's Orcs have long hairy arms, the strength of which is terrifying.

The two figures are, that is, mythological expressions of the same psychological category, but are presented from entirely different perspec-tives; indeed, the authors' descriptions of their creatures reveal, as well as anything else, their views of what their imaginations have summoned. Whereas Orc is a beautiful adolescent boy and quite properly naked, the Orcs have "hideous" faces and "foul breath," are "bow-legged," and wear "long hairy breeches of some unclean beast-fell," the scent of which causes "disgust" in Frodo.

Indeed Tolkien's revulsion from the Orcs is a chief motive force behind *The Lord of the Rings*; they *must* be pushed back into Mordor and held there. Tolkien wants Orc-hood sealed in precisely the same under-world of the mind from which Blake wants it to erupt; the one, that is, accepts the necessity of repression, the other argues that repression in any form is damaging to the soul.

Tolkien's mythological answer to Blackmur's fourth cultural fact, the explosion of populations, will be unacceptable to most moderns, though it is the only one Tolkien's own church can sanction: the orderly sexual restraint of the hobbits. Whereas the Orcs breed rapidly, the hobbits marry late and do not even count as men until age thirty-three. And whereas the Orcs are covered with hair, in part to represent their sexual voraciousness and animality, the hobbits' body hair has been displaced downward; their secondary sexual characteristic is located in the most apt of symbolic places, the feet (they have no beards).

The hobbits' homeland, the tradition-bound, backward-looking Shire, is an idealized version of preindustrial England that clearly grows out of Tolkien's own conservative, nostalgic view of the land of his youth. He has written:

> Not long ago—incredible though it may seem—I heard a clerk
> of Oxenford declare that he "welcomed" the proximity of

mass-production robot factories, and the roar of self-obstruc-
tive mechanical traffic, because it brought his university into
"contact with real life." He may have meant that the way men
were living and working in the twentieth century was
increasing in barbarity at an alarming rate, and that the loud
demonstrations of this in the streets of Oxford might serve as a
warning that it is not possible to preserve for long an oasis of
sanity in a desert of unreason by mere fences, without actual
offensive action (practical and intellectual). I fear he did not . . .
The notion that motorcars are more "alive" than, say, centaurs
or dragons is curious; that they are more "real" than, say horses
is pathetically absurd.

In *The Lord of the Rings*, this attitude is dramatized when Frodo and his
companions return to the Shire after the destruction of the Ring only to find
that in their absence Saruman has industrialized the homeland. Tolkien's
description of Hobbiton might have come out of a D. H. Lawrence novel:

> The great chimney rose up before them; and as they drew near
> the old village across the water, through rows of new mean
> houses . . . they saw the new mill in all its frowning and dirty
> ugliness: a great brick building straddling the stream, which it
> fouled with a steaming and stinking outflow.

Here is the point at which the polarity between Blake's and Tolkien's
visions of life begins to turn back into a parallel, for Blake too was appalled
at the effects of the Industrial Revolution on the life of his England and
condemned what he called the "dark Satanic Mills." Both men would oppose
the life-deadening and life-denying aspects of the modern world, both would
oppose what Freud calls Thanatos, the death instinct. Blake mythicizes that
aspect of man's makeup with a group of twelve lost creatures called the Sons
of Albion, who personify an "Abstract objecting power that Negatives everything". (*Jerusalem*); Tolkien feels that his myth of Sauron expresses an
impulse in the cosmos itself, an even greater malice of which he is but the
"servant or emissary." Both men assume that the struggle against evil is an
inevitable part of life: Blake always felt that "Without Contraries is no
progression" (*The Marriage of Heaven and Hell*), and Tolkien acknowledges
that there may always be Saurons to fight. The difference lies in the ground
on which they stand to combat the evil, the assumptions from which they
start. Blake assumes that the fundamental struggle is between Thanatos and

desirably unfettered Eros, while Tolkien is convinced that unfettered Eros is the ally, even the servant, of Thanatos.

What we can perhaps be most thankful for is that each myth is altogether suitable to the age out of which it comes. The world of the French and American Revolutions, which Blake addressed, deeply needed the freeing explosion of Orc; the world Tolkien addresses, faced with the altogether unprecedented cultural facts described by Blackmur, needs another mythology, and Tolkien has given us the most useful one I know, though we are well advised to be critical in our acceptance of some parts of it.

1925–1948(ii): The Third Age

Enter Mr Baggins

Really that missing piece had been there all the time. It was the Suffield side of his own personality.

His deep feeling that his real home was in the West Midland country-side of England, had since his undergraduate days, defined the nature of his scholarly work. The same motives that had led him to study *Beowulf, Gawain*, and the *Ancrene Wisse* now created a character that embodied everything he loved about the West Midlands: Mr Bilbo Baggins, the hobbit.

We can see certain superficial precedents for this invention: the Snergs, the name Babbitt, and in Tolkien's own stories the original four-foot Tom Bombadil and the tiny Timothy Titus. But this does not tell us very much. The personal element is far more revealing. In the story, Bilbo Baggins, son of the lively Belladonna Took, herself one of the three remarkable daughters of the Old Took, descended also from the respectable and solid Bagginses, is middle aged and unadventurous, dresses in sensible clothes but likes bright colours, and has a taste for plain food; but there is something strange in his character that wakes up when the adventure begins. John Ronald Reuel Tolkien, son of the enterprising Mabel Suffield, herself one of the three remarkable daughters of old John Suffield (who lived to be nearly a hundred), descended also from the respectable and solid Tolkiens, was

From *Tolkien: A Biography* by Humphrey Carpenter. © 1977 by George Allen & Unwin Publishers Ltd.

middle aged and inclined to pessimism, dressed in sensible clothes but liked coloured waistcoats when he could afford them, and had a taste for plain food. But there was something unusual in his character that had already manifested itself in the creation of a mythology, and it now led him to begin this new story.

Tolkien himself was well aware of the similarity between creator and creation. 'I am in fact a hobbit,' he once wrote, 'in all but size. I like gardens, trees, and unmechanized farmlands; I smoke a pipe, and like good plain food (unrefrigerated), but detest French cooking; I like, and even dare to wear in these dull days, ornamental waistcoats. I am fond of mushrooms (out of a field); have a very simple sense of humour (which even my appreciative critics find tiresome); I go to bed late and get up late (when possible.) I do not travel much.' And as if to emphasise the personal parallel, Tolkien chose for the hobbits house the name 'Bag End', which was what the local people called his Aunt Jane's Worcestershire farm. Worcestershire, the county from which the Suffields had come, and in which his brother Hilary was at that time cultivating the land, is of all West Midland counties The Shire from which the hobbits come; Tolkien wrote of it: 'Any corner of that county (however fair or squalid) is in an indefinable way "home" to me, as no other part of the world is.' But the village of Hobbiton itself with its mill and river is to be found not in Worcestershire but in Warwickshire, now half hidden in the red-brick skirt of Birmingham but still identifiable as the Sarehole where Ronald Tolkien spent four formative years.

The hobbits do not owe their origins merely to personal parallels. Tolkien once told an interviewer: 'The Hobbits are just rustic English people, made small in size because it reflects the generally small reach of their imagination—not the small reach of their courage or latent power.' To put it another way, the hobbits represent the combination of small imagination with great courage which (as Tolkien had seen in the trenches during the First World War) often led to survival against all chances. 'I've always been impressed,' he once said, 'that we are here, surviving, because of the indomitable courage of quite small people against impossible odds.'

In some ways it is wrong to talk of hobbits as the 'missing piece' that was needed before the two sides of Tolkien's imagination during the nineteen-twenties and thirties could meet and fuse; at least chronologically wrong, because Tolkien probably began to write *The Hobbit* quite early in this period. It would be more accurate to say that not until the book was finished and published— indeed not until he began to write the sequel—did he realise the significance of hobbits, and see that they had a crucial role to play in his mythology. In itself *The Hobbit* began as merely another story for amusement. Moreover it nearly suffered the fate of so many others and remained unfinished.

While we can see quite clearly why Tolkien began to write the story, it proves impossible to say exactly when. The manuscript gives no indication of day, and Tolkien himself was unable to remember the precise origins of the book. In one account he said: 'I am not sure but I think the Unexpected Party (the first chapter) was hastily written before 1935 but certainly after 1930 when I moved to 20 Northmoor Road.' Elsewhere he wrote: 'On a blank leaf I scrawled "In a hole in the ground there lived a hobbit". I did not and do not know why. I did nothing about it, for a long time, and for some years I got no further than the production of Thror's Map. But it became *The Hobbit* in the early nineteen-thirties.' This recollection that there was a hiatus between the original idea and the composition of the main body of the story is confirmed by a note that Tolkien scribbled on a surviving page of the original Chapter One: 'Only page preserved of the first scrawled copy of *The Hobbit* which did not reach beyond the first chapter.' In 1937, shortly after the book was published, Christopher Tolkien recorded (in his letter to Father Christmas) this account of the book's origins: 'Daddy wrote it ages ago, and read it to John, Michael and me in our Winter "Reads" after tea in the evening; but the ending chapters were rather roughly done, and not typed out at all; he finished it about a year ago.' And writing to his publishers during the same year, Tolkien declared: 'My eldest boy was thirteen when he heard the serial. It did not appeal to the younger ones who had to grow up to it successively.'

These statements lead to the conclusion that the book was begun in 1930 or 1931 (when John, the eldest boy, was thirteen); certainly there was a completed typescript in existence (lacking only the final chapters) in time for it to be shown to C. S. Lewis late in 1932. However John and Michael Tolkien do not believe this to be the entire picture, for they have a clear memory of certain elements in the story being told to them in the study at 22 Northmoor Road, that is, before 1930. They are not certain that what they were listening to at that time was necessarily a *written* story: they believe that it may well have been a number of impromptu tales which were later absorbed into *The Hobbit* proper.

The manuscript of *The Hobbit* suggests that the actual writing of the main part of the story was done over a comparatively short period of time: the ink, paper, and handwriting style are consistent, the pages are numbered consecutively, and there are almost no chapter divisions. It would also appear that Tolkien wrote the story fluently and with little hesitation, for there are comparatively few erasures or revisions. Originally the dragon was called 'Pryftan', the name 'Gandalf' was given to the chief dwarf, and the wizard was called 'Bladorthin'. The dragon's name was soon changed to 'Smaug', from the Germanic verb *smugan* meaning 'to squeeze through a hole';

Tolkien called this 'a low philological jest'. But the name 'Bladorthin' was retained for some time, and it was not until the draft was well advanced that the chief dwarf was renamed 'Thorin Oakenshield' and the name 'Gandalf' (taken, like all the dwarf-names, from the Elder Edda) was given to the wizard, for whom it was eminently suitable on account of its Icelandic meaning of 'sorcerer-elf' and hence 'wizard'.

The story began, then, merely for personal amusement. Certainly Tolkien had at first no intention that the bourgeois comfortable world of Bilbo Baggins would be related in any way to the vast mythological landscape of *The Silmarillion*. Gradually, however, elements from his mythology began to creep in. Inevitably the dwarves suggested a connection, for 'dwarves' (spelt in that fashion) had played a part in the earlier work; and when in the first chapter of *The Hobbit* the wizard mentioned 'the Necromancer' there was a reference to the legend of Beren and Lúthien. Soon it was apparent that the journey of Bilbo Baggins and his companions lay across a corner of that Middle-earth which had its earlier history chronicled in *The Silmarillion*. In Tolkien's words this was 'the world into which Mr Baggins strayed'. And if the events of the new story were clearly set long after those of *The Silmarillion*, then, since the earlier chronicles recorded the history of the First and Second Ages of Middle-earth, it appeared that *The Hobbit* was to be a tale of the Third Age.

'One writes such a story,' said Tolkien, 'out of the leaf-mould of the mind'; and while we can still detect the shape of a few of the leaves—the Alpine trek of 1911, the goblins of the 'Curdie' books of George Macdonald, an episode in *Beowulf* when a cup is stolen from a sleeping dragon—this is not the essential point of Tolkien's metaphor. One learns little by raking through a compost heap to see what dead plants originally went into it. Far better to observe its effect on the new and growing plants that it is enriching. And in *The Hobbit* the leaf-mould of Tolkien's mind nurtured a rich growth with which only a few other books in children's literature can compare.

For it *is* a children's story. Despite the fact that it had been drawn into his mythology, Tolkien did not allow it to become overwhelmingly serious or even adult in tone, but stuck to his original intention of amusing his own and perhaps other people's children. Indeed he did this too consciously and deliberately at times in the first draft, which contains a large number of 'asides' to juvenile readers, remarks such as 'Now you know quite enough to go on with' and 'As we shall see in the end'. He later removed many of theses, but some remain in the published text—to his regret, for he came to dislike them, and even to believe that any deliberate talking down to children is a great mistake in a story. 'Never mind about the young!' he once wrote, 'I am not interested in the "child" as such, modern or otherwise, and certainly have no intention of meeting him/her half way, or a quarter of the way. It is a mistaken thing to do anyway, either useless (when applied to the stupid) or pernicious (when inflicted on the gifted).' But when he wrote *The Hobbit* he was still suffering from what he later called 'the contemporary delusions about "fairy-stories" and children'—delusions that not long afterwards he made a conscious decision to renounce.

The writing of the story progressed fluently until the passage not far from the end where the dragon Smaug is about to die. Here Tolkien hesitated, and tried out the narrative in rough notes—something he was often to do in *The Lord of the Rings* but seems to have done only rarely in *The Hobbit*. These notes suggest that Bilbo Baggins might creep into the dragon's lair and stab him. 'Bilbo plunges in his little magic knife,' he wrote. 'Throes of dragon. Smashes walls and entrance to tunnel.' But this idea, which scarcely suited the character of the hobbit or provided a grand enough death for Smaug, was rejected in favour of the published version where the dragon is slain by the archer Bard. And then, shortly after he had described the death of the dragon, Tolkien abandoned the story.

Or to be more accurate, he did not write any more of it down. For the benefit of his children he had narrated an impromptu conclusion to the story, but, as Christopher Tolkien expressed it, 'the ending chapters were rather roughly done, and not typed out at all'. Indeed they were not even written in manuscript. The typescript of the nearly finished story, made in the small neat typeface of the Hammond machine, with italics for the songs, was occasionally shown to favoured friends, together with its accompanying maps (and perhaps already a few illustrations). But it did not often leave Tolkien's study, where it sat, incomplete and now likely to remain so. The boys were growing up and no longer asked for 'Winter Reads', so there was no reason why *The Hobbit* should ever be finished.

One of the few people to be shown the typescript of *The Hobbit* was a graduate named Elaine Griffiths, who had been a pupil of Tolkien's and had become a family friend. Upon his recommendation she was engaged by the London publishers George Allen & Unwin to revise Clark Hall's translation of *Beowulf*, a popular undergraduate 'crib'. One day in 1936 (some time after *The Hobbit* had been abandoned) a member of Allen & Unwin's staff came down to Oxford to see Elaine Griffiths about the project. This was Susan Dagnall, who had read English at Oxford at the same time as Elaine Griffiths and indeed knew her well. From her she learnt of the existence of the unfinished but remarkable children's story that Professor Tolkien had written. Elaine Griffiths suggested that Susan Dagnall should go to Northmoor Road and try to borrow the typescript. Susan Dagnall went, met Tolkien, asked for the typescript, and was given it. She took it back to London, read it, and decided that it was certainly worthy of consideration by Allen & Uuwin. But it stopped short just after the death of the dragon. She sent the typescript back to Tolkien, asking him if he would finish it, and preferably soon, so that the book could be considered for publication in the following year.

Tolkien got down to work. On 10 August 1936 he wrote: '*The Hobbit* is now nearly finished, and the publishers clamouring for it.' He engaged his son Michael, who had cut his right hand badly on a school window, to help with the typing, using his left hand, The whole labour was finished by the first week in October, and the typescript was sent to Allen & Unwin's offices near the British Museaum, bearing the title *The Hobbit*, or *There and Back Again.*

The firm's chairman, Stanley Unwin, believed that the best judges of children's books were children, so he handed *The Hobbit* to his ten-year-old son Rayner, who read it and wrote this report:

> Bilbo Baggins was a hobbit who lived in his hobbit-hole and *never* went for adventures, at last Gandalf the wizard and his dwarves perswaded him to go. He had a very exiting time fighting goblins and wargs. at last they got to the lonley moun- tain; Smaug, the dragon who gawreds it is killed and after a terrific battle with the goblins he returned home—rich! This book, with the help of maps, does not need any illustrations it is good and should appeal to all children between the ages of 5 and 9.

The boy earned a shilling for the report, and the book was accepted for publication.

Despite what Rayner Unwin had written, it was decided that *The Hobbit* did need illustrations. Tolkien was modest about his talents as an artist, and when at the publishers' suggestion he submitted a number of drawings which he had made for the story he commented: 'The pictures seem to me mostly only to prove that the author cannot draw.' But Allen & Unwin did not agree, and they gladly accepted eight of his black and white illustrations.

Although Tolkien had some idea of the processes involved in the production of books, he was surprised by the number of difficulties and disappointments during the following months; indeed the machinations and occasionally the downright incompetence of publishers and printers continued to amaze him until the end of his life. *The Hobbit* maps had to be redrawn by him because his originals had incorporated too many colours, and even then his scheme of having the general map as an endpaper and

Thror's map placed within the text of Chapter One was not followed. The publishers had decided that both maps should be used as endpapers, and in consequence his plan for 'invisible lettering', which would appear when Thror's map was held up to the light, had to be abandoned. He also had to spend a good deal of time on the proofs—though that was entirely his fault. When the page-proofs arrived at Northmoor Road in February 1937 he decided that he ought to make substantial revisions to several parts of the book, for he had let the manuscript go without checking it with his usual thoroughness, and he was now unhappy about a number of passages in the story; in particular he did not like many of the patronising 'asides' to juvenile readers, and he also saw that there were many inconsistencies in the description of the topography, details which only the most acute and painstaking reader would notice, but which he himself with his passion for perfection could not allow to pass. In a few days he had covered the proofs with a host of alterations. With typical consideration for the printers he ensured that his revisions occupied an identical area of type to the original wording—though here he was wasting his time, for the printers decided to reset the entire sections that he had revised.

The Hobbit was published on 21 September 1937. Tolkien was a little nervous of Oxford reaction, especially as he was currently holding a Leverhulme Research Fellowship, and he remarked: 'I shall now find it very hard to make people believe that this is not the major fruits of "research" 1936–7.' He need not have worried: at first Oxford paid almost no attention.

A few days after publication the book received an accolade in the columns of *The Times*. 'All who love that kind of children's book which can be read and re-read by adults', wrote the reviewer, 'should take note that a new star has appeared in this constellation. To the trained eye some characters will seem almost mythopoeic.' The eye in question was that of C. S. Lewis, at that time a regular reviewer for *The Times Literary Supplement*, who had managed to get this notice of his friends' book into the parent journal. Naturally, he also reviewed the book in glowing terms in the *Supplement* itself. There was an equally enthusiastic reaction from many other critics, although some took a delight in pointing out the ineptness of the publisher's 'blurb' that compared the book to *Alice in Wonderland* simply because both were the work of Oxford dons; and there were a few dissenting voices, among them that of the reviewer who wrote (somewhat puzzlingly) in *Junior Bookshelf*: 'The courageous freedom of real adventure doesn't appear.'

The first edition of *The Hobbit* had sold out by Christmas. A reprint was hurried through, and four of the five coloured illustrations that Tolkien had drawn for the book were now included in it; he had apparently never offered them to Allen & Unwin, and it was not until they passed through the publisher's office on the way to Houghton Mifflin, who were to publish the book in America, that their existence was discovered. When the American edition was issued a few months later it too received approbation from most critics, and it was awarded the *New York Herald Tribune* prize for the best juvenile book of the season. Stanley Unwin realised that he had a children's best-seller in his list. He wrote to Tolkien: 'A large public will be clamouring next year to hear more from you about Hobbits!'

2. "The new *Hobbit*"

A few weeks after *The Hobbit* had been published Tolkien went to London and had lunch with Stanley Unwin to discuss a possible successor to the book. He found that the publisher, small, bright-eyed, and bearded, looked 'exactly like one of my dwarves, only I don't think he smokes.' Unwin certainly did not smoke, nor did he drink alcohol (he came from a strict Nonconformist family), and each man found the other rather strange. Unwin learnt that Tolkien had a large mythological work called *The Silmarillion* that he now wanted to publish, though Tolkien admitted that it was not very suitable as a successor to the adventures of Bilbo Baggins; he also said that he had several short stories for children, 'Mr Bliss', 'Farmer Giles of Ham', and 'Roverandom'; and there was an unfinished novel called 'The Lost Road'. Unwin asked Tolkien to send all of these manuscripts to his office in Museum Street.

They were sent, and they were read. The children's stories were all enjoyed, but none of them was about hobbits, and Stanley Unwin was certain that this was what the people who had enjoyed the first book wanted. As for 'The Lost Road', it was obviously unsuitable for a juvenile audience. But *The Silmarillion* presented a more complex problem.

The manuscript of this lengthy work—or rather, the bundle of manuscripts—had arrived in a somewhat disordered state, and the only clearly continuous section seemed to be the long poem 'The Gest of Beren and Lúthien'. So this poem was passed to a publisher's reader. The reader did not think much of it; in fact in his report he was very rude about the rhyming couplets. But he hastened to say that he found the prose version of the Beren and Lúthien story enthralling—Tolkien had presumably attached it to the poem for the purpose of completing the story, for the poem itself was unfinished. 'The tale here proceeds at a stinging pace,' the reader reported to Stanley Unwin, and continued enthusiastically (albeit in rather nonsensical terms of praise): 'It is told with a picturesque brevity and dignity that holds the reader's interest in spite of its eye-splitting Celtic names. It has something of that mad, bright-eyed beauty that perplexes all Anglo-Saxons in face of Celtic art.'

There is no evidence that any other part of *The Silmarillion* was read by Allen & Unwin at this juncture. Nevertheless Stanley Unwin wrote to Tolkien on 15 December 1937:

> *The Silmarillion* contains plenty of wonderful material; in fact it is a mine to be explored in writing further books like *The Hobbit* rather than a book in itself. I think this was partly your own view, was it not? What we badly need is another book with which to follow up our success with *The Hobbit* and alas! neither of these manuscripts (the poem and *The Silmarillion* itself) quite fits the bill. I still hope that you will be inspired to write another book about the Hobbit.

In his letter Unwin also passed on to Tolkien the reader's enthusiastic if misguided compliments about the section of *The Silmarillion* that he had seen.

Tolkien replied (on 16 December 1937):

> My chief joy comes from learning that *The Silmarillion* is not rejected with scorn. I have suffered a sense of fear and bereavement, quite ridiculous, since I let this private and beloved nonsense out; and I think if it had seemed to you to be nonsense I should have felt really crushed. But I shall certainly now hope one day to be able, or to be able to afford, to publish *The Silmarillion*! Your reader's comments afford me delight. I am sorry the names split his eyes—personally I believe (and here I believe I am a good judge) they are good, and a large part of the effect. They are coherent and consistent and made upon two related linguistic formulae, so that they achieve a reality not fully achieved by other name-inventors (say Swift or Dunsany!). Needless to say they are not Celtic! Neither are the tales.
>
> I did not think any of the stuff I dropped on you filled the bill. But I did want to know whether any of the stuff had any exterior or non-personal value. I think it is plain that quite apart from it, a sequel or successor to *The Hobbit* is called for. I promise to give this thought and attention. But I am sure you will sympathize when I say that the construction of elaborate and consistent mythology (and two languages) rather occupies the mind, and the Silmarils are in my heart. So that goodness knows what will happen. Mr Baggins began as a comic tale

among conventional and inconsistent Grimm's fairy-tale dwarves, and got drawn into the edge of it—so that even Sauron the terrible peeped over the edge. And what more can hobbits do? They can be comic, but their comedy is suburban unless it is set against things more elemental. But the real fun about orcs and dragons (to my mind) was before their time. Perhaps a new (if similar) line?

Stanley Unwin probably did not understand much of this letter; but in any case Tolkien was really thinking aloud and beginning to plan, for a mere three days later, on 19 December 1937, he wrote to Charles Furth, one of the editorial staff at Allen & Unwin: 'I have written the first chapter of a new story about Hobbits—"A long expected party".'

The new story began rather like the first hobbit tale. Mr Bilbo Baggins of Hobbiton gives a party to celebrate his birthday, and after making a speech to his guests he slips on the magic ring that he acquired in *The Hobbit*, and vanishes. The reason for his disappearance, as given in this first draft, is that Bilbo 'had not got any money or jewels left' and was going off in search of more dragon-gold. At this point the first version of the opening chapter breaks off, unfinished.

Tolkien had as yet no clear idea of what the new story was going to be about. At the end of *The Hobbit* he had stated that Bilbo 'remained very happy to the end of his days, and those were extraordinarily long'. So how could the hobbit have any new adventures worth the name without this being contradicted? And had he not explored most of the possibilities in Bilbo's character? He decided to introduce a new hobbit, Bilbo's son—and to give him the name of a family of toy koala bears owned by his children, 'The Bingos'. So he crossed out 'Bilbo' in the first draft and above it wrote 'Bingo'. Then another idea occurred to him, and he wrote it down in memorandum form (as he was often to do during the invention of this new story): 'Make *return of ring* a motive.'

The ring, after all, was both a link with the earlier book and one of the few elements in it that had not been fully developed. Bilbo had acquired it accidentally from the slimy Gollum beneath the Misty Mountains. Its power of making the wearer invisible had been exploited fully in *The Hobbit*, but it might be supposed to have other properties. Tolkien made some further notes: 'The Ring: whence its origin? Necromancer? Not very dangerous, when used for good purpose. But it exacts its penalty. You must either lose it, or *yourself*.' Then he rewrote the opening chapter, calling the hero 'Bingo Bolger-Baggins' and making him Bilbo's nephew rather than his son. He typed it out, and at the beginning of February 1938 he sent it to Allen & Unwin, asking if Stanley Unwin's son Rayner, who had written the original report on *The Hobbit*, would care to let him have an opinion on it.

Stanley Unwin wrote on 11 February that Rayner had read it and was delighted with it, and he told Tolkien: 'Go right ahead.'

Tolkien was encouraged, but he replied: 'I find it only too easy to write opening chapters—and at the moment the story is not unfolding. I squandered so much on the original "Hobbit" (which was not meant to have a sequel) that it is difficult to find anything new in that world.' Nevertheless he set to work again, and wrote a second chapter which he called 'Three's Company'. It told how Bingo with his cousins Odo and Frodo set off to make a journey across the countryside under the stars.

'Stories tend to get out of hand,' Tolkien wrote to his publisher a few weeks later, 'and this has taken an unpremeditated turn.' He was referring to the appearance, unplanned by him, of a sinister 'Black Rider' who is clearly searching for the hobbits. It was indeed the first of several unpremeditated turns that the story was to take. Unconsciously, and usually without forethought, Tolkien was bending his tale away from the jolly style of *The Hobbit* towards something darker and grander, and closer in concept to *The Silmarillion*.

A third chapter was written, untitled but in essence the same chapter that was eventually published as 'A Short Cut to Mushrooms'. Tolkien then typed out everything he had written (and rewritten), and once again sent it to Rayner Unwin for comment. Again the boy approved of it, though he said that there was 'too much hobbit talk', and asked what the book would be called.

What indeed? And, much more important, Tolkien still did not have a clear idea what it was all about. Nor did he have much time to devote to it. Besides the usual calls on his attention—lecturing, examining, administration, research—there was the additional worry of a mysterious heart condition that had been diagnosed in his son Christopher; the boy, who had recently followed his brothers to a Catholic boarding-school in Berkshire, was ordered to stay at home for many months and kept lying on his back, and his father devoted much time and care to him. Not for many weeks was the new story again considered. Tolkien had made a note at the end of the three chapters that he had already written: 'Bingo is going to do something about the Necromancer who is planning an attack on the Shire. They have to find Gollum, and find where he got the ring, for 3 are wanted.' But promising as this may have seemed at first, it did not immediately produce results, and on 24 July 1938 he wrote to Charles Furth at Allen & Unwin: 'The sequel to *The Hobbit* has remained where it stopped. It has lost my favour, and I have no idea what to do with it.'

Shortly afterwards news came of E. V. Gordon's death in hospital, and this blow contributed further to delay with the new story. Yet at about this time Tolkien began to organise his thoughts on the central matter of the Ring, and began to write some dialogue between Bingo and the elf Gildor, explaining the nature of it. It is, says the elf, one of a number of rings that were made by the Necromancer, and it seems that *he* is looking for it. The Black Riders, explains the elf, are 'Ring-wraiths' who have been made permanently invisible by other rings. Now at last ideas began to flow, and Tolkien wrote a passage of dialogue between Bingo and the wizard Gandalf in which it is determined that the Ring must be taken many hundreds of miles to the dark land of Mordor, and there cast into 'one of the Cracks of Earth' where a great fire burns. This was basis enough for the story to be continued, taking the hobbits to the house of Tom Bombadil. When this was done, on 31 August 1938, Tolkien wrote to Allen & Unwin that the book was 'flowing along, and getting quite out of hand. It had reached about Chapter VII and progresses towards quite unforeseen goals.' Then he went off with the family, including Christopher who was now in much better health, for a holiday at Sidmouth.

There he did a good deal of work on the story, bringing the hobbits to a village inn at 'Bree' where they meet a strange character, another unpremeditated element in the narrative. In the first drafts Tolkien described this person as 'a queer-looking brown-faced hobbit', and named him 'Trotter'. Later he was to be recast as a man of heroic stature, the king whose return to power gives the third volume of the book its title; but as yet Tolkien had no more idea than the hobbits who he was. The writing continued, bringing Bingo to Rivendell; and at about this time Tolkien scribbled on a spare sheet: 'Too many hobbits. Also Bingo Bolger-Baggins a bad name. Let Bingo = Frodo.' But below this he wrote: 'No—I am now too used to Bingo.' There was also the problem of why the Ring seemed so important to everyone—this had not yet been established clearly. Suddenly an idea occurred to him, and he wrote : 'Bilbo's ring proved to be the *one ruling Ring*—all others had come back to Mordor: but this one had been lost.'

The one ruling ring that controlled all the others; the ring that was the source and instrument of the power of Sauron, the Dark Lord of Mordor; the ring that must be carried to its destruction by the hobbits, or else the whole world will come under Sauron's domination. Now everything fell into place, and the story was lifted from the 'juvenile' level of *The Hobbit* into the sphere of grand and heroic romance. There was even a name for it: when next he wrote about it to Allen & Unwin, Tolkien referred to it as 'The Lord of the Rings'.

What had happened was almost inevitable. Tolkien had not really wanted to write any more stories like *The Hobbit*; he had wanted to get on with the serious business of his mythology. And that was what he could now do. The new story had attached itself firmly to *The Silmarillion*, and was to acquire the dignity of purpose and the high style of the earlier book. True, the hobbits were still hobbits, small people with fur on their feet and funny names like Baggins and Gamgee (the family joke bout 'Gaffer Gamgee' had led to the inclusion of a character of that name, and, more important, to the invention of his son 'Sam', who was to play a major part in the story). In a sense the hobbits had only been acquired by accident from the earlier book. But now, for the first time, Tolkien realised the significance of hobbits in Middle-earth. The theme of his new story was large, but it was to have its centre in the courage of these small people; and the heart of the book was to be found in the inns and gardens of The Shire, Tolkien's representation of all that he loved best about England.

Now that the full nature of the story had become apparent, there were fewer false starts or reconsiderations. Home from the Sidmouth holiday, Tolkien spent many hours during the autumn of 1938 continuing the tale, so that by the end of the year it was well into what eventually became Book II. Usually he worked at night, as was his habit, warmed by the idiosyncratic stove in his study grate at Northmoor Road, and writing with his dip-pen on the backs of old examination answers—so that much of *The Lord of the Rings* is interspersed with fragments of long-forgotten essays by undergraduates. Each chapter would begin with a scribbled and often illegible draft; then would come a rewriting in a fairer hand; and finally a typescript done on the Hammond machine. The only major change still to be made was in the matter of the hero's name. After a brief period in the summer of 1939 when he considered changing everything he had done so far and starting all over again with Bilbo as the hero—presumably on the principle that the hero of the first book ought to be the hero of the second—Tolkien went back to his intention of using the 'Bingo' character; but as the name 'Bingo' had now become quite unbearable to him in view of the serious nature the story had taken on, he changed it to 'Frodo', a name that already belonged to a minor character. And 'Frodo' it remained.

At about the time that Tolkien decided to call the book *The Lord of the Rings*, Chamberlain signed the Munich agreement with Hitler. Tolkien like many others at the time, was suspicious not so much of German intentions as of those of Soviet Russia; he wrote that he had 'a loathing of being on any side that includes Russia,' and added: 'One fancies that Russia is probably ultimately far more responsible for the present crisis and choice of moment than Hitler.' However this does not mean that the placing of Mordor (the seat of evil in *The Lord of the Rings*) in the East is an allegorical reference to contemporary world politics, for as Tolkien himself affirmed it was a 'simple narrative and geographical necessity'. Elsewhere he made a careful distinction between allegory and applicability: 'I cordially dislike allegory in all its manifestations, and always have done so since I grew old and wary enough to detect its presence. I much prefer history, true or feigned, with its varied applicability to the thought and experience of readers. I think that many confuse "applicability" with "allegory"; but the one resides in the freedom of the reader, and the other in the purposed domination of the author.' As C. S. Lewis wrote of *The Lord of the Rings*: 'These things were not devised to reflect any particular situation in the real world. It was the other way round; real events began, horribly, to conform to the pattern he had freely invented.'

Tolkien hoped to continue work on the book in the early months of 1939, but there were endless distractions, among them his commitment to deliver the Andrew Lang Lecture at the University of St Andrews at the beginning of March. For his subject he had chosen the topic originally promised to the undergraduate society at Worcester College a year previously: fairy-stories. It was appropriate to the occasion, being a subject that had much concerned Lang himself, and it was also much in Tolkien's mind while he was writing his new story. *The Hobbit* was clearly designed for children and *The Silmarillion* for adults, but he was aware that *The Lord of the Rings* was less easy to categorise. In October 1938 he wrote to Stanley Unwin that it was 'forgetting "children" and becoming more terrifying than *The Hobbit*'. And he added: 'It may prove quite unsuitable.' But he felt strongly that fairy-stories are not necessarily for children, and he decided to devote much of his lecture to the proof of this belief.

He had touched on the crucial point in the poem 'Mythopoeia' that he had written for C. S. Lewis many years before, and he decided to quote from it in the lecture:

> The heart of man is not compound of lies,
> but draws some wisdom from the only Wise,
> and still recalls Him. Though now long estranged,
> Man is not wholly lost nor wholly changed.
> Dis-graced he may be, yet is not de-throned,
> and keeps the rags of lordship once he owned:
> Man, Sub-creator, the refracted light
> through whom is splintered from a single White
> to many hues, and endlessly combined
> in living shapes that move from mind to mind.
> Though all the crannies of the world we filled

> with Elves and Goblins, though we dared to build
> Gods and their houses out of dark and light,
> and sowed the seed of dragons—'twas our right
> (used or misused). That right has not decayed:
> we make still by the law in which we're made.

'Man, Sub-creator' was in the one sense a new way of expressing what is often called 'the willing suspension of disbelief', and Tolkien made it the central argument of the lecture.

'What really happens', he wrote, 'is that the story-maker proves a successful "sub-creator". He makes a Secondary World which your mind can enter. Inside it, what he relates it "true": it accords with the laws of that world. You therefore believe it, while you are, as it were, inside. The moment disbelief arises, the spell is broken; the magic, or rather art, has failed. You are then out in the Primary World again, looking at the little abortive Secondary World from outside.'

He made a good many points in the lecture, perhaps too many for an entirely cogent argument. But at the end he asserted in powerful terms that there is no higher function for man than the 'sub-creation' of a Secondary World such as he was already making in *The Lord of the Rings*, and he gave expression to his hope that in one sense this story and the whole of his related mythology might be found to be 'true'. 'Every writer making a secondary world', he declared, 'wishes in some measure to be a real maker, or hopes that he is drawing on reality: hopes that the peculiar quality of this secondary world (if not all the details) are derived from Reality, or are flowing into it.' Indeed he went so far as to say that it was a specifically Christian venture to write such a story as he was now engaged upon. 'The Christian,' he said, 'may now perceive that all his bents and faculties have a purpose, which can be redeemed. So great is the bounty with which he has been treated that he many now, perhaps, fairly dare to guess that in Fantasy he may actually assist in the effoliation and multiple enrichment of creation.'

The lecture was delivered at St Andrews on 8 March 1939 (the date has been variously and erroneously given as 1938 and 1940); and afterwards Tolkien returned with a new enthusiasm to the story whose purpose he had justified. That story had been begun as a mere 'sequel' to *The Hobbit*, at the instigation of his publisher, but now, especially after the declaration of high purpose that he had made in the lecture, the Ring was as important to him as the Silmarils. In fact it was now clear that *The Lord of the Rings* was not so much a sequel to *The Hobbit* as a sequel to *The Silmarillion*. Every aspect of the earlier work was playing a part in the new story: the mythology itself, which provided both a historical setting and a sense of depth, the elvish languages that he had developed so painstakingly and thoroughly over more than twenty-five years, even the Fëanorian alphabet in which he had kept his diary from 1926 to 1933, and which he now used for elvish inscriptions in the story. Yet to his friends, Tolkien still referred to the story in modest terms as 'the new Hobbit' or 'the Hobbit sequel'.

Under this title it was read chapter by chapter to the Inklings, and was received with much enthusiasm; although not everyone who listened to the story was delighted by the 'high style' of prose that had begun to predominate in the book. Tolkien had moved from the comparatively colloquial approach of the opening chapters into a manner that was more and more archaic and solemn as he progressed. He was well aware of this; indeed it was entirely deliberate, and it was discussed by him at the time in print—just as the intentions of the book had been discussed in the St Andrews lecture. This time the context was his introduction to the revised Clark Hall translation of *Beowulf*. Elaine Griffiths had found herself unable to complete the revision, and after failing to find the time to get it done himself Tolkien had handed the task over to his colleague Charles Wrenn, who was then at the University of London. Wrenn completed the work speedily, but Allen & Unwin had to wait for many months before Tolkien could be persuaded to marshal his thoughts sufficiently to write the introduction that he had promised for the volume. When he did write it, this introduction proved to be a lengthy discussion of the principles of translation, and in particular an argument in favour of the adoption of a 'high style' when dealing with heroic matters. Consciously or unconsciously, he was really discussing *The Lord of the Rings*, which had at that time (the beginning of 1940) reached the middle of what was to become Book II.

In the introduction Tolkien declared, in justification of a high style: 'We are being at once wisely aware of our own frivolity if we avoid *hitting* and *whacking* and prefer "striking" and "smiting"; *talk* and *chat* and prefer "speech" and "discourse"; *well-bred, brilliant*, or *polite noblemen* (visions of snobbery columns in the Press, and fat men on the Riviera) and prefer the "worthy, brave and courteous men" of long ago.' From this time onwards he put these stylistic precepts more and more into practice in *The Lord of the Rings*. This was almost inevitable, for as the story grew grander in scale and purpose it adopted the style of *The Silmarillion*; yet Tolkien did not make any stylistic revision of the first chapters, which had been written in a much lighter vein; and he himself noted when reading the book again twenty-five years later: 'The first volume is really very different to the rest.'

The outbreak of war in September 1939 did not have any immediate major effect on Tolkien's life; but during this time, to his inevitable sorrow, family life changed as the boys left home. John, the eldest, who had read English at his father's old college, Exeter, was training for the Catholic priesthood in Rome, and was later evacuated with his fellow-students to Lancashire. Michael spent a year at Trinity College and then became an anti-aircraft gunner. Christopher, recovered from his illness, returned to school for a brief period before following his brother to Trinity. Only Priscilla, the youngest of the family, was still living at home. There was some disruption of the regular pattern of life at Northmoor Road: domestic help became scarce, evacuees and lodgers were sometimes accommodated, hens were installed in the garden to increase the supply of eggs, and Tolkien took turns of duty as an air raid warden, sleeping in the damp little hut that served as the local headquarters. There were, however, no German air attacks on Oxford; nor was Tolkien required, as were a number of dons, to undertake work for the War Office or other government departments.

As the war progressed, the character of the University changed greatly, for large numbers of service cadets were drafted to Oxford for 'short courses' before they took up their duties as officers; Tolkien organised a syllabus for naval cadets in the English School, and modified many of his lectures to suit the less specialist audiences. But in general terms life was much as it had been before the war, and his distress at the continuation of hostilities was almost as much for ideological as for personal reasons. 'People in this land', he wrote in 1941, 'seem not even yet to realize that in the Germans we have enemies whose virtues (and they are virtues) of obedience and patriotism are greater than ours in the mass. I have in this War a burning private grudge against that ruddy little ignoramus Adolf Hitler for ruining, perverting, misapplying, and making for ever accursed, that noble northern spirit, a supreme contribution to Europe, which I have ever loved, and tried to present in its true light.'

Many years later, Tolkien recalled that the writing of *The Lord of the Rings* halted for almost a year late in 1940, when it had reached the point at which the Company discovers Balin's tomb in Moria. If this is true—and other evidence would seen to confirm that there was a hiatus at about this time—it was only the first of several major delays or hesitations in the writing, none of them ascribable to any specific external cause.

When work was resumed, Tolkien drew up outlines for the end of the story—which he did not imagine was more than a few chapters away—and began to sketch the episode where two of the hobbits encounter Treebeard, the being who was the ultimate expression of Tolkien's love and respect for trees. When eventually he came to write this chapter (so he told Nevil Coghill) he modelled Treebeard's way of speaking, '*Hrum, Hroom*', on the booming voice of C. S. Lewis.

Allen & Unwin had originally hoped that the new story would be ready for publication a mere couple of years after they had issued *The Hobbit*. That hope had faded, and in 1942 even the original *Hobbit* had to go out of print when the warehouse stock of copies was burnt in the London blitz. But Stanley Unwin continued to take an interest in the progress of the 'new Hobbit', and in December 1942 he received a letter from Tolkien which reported: 'It is now approaching completion. I hope to get a little free time this vacation, and might hope to finish it off early next year. It has reached Chapter XXXI and will require at least six more to finish (these are already sketched).'

Yet Chapter XXXI (the original number of 'Flotsam and Jetsam') was only at the end of what became Book III; and in the event there were to be not six but thirty-one more chapters before the book was complete. Tolkien tried to tackle the story in the months that followed, and he wrote a little more of it. But by the summer of 1943 he had to admit that he was 'dead stuck'.

One cause of the difficulty was his perfectionism. Not content with writing a large and complex book, he felt he must ensure that every single detail fitted satisfactorily into the total pattern. Geography, chronology, and nomenclature all had to be entirely consistent. He had been given some assistance with the geography, for his son Christopher helped him by drawing an elaborate map of the terrain covered by the story. Tolkien himself had been making rough sketch-maps since beginning work on the book; he once said: 'If you're going to have a complicated story you must work to a map; otherwise you'll never make a map of it afterwards.' But the map in itself was not enough, and he made endless calculations of time and distance, drawing up elaborate charts concerning events in the story, showing dates, the days of the week, the hours, and sometimes even the direction of the wind and the phase of the moon. This was partly his habitual insistence on perfection, partly sheer revelling in the fun of 'sub-creation', but most of all a concern to provide a totally convincing picture. Long afterwards he said: 'I wanted people simply to get inside this story and take it (in a sense) as actual history.'

Name-making also involved much of his attention, as was inevitable, for the invented languages from which the names were constructed were both the mainspring of his mythology and in themselves a central activity of his intellect. Once again, the elvish languages Quenya and Sindarin, now more sophisticated than they had been when he began *The Silmarillion* twenty-five years earlier, played a principal role in name-making, and were used in the composition of elvish poems and songs. The story also called for the invention of at least the rudiments of several other languages, and all this took time and energy. Moreover he had reached a point where the story divided into several independent and in themselves complicated chains of events, and while he believed that it would only take him two or three chapters to get Frodo and Sam Gamgee to Mordor he could not yet face unravelling the complexities of the simultaneous events in Gondor and Rohan. It had taken him nearly six years to bring the story this far; how could he ever find the time and energy to finish it, let alone to complete and revise *The Silmarillion*, which still clamoured for attention? He was fifty-one, tired, and fearful that in the end he would achieve nothing. He had already gained a reputation for almost indefinite procrastination in his philological work, and this sometimes amused him, though it was often saddening to him; but as to never finishing his mythology, that was a dreadful and numbing thought.

One day at about this time Lady Agnew, who lived opposite in Northmoor Road, told him that she was nervous about a large poplar tree in the road; she said that it cut off the sun from her garden, and she feared for her house if it fell in a gale. Tolkien thought that this was ridiculous. 'Any wind that could have uprooted it and hurled it on her house', he said, 'would have demolished her and her house without any assistance from the tree.' But the poplar had already been lopped and mutilated, and though he managed to save it now, Tolkien began to think about it. He was after all 'anxious about my own internal Tree', his mythology; and there seemed to be some analogy.

One morning he woke up with a short story in his head, and scribbled it down. It was the tale of a painter named Niggle, a man who, like Tolkien, 'niggled' over details: 'He used to spend a long time on a single leaf, trying to catch its shape, and its sheen, and the glistening of dewdrops on its edges. Yet he wanted to paint a huge tree. There was one picture in particular which bothered him. It had begun with a leaf caught in the wind, and it became a tree; and the tree grew, sending out innumerable branches, and thrusting out the most fantastic roots. Strange birds came and settled on the twigs and had to be attended to. Then all round the tree, and behind it, through the gaps in the leaves and boughs, a country began to open out.'

In the story, which he called *Leaf by Niggle*, Tolkien expressed his worst fears for his mythological Tree. Like Niggle he sensed that he would be snatched away from his work long before it was finished—if it could ever be finished in this world. For it is in another and brighter place that Niggle finds his Tree finished, and learns that it is indeed a real tree, a true part of creation.

The story was not published for many months, but the actual business of writing it helped to exorcise some of Tolkien's fear, and to get him to work again on *The Lord of the Rings*; though the immediate impulse came from C. S. Lewis.

By the beginning of 1944 *The Lord of the Rings* had lain untouched for many months, and Tolkien wrote: 'I do not seem to have any mental energy or invention.' But Lewis had noticed what had happened, and he urged Tolkien to get going again and finish the story. 'I needed some pressure,' said Tolkien, 'and shall probably respond.' At the beginning of April he resumed work, beginning to write what eventually became Book IV, which takes Frodo and Sam Gamgee across the marshes towards Mordor where they hope to destroy the Ring by hurling it into the Cracks of Doom.

Christopher Tolkien had now been called up into the R.A.F., and had been sent to South Africa to train as a pilot (much to the regret of his father, who believed that aerial warfare was both immoral and excessively dangerous). Tolkien was already writing long letters to Christopher, and now these letters carried a detailed account of progress on the book, and of reading it to the Lewis brothers and Charles Williams in the White Horse, a pub they favoured at the time. Here are a few extracts from the letters:

Wednesday 5 April 1944: 'I have seriously embarked on an effort to finish my book, and have been sitting up rather late: a lot of rereading and research required. And it is a painful tricky business getting into swing again. A few pages for a lot of sweat; but at the moment they are just meeting Gollum on a precipice.'

Saturday 8 April: 'Spent part of day (and night) struggling with chapter. Gollum is playing up well on his return. A beautiful night with high moon About 2 a.m. I was in the warm silver-lit garden, wishing we two could go for a walk. Then went to bed.'

Thursday 13 April: 'I miss you hourly, and am lonely without you. I have friends, of course, but can seldom see them. I did see C.S.L. and Charles Williams yesterday for almost two hours. I read my recent chapter; it receive approbation. I have begun another. Shall have spare copies typed, if possible, and sent out to you. Now I will return to Frodo and Gollum for a brief spell.'

Friday 14 April: 'I managed to get an hour or two's writing, and have brought Frodo nearly to the gates of Mordor. Afternoon lawnmowing. Term begins next week, and proofs of Wales papers have come. Still I am going to continue "Ring" in every salvable moment.'

Tuesday 18 April: 'I hope to see C.S.L. and Charles W. tomorrow morning and read my next chapter—on the passage of the Dead Marshes and the approach to the Gates of Mordor, which I have now practically finished. Term has almost begun: I tutored Miss Salu for an hour. The afternoon was squandered on plumbing (stopping overflow) and cleaning out fowls. They are laying generously (9 again yesterday). Leaves are out: the white-grey of the quince, the grey-green of young apples, the full green of hawthorn, the tassels of flower even on the sluggard poplars.'

Sunday 23 April: 'I read my second chapter, Passage of the Dead

Marshes, to Lewis and Williams on Wed. morning. It was approved. I have now nearly done a third: Gates of the Land of Shadow. But this story takes me in charge, and I have already taken three chapters over what was meant to be one! And I have neglected too many things to do it. I am just enmeshed in it now, and have to wrench my mind away to tackle exam-paper proofs, and lectures.'

Tuesday 25 April: 'Gave a poor lecture, saw the Lewises and C.W. (White Horse) for 1/2 hour; mowed three lawns, and wrote letter to John, and struggled with recalcitrant passage in "The Ring". At this point I require to know how much later the moon gets up each night when nearing full, and how to stew a rabbit!'

Thursday 4 May: 'A new character has come on the scene (I am sure I did not invent him, I did not even want him, though I like him, but there he came walking into the woods of Ithilien): Faramir, the brother of Boromir— and he is holding up the "catastrophe" by a lot of stuff about the history of Gondor and Rohan. If he goes on much more a lot of him will have to be removed to the appendices—where already some fascinating material on the hobbit Tobacco industry and the Languages of the West have gone.'

Sunday 14 May: 'I did a certain amount of writing yesterday, but was hindered by two things: the need to clear up the study (which had got into the chaos that always indicates literary or philological preoccupation) and attend to business; and trouble with the moon. By which I mean that I found my moons in the crucial days between Frodo's flight and the present situation (arrival at Minas Morgul) were doing impossible things, rising in one part of the country and setting simultaneously in another. Rewriting bits of back chapters took all afternoon!'

Sunday 21 May: 'I have taken advantage of a bitter cold grey week (in which the lawns have not grown in spite of a little rain) to write: but struck a sticky patch. All that I had sketched or written before proved of little use, as times, motives, etc., have all changed. However at last with v. great labour, and some neglect of other duties, I have now written or nearly written all the matter up to the capture of Frodo in the high pass on the very brink of Mordor. Now I must go back to the other folk and try to bring things to the final crash with some speed. Do you think *Shelob* is a good name for a monstrous spider creature? It is of course only "She + lob" (=spider), but written as one, it seems to be quite noisome.'

Wednesday 31 May: 'I have done no serious writing since Monday. Until midday today I was sweating at Section Papers: and took my MSS. to the Press at 2 p.m. today—the last possible day. Yesterday: lecture—puncture, after fetching fish, so I had to foot it to town and back, and as bike-repairs are impossible I had to squander afternoon in a grimy struggle, which ended at last in my getting tyre off, mending one puncture in inner tube, and gash in outer, and getting thing on again. Io! triumphum!

'The Inklings meeting [held the previous Thursday night] was very enjoyable. Hugo was there: rather tired-looking, but reasonably noisy. The chief entertainment was provided by a chapter of Warnie Lewis's book on the times of Louis XIV (very good I thought it); and some excerpts from C.S.L.'s "Who Goes Home"—a book on Hell, which I suggested should have been called rather "Hugo's Home". I did not get back till after midnight. The rest of my time, barring chores in and out door, has been occupied by the desperate attempt to bring "The Ring" to a suitable pause, the capture of Frodo by Orcs in the passes of Mordor, before I am obliged to break off by examining. By sitting up all hours, I managed it: and read the last 2 chapters ('Shelob's Lair' and 'The Choices of Master Samwise') to C.S.L. on Monday morning. He approved with unusual fervour, and was actually affected to tears by the last chapter, so it seems to be keeping up.'

Book IV of *The Lord of the Rings* was typed and sent out to Christopher in South Africa. By this time Tolkien was mentally exhausted by his feverish burst of writing. 'When my weariness has passed,' he told Christopher, 'I shall get on with my story.' But for the time being he achieved nothing. 'I am absolutely dry of any inspiration for the Ring,' he wrote in August, and by the end of the year he had done nothing new except draft a synopsis for the remainder of the story. He meditated rewriting and completing 'The Lost Road', the unfinished story of time-travel that he had begun many years before, and he discussed with Lewis the idea of their collaborating on a book about the nature, function, and origin of Language. But nothing was done about either of these projects, and Lewis, referring some time later to the non-appearance of the book on Language, describe Tolkien as 'that great but dilatory and unmethodical man'. 'Dilatory' was not altogether fair, but 'unmethodical' was often true.

Tolkien made little if any progress on *The Lord of the Rings* during 1945. On 9 May the war in Europe came to an end. The next day Charles Williams was taken ill. He underwent an operation at an Oxford hospital, but died on 15 May. Even if Williams and Tolkien had not inhabited the same plane of thought, the two men had been good friends, and the loss of Williams was a bitter thing, a symbol that peace would not bring an end to all troubles—something that Tolkien knew only too well. During the war he had said to Christopher: 'We are attempting to conquer Sauron with the Ring', and now he wrote: 'The War is not over (and the one that is, or the part of it, has largely been lost). But it is of course wrong to fall into such a mood, for Wars are always lost, and The War always goes on; and it is no good growing faint.'

In the autumn of 1945 he became Merton Professor of English
Language and Literature, and hence a Fellow of Merton College, an insti-
tution that he found 'agreeably informal' after Pembroke. A few months
later the retirement of David Nichol Smith raised the question of whom to
appoint to the Merton Professorship of English Literature. Tolkien was
one of the electors, and he wrote: 'It ought to be C. S. Lewis, or perhaps
Lord David Cecil, but one never knows.' And in the event both these men
were passed over, and the chair was offered to and accepted by F. P. Wilson.
Though there is no reason to suppose that Tolkien did not support Lewis
in the election, the gap between the two friends widened a little after this;
or to be more accurate there was a gradual cooling on Tolkien's part. It is
impossible to say precisely why. Lewis himself probably did not notice it at
first, and when he did he was disturbed and saddened by it. Tolkien
continued to attend gatherings of the Inklings, as did his son Christopher
(who after the war resumed his undergraduate studies at Trinity college);
Christopher was first invited to the Inklings to read aloud from *The Lord of
the Rings*, as Lewis alleged he read better than his father, and later he
became an Inkling in his own right. But though Tolkien could regularly be
seen in the 'Bird and Baby' on Tuesday mornings and at Magdalen on
Thursday nights, there was not the same intimacy as of old between him
and Lewis.

In part the friendship's decay may have been hastened by Lewis's
sometimes stringent criticisms of details in *The Lord of the Rings*, particularly his comments on the poems, which (with the notable exception of the
alliterative verses) he tended to dislike. Tolkien was often hurt by Lewis's
comments, and he generally ignored them, so that Lewis later remarked of
him: 'No one ever influenced Tolkien—you might as well try to influence
a bander-snatch.' In part the increasing coolness on Tolkien's side was
probably also due to his dislike of Lewis's 'Narnia' stories for children. In
1949 Lewis began to read the first of them, *The Lion, the Witch and the
Wardrobe*, aloud to Tolkien. It was received with a snort of contempt. 'It
really won't do!' Tolkien told Roger Lancelyn Green. 'I mean to say:
"Nymphs and their Ways, The Love-Life of a Faun"!' Nevertheless Lewis
completed it, and when it and its successors were published in their turn,
'Narnia' found as wide and enthusiastic an audience as that which had
enjoyed *The Hobbit*. Yet Tolkien could not find it in his heart to reverse his
original judgement. 'It is sad', he wrote in 1964, 'that "Narnia" and all that
part of C.S.L.'s work should remain outside the range of my sympathy, as
much of my work was outside his.' Undoubtedly he felt that Lewis had in
some ways drawn on Tolkien ideas and stories in the books; and just as he
resented Lewis's progress from convert to popular theologian he was

perhaps irritated by the fact that the friend and critic who had listened to the tales of Middle-earth had as it were got up from his armchair, gone to the desk, picked up a pen, and 'had a go' himself. Moreover the sheer number of Lewis's books for children and the almost indecent haste with which they were produced undoubtedly annoyed him. The seven 'Narnia' stories were written and published in a mere seven years, less than half the period in which *The Lord of the Rings* gestated. It was another wedge between the two friends, and after 1954 when Lewis was elected to a new chair of Medieval and Renaissance Literature at Cambridge, and was obliged to spend much of his time away from Oxford, he and Tolkien only met on comparatively rare occasions.

With the end of the war *The Hobbit* was reprinted, and arrangements were made to publish *Farmer Giles of Ham*. In the summer of 1946 Tolkien told Allen & Unwin that he had made a very great effort to finish *The Lord of the Rings*, but had failed; the truth was that he had scarcely touched it since the late spring of 1944. He declared: 'I really do hope to have it done before the autumn,' and he did manage to resume work on it in the following weeks. By the end of the year he told his publishers that he was 'on the last chapters'. But then he moved house.

The house in Northmoor Road was too big for the family such as it now was, and was too expensive to maintain. So Tolkien put his name down for a Merton College house, and when one became available in Manor Road near the centre of Oxford he made arrangements to rent it. He, Edith, Christopher, and Priscilla moved in during March 1947; John was by now working as a priest in the Midlands, and Michael, married with an infant son, was a schoolmaster.

Almost immediately Tolkien realised that the new home was unbearably cramped. 3 Manor Road was an ugly brick house, and it was very small. He had no proper study, merely a 'bed-sitter' in the attic. It was agreed that as soon as Merton could provide a better house, the family would move again. But for the time being it would have to do.

Rayner Unwin, the son of Tolkien's publisher, who as a child had written the report that secured the publication of *The Hobbit*, was now an undergraduate at Oxford, and had made the acquaintance of Tolkien. In the summer of 1947 Tolkien decided that *The Lord of the Rings* was sufficiently near completion for him to be shown a typescript of the greater part of the story. After reading it, Rayner reported to his father at Allen & Unwin that it was 'a weird book' but nevertheless 'a brilliant and gripping story'. He remarked that the struggle between darkness and light made him suspect allegory, and commented: 'Quite honestly I don't know who is expected to read it: children will miss something of it, but if grown ups will not feel infra dig to read it many will undoubtedly enjoy themselves.' He had no doubt at all that the book deserved publication by his father's firm, and he suggested that it would have to be divided into sections, commenting that in this respect Frodo's ring resembled that of the Nibelungs.

Stanley Unwin passed these comments to Tolkien. The comparison of his Ring with the *Nibelungenlied* and Wagner always annoyed Tolkien; he once said: 'Both rings were round, and there the resemblance ceased.' Nor, of course, was he pleased by the suggestion of allegory; he replied : 'Do not let Rayner suspect "Allegory". There is a "moral", I suppose, in any tale worth telling. But that is not the same thing. Even the struggle between darkness and light (as he calls it, not me) is for me just a particular phase of history, one example of its pattern, perhaps, but not The Pattern; and the actors are individuals—they each, of course, contain universals, or they would not live at all, but they never represent them as such.' However he was on the whole very pleased by Rayner's enthusiasm for the book, and he concluded by saying: 'The thing is to finish the thing as devised, and then let it be judged.'

Yet even now he did not finish. He revised, niggled, and corrected earlier chapters, spending so much time at it that his colleagues came to regard him as lost to philology. But the final full stop was something he could not yet achieve.

During the summer of 1947 he drafted a revision to *The Hobbit* which would provide a more satisfactory explanation of Gollum's attitude to the Ring; or rather, an explanation that fitted better with the sequel. When this was written he sent it to Stanley Unwin asking for an opinion on it. Unwin mistakenly assumed that it was intended for inclusion in the next reprint of *The Hobbit* without any further discussion on the matter, and he passed it directly to his production department. Many months later, Tolkien was astonished to see the revised chapter in print when the page-proofs of the new impression were sent to him.

In the following months *The Lord of the Rings* at last reached its conclusion. Tolkien recalled that he 'actually wept' when writing the account of the heroes' welcome that is given to the hobbits on the Field of Cormallen. Long ago he had resolved to take the chief protagonists across the sea towards the West at the end of the book, and with the writing of the chapter that describes the setting sail from the Grey Havens the huge manuscript was nearly complete. Nearly, but not quite. 'I like tying up loose ends,' Tolkien once said, and he wished to make sure that there were no loose ends in his great story. So he wrote an Epilogue in which Sam Gamgee told his children what happened to each of the principal characters who did not sail West. It ended with Sam listening to 'the sigh and murmur of the Sea upon the shores of Middle-earth'.

And that *was* the end; but now Tolkien had to revise, again and again, until he was completely satisfied with the entire text, and this took many months. He once said of the book: 'I don't suppose there are many sentences that have not been niggled over.' Then he typed out a fair copy, balancing his typewriter on his attic bed because there was no room on his desk, and using two fingers because he had never learned to type with ten. Not until the autumn of 1949 was it all finished.

Tolkien lent the completed typescript to C. S. Lewis, who replied after reading it:

> My dear Tollers,
>
> *Uton herian holbytlas* indeed. I have drained the rich cup and satisfied a long thirst. Once it really gets under weigh the steady upward slope of grandeur and terror (not unrelieved by green dells, without which it would indeed be intolerable) is almost unequalled in the whole range of narrative art known to me. In two virtues I think it excels: sheer sub-creation—Bombadil, Barrow Wights, Elvers, Ents—as if from inexhaustible resources, and construction. Also in *gravitas*. No romance can repel the charge of 'escapism' with such confidence. If it errs, it errs in precisely the opposite direction: all victories of hope deferred and the merciless piling up of odds against the heroes are near to being too painful. And the long *coda* after the eucatastrophe, whether you intended it or no, has the effect of reminding us that victory is as transitory as conflict, that (as Byron says) 'there's no sterner moralist than pleasure', and so leaving a final impression of profound melancholy.
>
> Of course this is not the whole story. There are many passages I could wish you had written otherwise or omitted altogether. If I include none of my adverse criticisms in this letter that is because you have heard and rejected most of them already (*rejected* is perhaps too mild a word for your reaction on at least one occasion!). And even if all my objections were just (which is of course unlikely) the faults I think I find could only delay and impair appreciation: the substantial splendour of the

tale can carry them all. *Ubi plura nitent in carmine non ego paucis offendi maculis.*

I congratulate you. All the long years you have spent on it are justified.

Yours,
Jack Lewis

Tolkien himself did not think it was flawless. But he told Stanley Unwin: 'It is written in my life-blood, such as that is, thick or thin; and I can no other.'

JANE CHANCE NITZSCHE

The Lord of the Rings: *Tolkien's Epic*

The epic form has proved useful in reflecting the clash of value systems during periods of transition in literary history. In the Old English *Beowulf* Germanic heroism conflicts with Christianity: the chivalric pride of the hero can become the excessive *superbia* condemned in Hrothgar's moralistic sermon. Similar conflicts occur in other epic or romance-epics: between the chivalric and the Christian in the twelfth-century German *Nibelungenlied* and in Sir Thomas Malory's fifteenth-century *Morte d'Arthure*, between the classical and the Christian in the sixteenth-century *Faerie Queene* of Sir Edmund Spenser, and between chivalric idealism and modern realism in the late sixteenth-century Spanish epic-novel of Cervantes, *Don Quixote*. Tolkien's *Lord of the Rings* delineates a clash of values during the passage from the Third Age of Middle-earth dominated by the elves to the Fourth Age dominated by man. Such values mask very medieval notions of Germanic heroism and Christianity evidenced earlier by Tolkien in his *Beowulf* article.

In this sense *The Lord of the Rings* resembles *The Hobbit* which, as we have seen previously, must acknowledge a great thematic and narrative debt to the Old English epic, even though *The Hobbit*'s happy ending renders it closer to fantasy in Tolkien's definition than to the elegy with its tragic ending. The difference between them stems from form: the children's story narrated by the arrogant adult in *The Hobbit* has 'grown up' sufficiently to

From *Tolkien's Art: A 'Mythology for England'* by Jane Chance Nitzsche. © 1979 by Jane Chance Nitzsche.

require no fictionalised narrator in the text itself and a more expansive and flexible genre like the epic. Indeed, Randel Helms notes that

> we have in *The Hobbit* and its sequel what is in fact the same story, told first very simply, and then again, very intricately. Both works have the same theme, a quest on which a most unheroic hobbit achieves heroic stature; they have the same structure, the 'there and back again' of the quest romance, and both extend the quest through the cycle of one year, *The Hobbit* from spring to spring, the *Rings* from fall to fall.

Although Helms does not mention their relationship with medieval ideas or even with the *Beowulf* article, still, given this reworking of a theme used earlier in *The Hobbit*, *The Lord of the Rings* must also duplicate any medieval ideas from *The Hobbit* and elsewhere in Tolkien.

As an epic novel it constitutes then a *summa* of Tolkien's art—a full development of themes originally enunciated in the *Beowulf* article and fictionalised later in other works. It was, after all, begun in 1937—the same year *The Hobbit* was published and a year later than the *Beowulf* article—and completed in 1949, prior to the publication of many of the fairy-stories (1945–67) and the medieval parodies (1945–62). Its medial position in Tolkien's career indicates how its author might have articulated his major ideas generally and comprehensively in this mammoth work before delving into their more specialised aspects in the later fairy-stories and parodies.

As a synthesis then of Tolkienian ideas, both Germanic heroic or medieval and Christian, it reconciles value systems over which its critics have debated incessantly and singlemindedly. Some have explored its major medieval literary sources, influences, and parallels; others have explored its direct and indirect religious, moral, or Christian aspects. No one seems to have understood fully how the dual levels of the *Beowulf* article might apply to *The Lord of the Rings*, although Patricia Meyer Spacks suggests provocatively that at least one level does apply: Tolkien's view of the 'naked will and courage' of man necessary to combat chaos and death in the context of northern mythology (as opposed to Christianity) resembles the similar epic weapons of the hobbit-heroes of his trilogy. In addition no critic has seemed to notice that even in genre and form this work combines an explicitly medieval bias (as epic, romance, or *chanson de geste*) with an implicitly Christian one (as fantasy or fairy-story).

Its title, 'Lord of the Rings', introduces the ambiguity of being a lord, a person with power over but also responsibility for others. Elsewhere in Tolkien's critical and creative works the lord has been depicted as an excessively proud Germanic earl bent on the sacrifice of his men for his own ends or as a humble Elf-king modelled on Christ, intent on sacrificing himself for the sake of his followers. So in this epic Sauron typifies the Germanic earl in his monstrous use of his slaves as Gandalf typifies the Elf-king or Christ-figure in his self-sacrifice during the battle with the Balrog. But there are hierarchies of both monstrous and heroic lords in this epic, whose plenitude has frustrated critical attempts to discern *the* hero as either Aragorn, Frodo, or Sam. Aragorn may represent the Christian hero as Frodo and Sam represent the more Germanic hero of the subordinate warrior, yet all three remain epic heroes. The complexity of Tolkien's system of heroic and monstrous 'lords' in the trilogy becomes clearer through an examination of its structural unity.

In defining the parameters of the work's structure, Tolkien declares that 'The only units of any structural significance are the books. These originally had each its title.' Apparently he substituted titles for each of the three parts at the instigation of his publisher, although he preferred to regard it as a 'three-decker novel' instead of as a 'trilogy' in order to establish it as a single, unified work, not three separate works. Thus each of the three parts thematically and symbolically supports the crowning title, 'The Lord of the Rings', by revealing some aspect of the adversary or the hero through a related but subordinate title, and each part is itself supported thematically and symbolically by its two-book division. In *The Fellowship of the Ring* the focus falls upon the lord as both a hero and a monster, a divided self. Frodo as the 'lord' or keeper of the Ring in the first part mistakes the chief threat to the hobbit fellowship (a symbol of community) as physical and external (for example, the Black Riders) but matures enough to learn by the end of the second book that the chief threat exists in a more dangerous spiritual and internal form, whether within him as microcosm (the hero as monster) or within the Fellowship as macrocosm (his friend Boromir). *The Fellowship* as *Bildungsroman* echoes the development of the hero Bilbo in *The Hobbit*. *The Two Towers* shifts attention from the divided self of the hero as monster to the more specifically Germanic but also Christian monster seen in Saruman (representing intellectual sin in Book Three) and Shelob (representing physical sin in Book Four) who occupy or guard the two towers of the title. The evil Germanic lord often has a good warrior to serve him; the figure of the good servant merges with the Christian king as healer (Aragorn) who dominates *The Return of the King* on opposition to the Germanic destroyer (Denethor) in book Five, the consequences of whose reign lead to a 'Return' or regeneration in the macrocosm in Book Six. Ideas in this last part mirror Chapter Three's 'Christian King' appearing in fairy-stories and Chapter Four's 'Germanic

King' appearing in medieval parodies. The structure of the epic then reveals a hierarchy of heroes and monsters implied by its title but also summoned from Tolkien's other critical and creative works.

I *The Fellowship of the Ring*: the Hero as Monster

Because it links the wandering Fellowship with the Ring, a subtitle for the first part of the epic might be 'All that is gold does not glitter, / Not all those who wander are lost.' The Ring appears valuable because it glitters; the wandering Fellowship appears lost. But in reality the gold ring may not be as simply valuable as it appears, and the Fellowship may not be lost; further, the person to whom the lines refer, despite his swart exterior and wandering behaviour as Strider the Ranger, may be real gold and definitely not lost. As the king of light opposed to the Dark Lord, he will return as king after the Ring has been finally returned to Mount Doom, ending the aspirations of the Lord of the Rings. 'The Fellowship of the Ring' as a title stresses the heroic mission of his 'followers' to advance the cause of the good king. The band of gold represents by synecdoche the power of the evil Lord of the Rings to be countered by the 'band' of the Fellowship, whether the four hobbits in Book One or the larger Fellowship of hobbits, wizard, elf, dwarf, and man in Book Two. Thematically, then, the title and its 'subtitle' suggest that appearance does not equal reality. Because the Fellowship is burdened with the responsibility of bearing the Ring and because its presence attracts evil, the greatest threat to the Fellowship and its mission comes not from without but within. The hero must realise that he can become a monster.

The two books of the *Fellowship* trace the process of this realisation: the first book centres on the presentation of evil as external and physical, requiring physical heroism to combat it, and the second book centres on the presentation of evil as internal and spiritual, requiring a spiritual heroism to combat it. The hero matures by coming to understand the character of good and evil—specifically, by descending into an underworld and then ascending into an overworld, a natural one in the first book and a supernatural one in the second. The second book then functions as a mirror image of the first. These two levels correspond to the two levels—Germanic and Christian—of *Beowulf* and *The Hobbit*. For Frodo, as for Beowulf and Bilbo, the ultimate enemy is himself.

Tolkien immediately defines 'the hero as monster' by introducing the divided self of Gollum-Sméagol and then, to ensure the reader's understanding of the hero as monster, Bilbo-as-Gollum. The Cain-like Sméagol rationalises the murder of his cousin Déagol for the gold ring he holds because it is his birthday. He deserves a gift, something 'precious' like the Ring, because the occasion celebrates the fact of his birth, his special being.

The parable of Sméagol's fall illustrates the nature of evil as *cupiditas* or avarice in the classical and literal sense. But as the root of all evil (in the words of Chaucer's Pardoner) *cupiditas*, more generally and medievally represents that Augustinian selfishness usually personified as strong desire in the figure of Cupid. The two names of Gollum-Sméagol dramatise the fragmenting and divisive consequences of his fall into vice, the 'Gollum' the bestial sound of his swallowing as an expression of his gluttony and greed, the 'Sméagol' in its homorymic similarity to Déagol as a sound relating him to a group of others like him to establish his common hobbitness. For later his resemblance to the hobbits is revealed when good overpowers the evil in him and, as he witnesses his master Frodo asleep in Sam's lap, reaches out a hand to touch his knee in a caress. At that moment he seems 'an old weary hobbit, shrunken by the years that had carried him far beyond his time, beyond friends and kin, and the fields and streams of youth, an old starved pitiable thing.' But also Tolkien takes care to present the good hobbit and heroic Bilbo as a divided self, 'stretched thin' into a Gollum-like being because of his years carrying the Ring. The scene opens after all with Bilbo's birthday party, to re-enact the original fall of Gollum. The role of Déagol is played by Bilbo's nephew Frodo: on Bilbo's birthday, instead of receiving a gift, Bilbo, like Gollum, must give away a gift—to the other hobbit relatives and friends, and to Frodo, recipient of the Ring. But at the moment of bequest Bilbo retreats into a Gollum-like personality illustrated by similar speech patterns: 'It is mine, I tell you. My own. My precious. Yes, my precious.' Bilbo refuses to give away the Ring because he feels himself to be more deserving and Frodo less deserving of carrying it. Later the feeling is described as a realisation of the Other as monstrous (presumably with the concomitant belief in the self as good). In the parallel scene at the beginning of Book Two, Bilbo wishes to see the Ring so he reaches out a hand for Frodo to give it to him; Frodo reacts violently because 'a shadow seemed to have fallen between them, and through it he found himself eyeing a *little wrinkled creature with a hungry face and bony groping hands*. He felt a desire to strike him' (my italics). The Ring then appropriately symbolises that wedding of self to self, of Gollum to Sméagol, in lieu of a wedding of self to Other.

The wedding of self to Other, as an expression of *caritas* hinted at in Gollums' momentary return to hobbitness when he almost loves his master Frodo, is symbolised by the 'band' of the Fellowship to which each member belongs. Such *caritas* opposes the view of the Other as monstrous. Even Frodo at first sees monstrous Gollum as despicable: 'What a pity that Bilbo did not stab that vile creature, when he had a chance!' But just as the hero can become monstrous so can the monster become heroic: it is Gollum who helps Frodo and Sam across the Dead Marshes and, more important, who inadvertently saves Frodo from himself and also saves Middle-earth by biting

the Ring off Frodo's finger as they stand on the precipice of Mount Doom in
the third part. So Gandalf cautions him to feel, not wrath or hatred, but love
as pity: 'Pity? It was Pity that stayed his hand. Pity, and Mercy: not to strike
without need.' Gandalf explains:

> Many that live deserve death. And some that die deserve life.
> Can you give it to them? Then do not be too eager to deal out
> death in judgment. For even the very wise cannot see all ends.
> I have not much hope that Gollum can be cured before he dies,
> but there is a chance of it. And he is bound up with the fate of
> the Ring. My heart tells me that he has some part to play yet,
> for good or ill, before the end; and when the act comes, the pity
> of Bilbo may rule the fate of many—yours not least.

This pity as charity or love binding one man to another cements together
the 'fellowship' of the hobbits and later the differing species; the 'chain' of
love it creates contrasts with the chains of enslavement represented by
Sauron's one Ring. Called a 'fair chain of love' in the Middle Ages, it
supposedly bound one individual to another and as well bound together the
macrocosm of the heavens: Boethius in *The Consolation of Philosophy* terms
it a 'common bond of love by which all things seek to be held to the goal
of good'. After describing the love that 'binds together people joined by a
sacred bond; love binds sacred marriages by chaste affections; love makes
the laws which join true friends', Boethius wistfully declares, 'O how happy
the human race would be, if that love which rules the heavens ruled also
your souls!' The chain of enslavement, in contrast, involves a hierarchy of
power, beginning with the

> One Ring to rule them all, One Ring to find them,
> One Ring to bring them all and in the darkness bind them

and encompassing the seven dwarf-rings (could they be found) and the nine
rings of the 'Mortal Men doomed to die', the Ringwraiths. If love binds
together the heavens and the hierarchy of species known as the Great Chain
of Being in the Middle Ages, which included angels, man, beasts, birds, fish,
plants, and stones, then hate and envy, pride and avarice bind together the
hierarchy of species under the aegis of the One Ring of Sauron the fallen
Vala. Only the 'Three Rings for the Elven-kings under the sky'—the loftiest
and most noble species—were never made by Sauron because, says Elrond,
the elves 'did not desire strength or domination or hoarded wealth, but
understanding, making, and healing, to preserve all things unstained.'
Tolkien intentionally contrasts the hierarchy of good characters linked by the

symbolic value of fellowship into an invisible band or chain of love with the hierarchy of evil characters and fallen characters linked by the literal rings of enslavement—a chain of sin. It is for this reason that the miniature Fellowship of hobbits in the first book draws together in love different representatives from hobbit 'species' or families—Baggins, Took, Brandybuck, Gamgee—as the larger Fellowship in the second book draws together representatives from different species—the four hobbit representatives, Gimli the dwarf, Strider and Boromir the men, Legolas the elf, and Gandalf the Wizard. In both cases, however, these representatives are all young—the heirs of the equivalents of the 'old men' who must revitalise and renew Middle-earth because it too has become 'old' and decrepit, governed by the spiritually old and corrupt influence of Sauron. Symbolically, then, these 'heirs' as young men represent vitality, life, newness: Frodo is Bilbo's nephew and heir, Gimli is Gloin's, Legolas is Thranduil's, Strider is Isildur's, Boromir is Denethor's, and the remaining hobbits are the still youthful children of their aged fathers. Only Gandalf as the good counterpart to Sauron is 'old'. In part he constitutes a spiritual guide for Frodo, especially in Book Two, as Aragorn-Strider constitutes a physical one in Book One.

The necessity for the young figure to become the saviour hero (like the *novus homo*) of the old is introduced by Tolkien in the first pages of *The Fellowship*. Note the spiritual oldness of the hobbit 'fathers' of the miniature Fellowship who view the different or queer as alien, evil, monstrous, dangerous: they lack charity, pity, understanding. They condemn the Brandybucks of Buckland as a 'queer breed' for engaging in unnatural (for hobbits at least) activities on water. Yet these old hobbits are not evil, merely 'old'. Even the Gaffer vindicates Bag End and its 'queer folk' by admitting: 'There's some not far away that wouldn't offer a pint of beer to a friend, if they lived in a hole with golden walls. But they do things proper at Bag End.' His oldness is characteristic of the Old Law of Justice ('proper') rather than the New Law of Mercy. The also lack imagination, an awareness of the spirit rather than the letter. Sam's father expresses a literalism and earthiness similar to Sauron's: *'Elves and Dragons! I says to him. Cabbages and potatoes are better for me and you.'* This 'Old Man' Tolkien casts in the role as the Old Adam for whom Christ as the New Adam will function as a replacement and redeemer: a gardener like Adam at Bag End, he condemns that of which he cannot conceive for that of which he can, cabbages and potatoes, and presents his condemnation in the appropriately-named inn of the 'Ivy Bush'. His son Sam in effect will become the New Adam of the Shire by the trilogy's end. Generally, however, earth-bound hobbits (inhabiting holes under ground) display a similar lack of imagination symbolised by their delight in the pyrotechnic dragon created by Gandalf—they may not be able to imagine elves and dragons but they love what they can *see*, a 'terribly life-like' dragon leaving nothing to the imagination. This dragon, however, poses no threat to their lives—in fact, it represents the 'signal for supper'.

The 'new man' represented by the hobbits Frodo, Sam, Merry, and Pippin then must overcome a natural inclination toward 'oldness', toward the life of the senses inherent in the hobbit love of food, comfort, warm shelter, entertainment, good tobacco. All of them do so by the trilogy's end, but only Frodo as Ring-bearer actually changes dramatically and centrally by the end of *The Fellowship*. His education, both verbal and experiential, begins with the gift of the Ring after Bilbo's Birthday Party.

Designated as Bilbo's heir and recipient of the Ring in the Birthday Party in the first book he is also designated as the official Ring-bearer after the Council of Elrond in the second book, to which it is parallel. In the first book Gandalf relates the history of Gollum's discovery of the ring and Bilbo's winning of it, and he explains its nature and properties; in the second book at this similar gathering the history of the Ring from its creation by Sauron to the present and the roles therein of various species is related. The birthday party that allows Bilbo to 'disappear' as if by magic from the Shire is like the Council that allows Frodo and other members of the Fellowship to 'disappear' as if by magic from Middle-earth—and the searching Eye of Sauron, for he will never imagine them carrying the Ring *back* to Mordor. Further, the distribution of gifts to friends and relatives after the party resembles the Council's decision to give back the 'gift' of the Ring to its 'relative', the mother lode of Mount Doom. The gifts in each episode make explicit the flaws of the recipient: Adelard Took for example, receives an umbrella because he has stolen so many from Bilbo. In a sense Sauron too will indirectly receive exactly what he has always wanted and has continually tried to usurp or steal—the Ring. The point of these parallels should be clear: the concept of the divided self or the hero as monster was revealed in the symbolic Birthday Party through the figures of Gollum-Sméagol, Bilbo-Gollum, Frodo-Gollum—the hero as monster suggested by the notion of the 'birthday'. For the reader, Tolkien warns that the most dangerous evil really springs from inside, not from outside. This message introduced at the beginning of the volume is what Frodo must learn by its end. The 'Council of Elrond', its very title suggesting egalitarian debate among members of a community rather than group celebration of an individual, symbolically poses the converse message that the most beneficial good similarly springs from the inside but must be directed toward the community rather than oneself. The humblest member of the Council—the insignificant hobbit Frodo—is ultimately chosen to pursue the mission of the Ring because he *is* insignificant. His insignificance in the community there contrasts with Bilbo's significance as a member of the Shire community. However, as 'The Birthday Party' indicated the presence of evil among relatives (the greedy and self-aggrandising Sackville-Bagginses) so The 'Council of Elrond' indicates the potential of evil threatening the Fellowship from within through the greed and self-aggrandisement of some of its members—men.

In the first book Frodo comes to understand evil as external and physical through the descent into the Old Forest, a parallel underworld to the supernatural underworld of Moria in the second book. Old Man Willow and the barrow-wights both represent the natural process of death caused, in Christian terms, by the Fall of man. Originally the Old Forest consisted of the 'fathers of the fathers of trees' whose 'countless years had filled them with pride and rooted wisdom, and with malice', as if they had sprung from the one Tree of Knowledge of Good and Evil in Eden. The ensuing history of human civilisation after the Fall of Adam and Eve resulted in similar falls and deaths: 'There was victory and defeat; and towers fell, fortresses were burned, and flames went up into the sky. Gold was piled on the biers of dead kings and queens; and mounds covered them and the stone doors were shut; and the grass grew over all.' As Old Man Willow and his malice represents the living embodiment of the parent Tree of Death, so the barrow-wights represent the ghostly embodiment of the dead parent civilisations of men: 'Barrow-wights walked in the hollow places with a clink of rings on cold fingers, and gold chains in the wind'. The hobbits' first clue to the character of the *Old* Forest (note again Tolkien's emphasis on oldness) resides in the falling of the hobbits' spirits—a 'dying' of merriment—when they first enter. Their fear, depression, and gloom are followed by the deathlike sleep (again, a result of the Fall) as the chief weapon of Old Man Willow. All growth in Nature is abetted by sleep and ends in death, usually after oldness (again, the Old Man Willow figure). The barrow-wights who attack the hobbits later in the Old Forest are also linked to the earth like the roots of Old Man Willow but here through the barrow, a man-made grave which they inhabit as ghosts. The song of the barrow-wights invokes coldness and death, and specifically the 'bed' of the human grave:

> Cold be hand and heart and bone,
> and cold be sleep under stone:
> never more to wake on stony bed,
> never, till the Sun fails and the Moon is dead.
> In the black wind the stars shall die,
> and still on gold here let them lie.

The attacks of the Old Man Willow and the Barrow-wights on the hobbits are stopped by Tom Bombadil who, along with his mate Goldberry, personify their complementary and positive counterparts in Nature. The principle of growth and revivification of all living things balances the process of mutability and death: what Goldberry lauds as 'spring-time and summer-time, and spring again after!', omitting autumn and winter as antithetical seasons. Tom Bombadil as master of trees, grasses, and the living things of the land complements the 'fair river-daughter' dressed in a gown 'green as young reeds, shot with silver like beads of dew', her feet surrounded by water-lilies. Because their role in Nature involves the maintenance of the existing order, their songs often praise the Middle-earth equivalent of the medieval Chain of Being:

> Let us sing together
> Of sun, stars, moon and mist, rain and cloudy weather,
> Light on the budding leaf, dew on the feather,
> Wind on the open hill, bells on the heather,
> Reeds by the shady pool, lilies on the water:
> Old Tom Bombadil and the River-daughter!

As the Old Forest depresses the hobbits, Tom Bomdadil cheers them up so much that, by the time they reach his house, 'half their weariness and all their fears had fallen from them'. It is no accident that Tom Bombadil always seems to be laughing and singing joyously.

Frodo learns from the descent into this underworld of the Old Forest that the presence of mutability, change, and death in the world is natural and continually repaired by growth and new life. In the second book he learns through a parallel descent into the Mines of Moria that the spiritual form of death represented by sin stems from within the individual but is redeemed by the 'new life' of wisdom and virtue counselled by Galadriel, the supernatural equivalent of Tom Bombadil who resides in the paradisal Lothlórien. The descent also involves a return to the tragic past of the dwarves, who fell because of the 'oldness' of their kings, their avarice; the ascent involves an encounter with the eternal present of Lothlórien, where all remains new and young, and filled with the healing spirit of elven mercy and *caritas*.

The dwarves led by both Durin and later Balin fell because of their greed for the jewels mined in Moria—its depths a metaphorical equivalent of Old Man Willow's buried roots and the deep barrows inhabited by the wights. But unlike the death pervading the Old Forest, the death represented by the Mines is voluntary, because spiritual: it exists in the form of avarice. Gandalf declares that 'even as *mithril* was the foundation of their wealth, so also it was their destruction: they delved too greedily and too deep, and disturbed that from which they fled, Durin's Bane.' Durin's Bane, the Balrog, monstrously projects their internal vice, which resurfaces later to down other dwarves including Balin. It is no accident that he dies at Mirrormere, a very dark mirror in which he is blind to himself. His mistaken goal of *mithril* and jewels contrasts with that of the elves of Lórien, whose Galadriel possesses a clear mirror of wisdom.

Lórien of the Blossom boasts an Eternal Spring where 'ever bloom the winter flowers in the unfading grass', a 'vanished world' where the shapes and colours are pristine and new, for 'No blemish or sickness or deformity could be seen in anything that grew upon the earth. On the land of Lórien there was not stain'. In this paradise of restoration, like that of Niggle in 'Leaf by Niggle', time almost ceases to pass and seems even to reverse so that 'the grim years were removed from the face of Aragorn, and he seemed clothed in white, a young lord tall and fair.' Evil does not exist in this land or in Galadriel unless brought in from the outside. The physical and spiritual regeneration or 'life' characteristic of these elves is embodied in their lembas, a food that restores spirits and lasts exceedingly long—a type of communion offered to the weary travellers. Other gifts of the Lady Galadriel—the rope, magic cloaks, golden hairs, phial of light, seeds of elanor—later aid them either physically or spiritually at times of crisis in their quest almost as Christian grace in material form. Like Adam and Eve forced to leave Paradise for the wilderness, although taking with them its memory as a 'paradise within, happier far'. in Miltonic terms, the travellers leave Lórien knowing 'the danger of light and joy'. Legolas reminds Gimli the dwarf that 'the least reward that you shall have is that the memory of Lothlórien shall remain ever clear and unstained in your heart, and shall neither fade nor grow stale'. Gimli's dwarfish and earth-bound nature compels him to deny the therapeutic value of memory: 'Memory is not what the heart desires. That is only a mirror, be it clear as Kheled-zâram'. The mirror to which he refers in Westron is called 'Mirrormere' and, instead of reflecting back the faces of gazers, portrays only the reflection of a crown of stars representing Durin's own desire. In contrast is the Mirror of Galadriel with its vision of the Eternal Present connoting supernatural wisdom, for it invites the gazer to 'see' or understand himself, however unpleasant. Gimli is wrong, memory *is* a mirror and reflects back the consolation of truth, at least for elves, whose 'memory is more like to the waking world than to a dream. Not so for Dwarves.'

This lesson in natural and supernatural evil and good also functions as a mirror for Frodo to see himself. He must learn there is both dwarf and elf in his heart, a Mines of Moria and Lothlórien buried in his psyche.

Having learned, he must then exercise free will in choosing either good or evil, usually experienced in terms of putting on or taking off the Ring at times of external or internal danger. While his initial exercises are fraught with mistakes in judgement, the inability to distinguish impulse from deliberation or an external summons from an internal decision, eventually he does learn to control his own desires and resist the will of others. Told by Gandalf to fling the Ring into the fire after just receiving it, 'with an effort of will he made a movement, as if to cast it away—but he found that he had put it back in his pocket.' As he practises he grows more adept but still slips—as when at the Inn of the Prancing Pony his singing and dancing attempt to divert the attention of Pippin's audience from the tale of Bilbo's birthday party allows him to become so 'please with himself' that he puts on the Ring by mistake and becomes embarrassingly invisible. The physical dangers he faces in these encounters culminate in the attack of the Black Riders one night and later at the Ford. The Ring in the first instance so controls his will that 'his terror was swallowed up in a sudden temptation to put on the Ring. The desire to do this laid hold of him, and he could think of nothing else—at last he slowly drew out the chain, and slipped the Ring on the forefinger of his left hand.' As a consequence he can see the Ringwraiths as they really are but unfortunately so can they see him, enough to wound him in the shoulder. The worst test in the first book involves the encounter at the Ford. Counselled first by Gandalf to 'Ride' from the Black Rider attacking them, he is counselled silently by the Riders to wait. When his strength to refuse diminishes he is saved first by Glorfindel, who addresses his horse in Elvish to flee, and again by Gandalf, who drowns the horses of the Black Riders when they prevent Frodo's horse from crossing the Ford. While he fails these major tests in the first book and must rely on *dei ex machina* to save himself, his newly established valour and courage represent the first steps toward attaining the higher form of heroism expressed by wisdom and self-control in the second book.

The physical heroism of Frodo combats physical dangers in Book One—his cry for help when Merry is caught by Old Man Willow, his stabbing of the barrow-wight's hand as it approaches the bound Sam, his dancing and singing to protect Pippin and their mission from discovery, his stabbing of the foot of one Rider during the night-attack, and his valour (brandishing his sword) and courage (refusing to put on the Ring, telling the Riders to return to Mordor) at the edge of the Ford. But this last incident reveals his spiritual naïveté: he believes physical gestures of heroism will ward off the Black Riders. Only after his education in the second book, which details supernatural death and regeneration instead of its more natural and physical forms as in the first book, does he begin to understand the necessity of *sapientia* in addition to that heroism expressed by the concept of *fortitudo*. In the last chapter, 'The Breaking of the Fellowship', he faces a threat from the proud and avaricious Boromir *within* the macrocosm of the Fellowship. Fleeing from him he puts on the Ring to render himself invisible and safe. But this unwise move allows him to see, as he sits, symbolically, upon Amon Hen, or the Hill of the Eye of the Men of Númenor, Sauron's own searching Eye. What results is a second internal danger—the threat from within Frodo the microcosm. A battle is staged within his psyche, and he is pulled first one way, then another, until Frodo, as a fully developed moral hero, exercises the faculty of free will with complete self-control:

> He heard himself crying out: *Never, never*! Or was it: *Verily I come, I come to you*? He could not tell. Then as a flash from some other point of power there came to his mind another thought: *Take if off! Take if off! Fool, take if off! Take off the Ring*!
>
> The two powers strove in him. For a moment, perfectly balanced between their piercing points, he writhed, tormented. Suddenly he was aware of himself again. Frodo, neither the Voice nor the Eye: free to choose, and with one remaining instant in which to do so. He took the Ring off his finger.

In this incident parallel to the encounter of the Riders at the Ford in the last chapter of the first book Frodo here rescues *himself* instead of being rescued by Glorifindel or Gandalf. Further, in proving his moral education by the realisation he must wage his own quest alone to protect both their mission and the other members of the Fellowship, he displays *fortitudo et sapientia* and *caritas*—hence he acts as that saviour of the Fellowship earlier witnessed in the figures of Tom Bombadil and Strider in the first book and Gandalf and Galadriel in the second. His education complete, Frodo can now function as a hero for he understands he may, at any time, become a monster.

The turning point in the narrative allows a shift in Tolkien's theme and the beginning of the second part of the epic novel in *The Two Towers*. The remaining members of the Fellowship are divided into two separate groups in this next book, division symbolising thematically not only the nature of conflict in battle in the macrocosm but also the psychic fragmentation resulting from evil. It is no mistake that the title is 'The *Two* Towers'—the double, again, symptomatic of the divided self. There are not only two towers but two monsters.

II *The Two Towers*: the Germanic King

The two towers of the title belong to Saruman and in a sense to Shelob because the quest of the remainder of the Fellowship in Book Three culminates in an attack on Orthanc and the quest of Frodo and Sam in Book Four leads to their 'attack' on Cirith Ungol, the sentry tower at the border of Mordor guarded by the giant spider. Both Orthanc and Cirith Ungol copy the greatest tower of all, the Dark Tower of Sauron described as a 'fortress, armoury, prison, furnace . . . secure in its pride and its immeasurable strength'. This second part of *The Lord of the Rings* through these two monsters represented by their towers defines the nature of the evil monster in greater detail than in the first part. Thus it introduces the notion of the Christian deadly sins embodied in the monsters, which must be combated by very Germanic heroes.

The tower image is informed by the Tower of Babel in Genesis 11. In this biblical passage at first 'Throughout the earth men spoke the same language, with the same vocabulary', but then the sons of Noah built a town and 'a tower with its top reaching heaven'. They decided, 'Let us make a name for ourselves, so that we may not be scattered about the whole earth.' Their desire to reach heaven and 'make a name' for themselves represents the same desire of Adam and Eve for godhead. Because they believe 'There will be nothing too hard for them to do', the Lord frustrates their desire by 'confusing' their language and scattering them over the earth.

The selfishness, or *cupiditas*, symbolised by the Tower of Babel shows how a preoccupation with Self at the expense of the Other or of God can lead to confusion, alienation, division. The Two Towers in Tolkien's work further break down this idea of *cupiditas* as perversion of self. The Tower of Saruman, or Orthanc, means 'Mount Fang' in Elvish but 'Cunning Mind' in the language of the Mark to suggest perversion of the mind; the Tower of Shelob, or Cirith Ungol, means 'Pass of the Spider' to suggest perversion of the body. While the creation of the Tower of Babel results in differing languages to divide the peoples, the two towers in Tolkien express division in a more microcosmic sense, in terms of the separation and perversion of the two parts of the self. Saruman's intellectual perversion has shaped his tower (formerly inhabited by the wardens of Gondor) to 'his shifting purposes, and made it better, as he thought, being deceived—for all those arts and subtle devices, for which he forsook his former wisdom, and which fondly he imagined were his own, came but from Mordor.' Specifically his pride and envy of Sauron impel him to achieve ever more power as his avarice impels him to seek the Ring and conquer more lands and forests through wrathful wars. Like Saruman, Shelob 'served none but herself' but in a very different, more bestial way by 'drinking the blood of Elves and Men, bloated and grown fat with endless brooding on her feasts, weaving webs of shadow; for all living things were her food, and her vomit darkness.' Her gluttony is revealed in her insatiable appetite, her sloth in her demands that others bring her food, her lechery in her many bastards (perhaps appropriately and symbolically quelled by Sam's penetration of her belly with his sword). Never can she achieve the higher forms of perversion manifested by Saruman: 'Little she knew of or cared for towers, or rings, or anything devised by mind or hand, who only desired death for all others, mind and body, and for herself a glut of life, alone, swollen till the mountains could not longer hold her up.' Guarding the gateway to Mordor at Cirith Ungol she suggests another guardian—of the gateway to Hell. In *Paradise Lost* Satan's daughter Sin mated with her father to beget Death, the latter of whom pursued her lecherous charms relentlessly and incessantly. In this case Shelob is depicted not as Satan's daughter but as Sauron's cat.

Tolkien shows the analogy between the two monsters and their towers by structuring their books similarly. The perversion of mind embodied in Saruman is expressed by the difficulty in communication through or understanding of words or gestures in Book Three and the perversion of body personified in Shelob is expressed by the difficulty in finding food and shelter, hospitality, in Book Four. Specifically Wormtongue, Grishnákh, and Saruman all display aspects of the higher sins of pride, avarice, envy, and wrath through their incomprehension or manipulation of language. Gollum and Shelob both illustrate the lower sins of gluttony, sloth, and lechery. Each book centres on the adventures of only part of the Fellowship, the nobler members in Book Three (Legolas, Gimli, Aragorn, and Merry and Pippin) and the more humble members in Book Four (Sam and Frodo). In each book too the adventures progressively become more dangerous, the enemies encountered more vicious.

The Uruk-hai in Book Three illustrate the disorder and contention caused by the literal failure to understand languages. When Pippin first awakens after being captured, he can understand only some of the orcs' language: 'Apparently the members of two or three quite different tribes were present, and they could not understand one another's orc-speech. There was an angry debate concerning what they were to do now: which way they were to take and what should be done with the prisoners.' The debate advances to quarrel and then to murder when Saruman's Uglúk of the Uruk-hai kills two of Sauron's orcs led by Grishnákh. The parable suggests that the tongues of different species or peoples create misunderstandings and hence conflict, disorder, death, because of the inability to transcend selfish interests. Because they do not adhere to a common purpose their enmity allows the hobbits their freedom when Grishnákh's desire for the Ring overcomes his judgement and he unties the hobbits just before his death.

This literal failure to communicate is followed in Book Three by a description of a deliberate manipulation of language so that misunderstanding will occur. Worm*tongue*'s ill-counsel renders the king impotent and his people leaderless. As a good counsellor Gandalf begs Théoden to 'come out before your doors and look abroad. Too long have you sat in shadows and trusted to twisted tales and crooked promptings.' When Théoden spurns the 'forked tongue' of the 'witless worm' (the Satanic parallels are intentional) in exchange for wise counsel he leaves the darkness, stands erect, and drops his staff to act as 'one new-awakened'. Without manipulating a belittling language into death and despair-dealing weapons, like Wormtongue, Gandalf wisely counsels life and hope. Such good words unite the Rohirrim and the Fellowship in a common purpose—fighting Saruman—rather than one which divides, like that of the quarrelsome Uruk-hair and orcs.

As Gandalf awakens Théoden from a sleep caused by evil counsel, Merry and Pippin awakens Treebeard from no counsel at all, he has so sleepily neglected his charge as Shepherd of the Trees. While Treebeard has been used as a source of information by Saruman, the latter has not reciprocated, even evilly: 'his face, as I remember it . . . became like windows in a stone wall: windows with shutters inside'. But Treebeard must realise the threat to Fangorn posed by Saruman, who 'has a mind of metal and wheels; and he does not care for growing things, except as far as they serve him for the moment'. He has abused Nature's growing things by destroying the trees and twisted human nature by creating mutants and enslaving the will of men like Théoden to obtain his will. In the Entmoot, an orderly civilised debate in contrast to the quarrels of the orcs and the one-sided insinuations of Wormtongue, language serves properly to unite the ents by awakening them to Saruman's threat. These talking trees—signifying the principle of reason and order inherent in Nature as the higher complement to the principle of life and growth signified by Tom Bombadil—join with the men of Rohan (as Riders complementary to the Rangers we met in the figure of Strider in the first book) to combat the evil represented by 'Cunning Mind'.

These episodes delineating the problem of language and communication as an attempt to join with or separate from the Other culminate in the most important one in the chapter entitled 'The Voice of Saruman', in which, in the final debate between the fallen and the reborn wizards, Saruman fails to use language cunningly enough to obtain his end and hence he loses, literally and symbolically, that chief weapon of the 'cunning mind', the palantir ('far-seer'). Unctuous Saruman almost convinces the group that he is a gentle man much put upon who only desires to meet the mighty Théoden. But Gimli wisely perceives that 'The words of this wizard stand on their heads . . . In the language of Orthanc help means ruin, and saving means

slaying, that is plain.' In addition Éomer and Théoden resist the temptation
to believe the wily ex-wizard so that his truly corrupt nature is then revealed
through the demeaning imprecations he directs toward the house of Eorl.

The emphasis upon language in this book shows that human speech
can reflect man's highest and lowest aspirations: good words can express the
love for another as cunning words can seek to subvert the other for the
speaker's own selfish ends. The archetypal Word is Christ as the Incarnation
of God's love; but words or speech in general, according to St Thomas
Aquinas in his essay 'On Kingship', naturally distinguishes man from the
beast because it expresses his rational nature. However, the misuse of man's
reason to acquire knowledge forbidden by God leads to his spiritual degen-
eration and the dehumanisation of other men. On the one hand such behaviour marks Saruman as a perverted wizard accompanied by his equally
perverted servant Wormtongue—their perversion makes them monstrous.
On the other hand this book is filled with examples of the heroes' difficulty
in communicating with others and understanding the signs and signals of
another's language, to underscore the extent of Saruman's perversion.

Thus, for example, when Aragorn, Legolas, and Gimli find the hobbits
missing but their whereabouts unknown they face an 'evil choice' because of
this lack of communication, just as Merry and Pippin, once captured, almost
succumb to despair because they do not know where they are or where they
are going. In their attempt to pursue the hobbits, the remainder of the
Fellowship must learn to 'read' a puzzling sign-language: the letter S embla-
zoned on a dead orc's shield (killed in Boromir's defence of the hobbits), the
footprints of Sam leading *into* the water but not back again, the heap of dead
orcs without any clue to the hobbits' presence, the appearance of a strange
old man bearing away their horses, the mystery of the bound hobbits'
apparent escape. All of these signs or riddles can be explained, and indeed, as
Aragorn suggests, 'we must guess the riddles, if we are to choose our course
rightly'. Man's quest symbolically depends on his correct use of his reason;
the temptation is to know more than one should by consulting a magical
device like the *palantir*.

If Book Three demonstrates the intellectual nature of sin then Book
Four demonstrates its physical nature. Although the structure of Shelob's
tower of Cirith Ungol ends this book as Orthanc ends the Third, it is never
described in this part. Instead another tower—Minas Morgul—introduces
the weary group to the land they approach at the book's end. In appearance
it resembles a human corpse:

> Paler indeed than the moon ailing in some slow eclipse was the
> light of it now, wavering and blowing like a noisome exhalation

of decay, a *corpse-light*, a light that illuminated nothing. In the
walls and tower windows showed, like countless black holes
looking inward into emptiness; but the topmost course of the
tower revolved slowly, first one way and then another, *a huge
ghostly head* leering into the night. (my italics)

The holes might be a skull's. As a type of corpse it focuses attention on the
human body, whose perverse desires preoccupy Tolkien in this book.

So Gollum's obsession with fish and dark things of the earth disgusts
Frodo and Sam: his name as the sound of swallowing aptly characterises his
monstrously gluttonous nature. Again, when he guides them across the Dead
Marshes it is dead bodies from the battle between Sauron and the Alliance in
the Third Age, or their appearance, which float beneath the surface and
tempt Gollum's appetite. But the hobbits' appetites result in trouble too: they
are captured by Faramir when the smoke of the fire for the rabbit stew
cooked by Sam and generously intended for Frodo is detected (just as
Gollum is captured by Frodo at Faramir's when he hunts fish in the
Forbidden Pool). Faramir's chief gift to the weary hobbits is a most welcome
hospitality, including food and shelter as a respite from the barren wasteland
they traverse. Finally, the hobbits are themselves intended as food by Gollum
for the insatiable spider Shelob. Truly the monster (whether Gollum or
Shelob) is depicted as a glutton just as the hero, past, present, or future (the
corpse, the hobbits, Faramir), is depicted as food or life throughout this
book. Physical life can end without food to sustain the body; it can also end,
as the previous book indicated, because of an inaccurate interpretation of
language to guide rational judgement.

These monsters representing sin are opposed by heroes represented
as Germanic kings and warriors. As we have seen, Théoden the weak leader
of Rohan is transformed by Gandalf's encouragement into a very heroic
Germanic king in Book Three, unlike the proud Beorhtnoth of 'The Battle
of Maldon'. In Book Four the Germanic warrior or subordinate (chiefly
Sam) vows to lend his aid to his master out of love and loyalty like the old
retainer Beorhtwold in 'The Battle of Maldon'. The bond between the king
as head of a nation and the reason as 'lord' of the individual corresponds to
that between the subordinate warrior as servant of the king and the subordinate body.

To enhance these Germanic correspondences Tolkien describes Rohan
as an Old English nation complete with appropriate names and includes a
suspicious hall-guardian named Hama very similar to one in *Beowulf* and an
ubi sunt poem modelled on a passage from the Old English 'Wanderer':

Where now the horse and rider? Where is the horn that
was blowing?
Where is the helm and the hauberk, and the bright hair
flowing?

Where went the horse, where went the man? Where went
the treasure-giver?

Where went the seats of banquets? Where are the hall-
joys?

In addition throughout Book Three Tolkien stresses the physical heroism of
the Rohirrim and the Fellowship in the battle at Helm's Deep, which resembles those described in 'The Battle of Maldon', 'Brunnanburh', and 'The
Fight at Finnsburg'. But in Book Four the heroism of the 'warrior' depends
more on love and loyalty than on expressions of valour in battle.

Four major subordinates emerge, Gollum, Sam, Frodo, and Faramir.
Each offers a very Germanic oath of allegiance to his master or lord: Gollum
in pledging not to run away if he is untied swears by the Ring that 'I will
serve the master of the Precious'. So Frodo becomes a lord, 'a tall stern
shadow, a mighty lord who hid his brightness in grey cloud, and at his feet a
whining dog'. Gollum must also swear an oath to Faramir never to return to
the Forbidden Pool or lead others there. Sam similarly serves his master
Frodo but like Gollum betrays him, not to Shelob but to Faramir, by cooking
the rabbit stew. Likewise Frodo the master seems to betray his servant
Gollum by capturing him at the Forbidden Pool even though he has actually
saved him from death at the hands of Faramir's men, because 'The servant
has a claim on the master for service, even service in fear'. Finally, because
Faramir has granted Frodo his protection Frodo offers him his service, while
simultaneously requesting a similar protection for Frodo's servant Gollum:
'take this creature, this Sméagol, under your protection'. Ultimately even
Faramir has vowed to serve his father and lord, Denethor, by protecting this
isolated post. In the next part of the epic Denethor will view Faramir's service
as incomplete, a betrayal. Because he has not died instead of his brother
Boromir, he will seem to fail just as the warriors lying in the Dead Marshes
have apparently succeeded only too well, given the fact of their death in
battle. While the exchange of valour or service for protection by a lord dupli-
cates the Germanic contract between warrior and king, the exchange in *The
Two Towers* seems fraught with difficulty either because of the apparent laxity
of the lord or the apparent disloyalty of the subordinate.

The enemy, interestingly enough, functions primarily as a symbolic perversion of Christian rather than Germanic values, but still there is some correspondence between the *ofermod* of the Germanic king and the *superbia* of the Christian, both leading to other, lesser sins. The Germanic emphasis in this volume does continue in the next part of the epic, but ultimately merges with a more Christian definition of both servant and king.

III *The Return of The King*: the Christian King

This part of *The Lord of the Rings* sees the climax of the struggle between good and evil through battle between the Satanlike Dark Lord and the Christlike true king, Aragorn. Because he 'returns' to his people to accept the mantle of responsibility the volume is entitled 'The Return of the King', with emphasis upon kingship in Book Five and return in Book Six. Dramatic foils for the Christian king as the good steward are provided in Book Five by the good and bad Germanic lords Théoden and Denethor, whose names suggest anagrams of one another. The good Germanic subordinates Pippin and Merry, whose notion of service echoes that of the good Christian, similarly act as foils for the archetypal Christian servant Sam, whose exemplary love for his master Frodo transcends all normal bounds in Book Six. Finally, the concept of renewal attendant upon the return of the king pervades the latter part of the sixth book as a fitting coda to the story of the triumph of the true king over the false one.

The contrast between the two Germanic lords is highlighted early in Book Five by the offers of service presented respectively by Pippin to Denethor in Chapter One and by Merry to Théoden in Chapter Two. As the Old Man, the Germanic king more interested in glory and honour than in his men's welfare, Denethor belittles Pippin because he assumes smallness of size equals smallness of service. This literalistic mistake has been made earlier by other 'Old Men', especially *Beowulf* critics, the narrator of *The Hobbit*, and Nokes in 'Smith of Wootton Major'. Why, Denethor muses, did the 'halfling' escape the orcs when the much larger Boromir did not? In return for the loss of his son Pippin feels moved—by pride—to offer in exchange himself, but as an eye-for-an-eye, justly-rendered payment of a debt: 'Then Pippin looked the old man in the eye, for pride stirred strangely within him, still stung by the scorn and suspicion in that cold voice. "Little service, no doubt, will so great a lord of Men think to find in a hobbit, a halfling from the northern Shire; yet such as it is, I will offer it, in payment of my debt."' His offer is legalised by a contractual vow binding him both to Gondor and the Steward of the realm either until death takes him or his lord releases him. The specific details of the contract invoke the usual terms of the bond between lord and warrior according to the Germanic *comitatus* ethic: he must not 'fail to reward that which is given: fealty with love, valour with honour, oath-breaking with vengeance'.

Merry's vow to Théoden, in contrast, expresses a voluntary love for rather than involuntary duty to his king characteristic of the ideal Germanic subordinate in Tolkien's 'Ofermod' commentary. And Théoden, unlike Denethor, represents the ideal Germanic lord who truly loves instead of using his men. Viewing Merry as an equal he invites him to eat, drink, talk, and ride with him, later suggesting that as his esquire he ride on a hill-pony especially found for him. Merry response to this loving gesture with one equally loving and spontaneous. 'Filled suddenly with love for the old man, he knelt on one knee, and took his hand and kissed it. "May I lay the sword of Meriadoc of the Shire on your lap, Théoden King?" he cried. "Receive my service, if you will!" In lieu of the legal contract of the lord Denethor and the servant Pippin there is a verbal promise of familial love: '"As a father you shall be to me," said Merry'.

These private vows of individual service to the governors of Gondor and Rohan are followed in Chapters Two and Three by more public demonstrations of national or racial service. In the first incident the previous Oathbreakers of the past—the Dead of the Grey Company—redeem their past negligence by bringing aid to Aragorn in response to his summons. This contractual obligation fulfilled according to the letter of prophecy, Théoden and his Rohirrim can fulfil their enthusiastic and loving pledge of aid by journeying to Gondor. They themselves are accompanied by the Wild Men in Chapter Five as a symbolic corollary to their spontaneity, love, and enthusiasm—the new law of the spirit.

In addition two oathmakers of Rohan literally violate their private vows of individual service but actually render far greater service than any outlined in a verbal contract. When Éowyn relinquishes her duty to Théoden of taking charge of the people until his return by disguising herself as Dernhelm so that she may fight in battle, she also allows Merry to relinquish his vow to Théoden when he secretly rides behind her into battle. But when Théoden is felled by the Nazgûl Lord it is she who avenges him—Dernhelm 'wept, for he had loved his lord as a father' as well as Merry—('"King's man? King's man!" his heart cried within him. "You must stay by him. As a father you shall be to me, you said" .' Dernhelm slays the winged creature ridden by the Lord of Nazgûl; Merry helps her slay the Lord. The service they render, a vengeance impelled by pity and love for their lord, is directed not only to the dead king and father Théoden, or to Rohan and Gondor, but to all of Middle-earth. Interestingly, her bravery in battle arouses Merry's: 'Pity filled his heart and great wonder, and suddenly the slow-kindled courage of his race awoke. He clenched his hand. She should

not die, so fair, so desperate! At least she should not die alone, unaided.'
Simple love for another results in Merry's most charitable and heroic act.
The subordinates have completely fulfilled the spirit, if not the letter, of their
pledges of allegiance to their lords.

Tolkien also compares and contrasts the lords of Book Five. The evil
Germanic lord Denethor is matched by the good Germanic lord Théoden;
both contrast with the Christian lord Aragorn. Denethor fails as a father, a
master, a steward, and a rational man. In 'The Siege of Gondor' (Chapter
Four) and later in 'The Pyre of Denethor' (Chapter Seven) Denethor reveals
his inability to love his son Faramir when, Lear-like, he measures the quality
and quantity of his worth. He prefers the dead Boromir to Faramir because
of the former's great courage and loyalty to him. 'Boromir was loyal to me
and no wizard's pupil. He would have remembered his father's need, and
would not have squandered what fortune gave. He would have brought me a
mighty gift'. So he chastises Farmir for his betrayal: 'have I not seen your eye
fixed on Mithrandir, seeking whether you said well or too much? He has long
had your heart in his keeping.' In the early chapters he reveals his failure as
a master: he assumes the service of a small individual like Pippin must be
domestic and menial in character, involving waiting on him, running errands,
entertaining him. As a steward of Gondor he fails most egregiously by
usurping the role of lord in misguided zeal for power and glory and by using
his men to further his own ends. He views this act in monetary terms: the
Dark Lord 'uses others as his weapons. So do all great lords, if they are wise,
Master Halfling. Or why should I sit here in my tower and think, and watch,
and wait, spending even my sons?' Unlike Théoden he remains secure in his
tower while his warriors die in the siege of Gondor. Most significantly he
fails to exhibit that rational self-control typical of man and often described in
the Middle Ages through the metaphor of kingship. Such unnatural behaviour results in despair and irrationality, and he loses his head. When he
nurses his madness to suicide and adds even his son Faramir to the pyre he
is termed a 'heathen' by Gandalf, like those kings dominated by the Dark
Power, 'slaying themselves in pride and despair, murdering their kin to ease
their own death'. As he succumbs to his pride he refuses to 'be the dotard
chamberlain of an upstart. . . . I will not bow to such a one, last of a ragged
house long bereft of lordship and dignity.' Symbolically the enemy hurls back
the heads of dead soldiers branded with the 'token of the Lidless Eye' to
signal the loss of reason and hope—the loss of the 'head'—and the assault of
despair on this city and its steward.

Théoden and Aragorn epitomise in contrast the good king. As a
Germanic king Théoden serves primarily heroically after his contest with
Wormtongue, giving leadership in battle and loving and paternal treatment

of his warriors outside it, as we have seen with Merry. So he rides at the head of his troop of warriors as they near the city and provides a noble and inspiring example for them to follow:

> Arise, arise . . .
> Fell deeds awake fire and slaughter!
> spear shall be shaken, shield be splintered,
> a sword-day, a red day, ere the sun rises!
> Ride now, ride now! Ride to Gondor!

The alliterative verse echoes the Old English heroic lines of 'The Battle of Maldon' in both its form and content.

Aragorn differs from Théoden in his role as Christian king because of his moral heroism as a healer rather than his valour as a destroyer. Ioreth, the Gondors' wise-woman, declares '*The hands of the king are the hands of a healer, and so shall the rightful king be known.*' In 'The Houses of Healing' (Chapter Eight) Aragorn carries the herb *kingsfoil* to the wounded Faramir, Éowyn, and Merry to revive and awaken each of them in highly symbolic acts. Also known as *athelas*, *kingsfoil* brings 'Life to the dying': its restorative powers, of course, transcend the merely physical. It represents Life itself juxtaposed to Death, similar to the restorative powers of the paradisal Niggle in 'Leaf by Niggle'. Indeed, when he places the leaves in hot water, 'all hearts were lightened. For the fragrance that came to each was like a memory of dewy mornings of unshadowed sun in some land of which the fair world in Spring is itself but a fleeting memory.' In awakening Faramir, Aragorn as well awakens knowledge and love so that he responds in words similar to those of a Christian disciple: 'My lord, you called me. I come. What does the king command?' Instead of responding rationally to the king, Éowyn awakens from her deathlike sleep to enjoy her brother's presence and to mourn her father's death. Merry awakens hungry for supper. The revival of self witnessed in these three incidents symbolises the renewal of the three human faculties, rational, appetitive, and sensitive.

Structurally Tolkien supports his thematic contrasts and parallels. The House of Healing visited in Chapter Eight occurs back-to-back with Chapter Sevens' House of the Dead in which Denethor commits fiery suicide. More than physical, his death is chiefly spiritual. Both a spiritual and physical rebirth follow Aragorn's laying on of *kingsfoil* in the House of Healing. But so this ritualistic and epiphanic act readies the narrative for the final symbolic Christian gesture of all the free peoples in the last two chapters. In 'The Last Debate' they decide to sacrifice themselves, if necessary, out of love for their world in the hope that their action will distract Sauron long enough for Sam and Frodo to reach Mount Doom. As an entire community of 'servants' they each alone act as freely, spontaneously, and charitably as did Merry or Éowyn toward Théoden earlier. Aragorn declares that 'As I have begun, so I will go on. . . . Nonetheless I do not yet claim to command any man. Let others choose as they will.' Even the title of 'The Last Debate' portrays the egalitarian spirit of the group. In contrast in the last chapter, 'The Black Gate Opens', only one view—that of the Dark Lord, voiced by his Mouth, the Lieutenant—predominates. Sauron too demands not voluntary service but servitude: the Lieutenant 'would be their tyrant and they his slaves'. Finally, the arrogance of Sauron's 'Steward' functions antithetically to the humility and love of the good 'servants'. Mocking and demeaning them, he asks if 'any one in this rout' has the 'authority to treat with me? . . . Or indeed with wit to understand me?' His stentorian voice grows louder and more defensive when met with the silence of Aragorn, whom he has described as brigand-like. This attack of the free peoples on the Black Gate of Mordor parallels that of Sauron's orcs on the Gate of Gondor in Chapter Four, but differs in that the former consists not so much of physical attack as a spiritual defence. When the peoples realise the Lieutenant holds Sam's short sword, the grey cloak with its elven brooch, and Frodo's mithril-mail they almost succumb to despair—Sauron's greatest weapon, as witnessed in the siege of Gondor. But Gandalf's steely self-discipline and wisdom so steadies their nerves that they are buoyed by his refusal to submit to the Mouth's insolent terms. Well that he does, for Sauron then surrounds them on all sides, betraying his embassy of peace. They are saved from physical destruction by the eagles as *dei ex machina* and from spiritual destruction by Frodo, Sam, and Gollum as they near Mount Doom in Book Six.

The Ring finally reaches its origin in the first three chapters of Book Six. Initiating the idea of 'Return' this event introduces a tripartite division of the book in narrative and theme. In Chapters Four to Seven Aragorn returns as king of his people, after which his marriage to Arwen, in addition to Faramir's to Éowyn, symbolises the renewal of society through the joining of different species, man and elf, and of different nations, Rohan and Gondor. A later marriage symbolises a more natural form of rejuvenation, for Sam as gardener marries an appropriately named Rosie Cotton to illustrate further the fertility emblazoning the reborn Shire. Finally, in the third part (Chapter Eight) Frodo and his hobbits return to the Shire, where the false 'mayor' Sharkey is ousted and a new one, Sam, elected. In the last chapter Tolkien hints at more supernatural forms of return and rebirth. On one level those chosen few 'return' to the Grey Havens, where they seem to acquire an immortality reminiscent of Christianity. But on another level others of a less spiritual cast must return to the duties of the natural world. So Sam returns at the very end, a 'king' who must continue to serve his 'people', his family, and his 'kingdom', the Shire, by remaining in this world: '"Well, I'm back," he said.'

Throughout the first part of Book Six before the Ring has been returned and Sauron similarly 'returns' to a grey smoke (in contrast to the Grey Havens reached by Frodo and Gandalf at the end), Sam exemplifies the ideal Christian-king-as-servant theme enunciated in the last part. Physically he provides food for Frodo as he weakens, offers him his share of the remaining water, carries him bodily over rough terrain, and lifts his spirits. But spiritually he serves Frodo through the moral character which reveals him to be, as the most insignificant hobbit and character in the epic, the most heroic. He will become an artist by the work's end, but even during the trek across Mordor his sensitivity to spiritual reality is expressed by his understanding of the beauty beneath the appearance of waste, of light beyond darkness, of hope beyond despair. This insight is triggered by the appearance of a star above: 'The beauty of it smote his heart, as he looked up out of the forsaken land, and hope returned to him. For like a shaft, clear and cold, the thought pierced him that in the end the Shadow was only a small and passing thing: there was light and high beauty for ever beyond its reach. . . . Now, for a moment, his own fate, and even his master's ceased to trouble him.' Strangely he remains the only character who has worn the Ring but who is never tempted to acquire it by overpowering his master. Yet like Frodo earlier he refuses to kill the detested Gollum when an opportunity arises because of his empathy for this 'thing lying in the dust, forlorn, ruinous, utterly wretched'. Having borne the Ring himself, he finally understands the reason for Gollum's wretchedness. This charitable refusal permits Gollum as a foil for the good servant to serve his master and Middle-earth in the most ironic way imaginable; when Frodo betrays himself enough to keep the Ring at the last moment, Gollum bites off both Ring and finger only to fall into the furnace of Mount Doom, the most ignominious 'servant' finally achieving the coveted role of 'Lord of the Rings', the least dangerous adversary finally felling the most dangerous—Sauron.

In the last two parts the reunion of the entire Fellowship and all the species, the coronation of the king and the double weddings mark the restoration of harmony and peace to Middle-earth. Symbolically the Eldest of Trees blooms again to replace the barren and withered Tree in the Court of the Fountain. A new Age—the Age of Man, the fourth Age—begins. Even in the Shire rejuvenation occurs: note the domestic image implied by the title of Chapter Eight, 'The Scouring of the Shire'.

In a social sense the Shire must be washed and purified of the reptilian monsters occupying it. Once Sharkey and Worm have disappeared, Sam the new Mayor as gardener can replenish its natural stores as well. After he

plants the seed given him by Galadriel, new trees, including a mallorn with
silver bark and gold flowers, burst into bloom in the spring. The lush growth
introduces a season or rebirth in Shire year 1420 through sunshine, rain in
moderation,

> an air of richness and growth, and a gleam of beauty beyond
> that of mortal summers that flicker and pass upon this Middle-
> earth. All the children born or begotten in that year, and there
> were many, were fair to see and strong, and most of them had
> a rich golden hair that had before been rare among hobbits.
> The fruit was so plentiful that young hobbits very nearly
> bathed in strawberries and cream. . . . And no one was ill, and
> everyone was pleased, except those who had to mow the grass.

Sam as gardener becomes a natural artist who fuses together the Niggle and
Parish of 'Leaf by Niggle'.

The ending of this epic may seem optimistic. But as the Second Age
has passed into the Third, so now the Third passes into the Fourth, a lesser
one because dominated by man, a lesser species than the elf. Also, as Sauron
replaced Morgoth, perhaps an even Darker Lord will replace Sauron in the
future. Yet Tolkien's major interest does not lie in predicting the future or in
encouraging man to hope for good fortune. He wishes to illustrate how best
to conduct man's life, both privately and publicly, by being a good servant
and a good king, despite the vagaries of fortune, the corruption of others,
and the threat of natural and supernatural death.

So this epic constitutes a sampler of Tolkienian concepts and forms
realised singly and separately in other works. The critic as monster depicted
in the *Beowulf* article reappears as Tolkien the Critic in the foreword to *The
Lord of the Rings*, a 'grown up' version of Tolkien the narrator in *The Hobbit*.
The hero as monster finds expression, as it has earlier in Bilbo, in Frodo, who
discovers the landscape of the self to be a harsher terrain than that of
Mordor. The series of monsters typifying the deadly sins—Saruman,
Shelob—ultimately converge with the evil Germanic king of the trilogy—
Denethor—combining ideas of the 'King under the Mountain' in *The Hobbit*
with the idea of the Germanic king presented in 'The Homecoming' and
other medieval parodies. The good Germanic hero-as-subordinate, too,
from *The Hobbit* and the medieval parodies, converges with the Christian
concept of the king-as-servant from the fairy-stories, in the last two volumes
of the trilogy. In addition the genres and formal constructs Tolkien most
loves reappear here. The preface, lecture, or prose non-fiction essay is transformed into the Foreword; the 'children's story' for adults is expanded into

the adult story of the epic, also for children; the parody of medieval literature recurs not only in the epic or romance form used here but also in the
presentation of the communities of Rohan and Gondor; the fairy-story with
its secondary world of Faërie governed by a very Christian Elf-king is translated into elven form here. Thus all of Tolkien's work manifests a unity, with
understanding of its double and triple levels, in this respect like the distinct
dual levels, Germanic and Christian, of *Beowulf* first perceived in Tolkien's
own *Beowulf* article. So the Tolkien reader, like Bilbo in *The Hobbit* and Sam
in *The Lord of the Rings*, must return to the beginning—not to the Shire, but
to the origin of the artist Tolkien—in 'Beowulf: The Monsters and the
Critics'.

JARED LOBDELL

Defining The Lord of the Rings:
An Adventure Story in the Edwardian Mode

We shall not cease from exploration
And the end of all our exploring
Will be to arrive where we started
And know the place for the first time. . . .
And all shall be well and
All manner of thing shall be well.

T. S. Eliot, "Little Gidding"

"Beyond the Wild Wood comes the Wide World," said the Rat.
Kenneth Grahame, *The Wind in the Willows*

It is not at all certain that the game of *Quellenforschung* ("source-hunting")
is worth playing with *The Lord of the Rings*, or indeed with most literary
creations. Exceptions can be made, of course, for the asking of questions such
as "What did Chaucer really do to *Il Filostrato*?" or for the game-playing
demanded by *The Waste Land*, but there may well be truth to the suspicion
that the game in general is not worth the candle. Yet the search for sources
can be part of a search for influences, and the search for influences can be
both valid and helpful—as when we look for Vergil's influence on Milton or
the influence of the ballads on Coleridge. But we must be looking at both
form and subject matter.

Now of course Vergil is an influence on Milton, but is not his source.
The influence of the ballads on *The Rime of the Ancient Mariner* is obvious,

From *England and Always: Tolkien's World of the Rings* by Jared Lobdell. © 1981 by William
B. Eerdmans Publishing Co.

but it would be a brave man who considered them Coleridge's sources. Nevertheless, if there were a number of secondary epics that might have influenced Milton, we should, I think, be justified in looking to see which of them served as a source, in order to see which was most likely to have served as an influence. Similarly, if we were interested in finding out which ballads influenced Coleridge, we might well look through the ballad corpus for parallels—sources and analogues—for the *Rime*.

This is essentially the kind of endeavor I am engaged in here, for *The Lord of the Rings*. I want to know what kind of work Tolkien set out to write. To which of the great pre-existing forms of literary creation, so different in the expectations they excite and fulfill (the reader may recognize Professor Lewis's words here), so diverse in their powers, is *The Lord of the Rings* designed to contribute? Since we do not have available to us any writings in which Professor Tolkien set down the answer to that question, and since (despite the intentional fallacy) it is indeed "the first qualification for judging any piece of workmanship, from a corkscrew to a cathedral, to know what it is," I think my endeavor is justified. There may of course be better ways than mine to find out what *The Lord of the Rings* is designed to be, but this way seems to be both promising and untrod.

There are two sets of clues to which we should pay particular heed in search for those whose writing influenced the form of *The Lord of the Rings*, and both sets have been largely overlooked. The first set is composed primarily of Tolkien's own comments and secondarily of those few passages in his work where he obviously echoes another author. The second set is composed of the subjective reactions and literary tastes of those readers of *The Lord of the Rings* who have at least a passing familiarity with the English literature of the period in which Tolkien grew up. The first set of clues provides material for answering the question, "Who, according to what Tolkien wrote, may be considered to have influenced him?" The second provides material for answering the question, "Who wrote the kind of book that affects us in the way *The Lord of the Rings* affects us and, the dates being right, may therefore have written the kind of book Tolkien would be likely to have read?" (The implicit assumption here is that authors write the kind of book they like to read.)

If we are to make use of both sets of clues, it is of course necessary for us to have some idea of the way Tolkien's mind worked. I suspect there has not been much of value written on this subject, but we can at least make a stab at gaining information sufficient to proceed with our inquiry. We can begin by quoting Tolkien's reaction to the tale of the juniper tree.

"The beauty and horror" of the tale, he says, "with its exquisite and tragic beginning, the abominable cannibal stew, the gruesome bones, the gay and vengeful bird-spirit coming out of a mist that rose from the tree, has remained with me since childhood; and yet always the chief flavour of that tale lingering in the memory was not beauty or horror, but distance and a great abyss of time, not measurable even by *twe tusend Johr*." And, as I hope to demonstrate, we can see in some of Tolkien's other reading the impress of that dark backward and abysm of time. At the same time, we can see in his childhood reading of dictionaries a fascination with languages. Indeed, his mind was chiefly attuned to languages and the past—which is not, I should emphasize, the same thing as being interested in words and history.

I shall have occasion to refer to this again, but it may be a good thing to mention here Tolkien's reference to the remark of Sjera Tomas Saemundsson: "Languages are the chief distinguishing marks of peoples. No people in fact comes into being until it speaks a language of its own; let the languages perish and the peoples perish too, or become different peoples." The languages are more than the words. And, in the same way, the past is more than its history. History is only the facts, or a presentation of the facts, accidentally left to us from the past. We cannot get into the real forest of the past; that is part of what the word "past" means.

It must also be made clear that to give the direction of Tolkien's mind is not yet to explain how his mind worked, only to give what mathematicians might call the parameters of its working. The important thing for us to remember here is that while grammar studies the rules of language, and history studies the rules of the past (one might argue that history is the grammar of the past), Tolkien's reactions to these things were not those of a grammarian. He described *The Lord of the Rings* as containing "in the way of presentation that I find most natural, much of what I personally have received from the study of things Celtic." And he once remarked that "his typical response upon reading a medieval work was to desire not so much to make a philological or critical study of it as to write a modern work in the same tradition."

In Tolkien's professional life the intersection of language and the past came in the realm of philology. In the inward life of his imagination, it came in his creation of a new version of middle-earth. There have, of course, been other versions of middle-earth, from the Midgard of the Norsemen to Langland's fair field full of folk: as Tolkien has reminded us, middle-earth is not his creation, though he created the "Middle Earth" of *The Lord of the Rings*. That act of creation was necessary before a story could be written about his Middle Earth, but it is the story, and not the creation, that is our subject here.

We know that *The Lord of the Rings* was not the first or even the second story whose events took place within the bounds of Tolkien's Middle Earth. It is not even certain it was the third story. We know also that Tolkien wrote other stories as his children were growing up, and it may be that these would repay our attention by giving us additional clues for our endeavor (one of these stories, "Mr. Bliss," has been spoken of as "Thurber without the bitterness"). But since we do not have these additional clues, we may reasonably turn to the clues we have, to see where they will lead us.

First, we may look at the writers whose influence Tolkien himself acknowledged or to whose works he referred, or whose works he conspicuously echoed. The list is not long, and the first name on it, Sir Henry Rider Haggard, is almost certainly the most important. Indeed, in a telephone conversation with the American journalist Henry Resnick, Tolkien said this of Haggard's *She*: "I suppose as a boy *She* interested me as much an anything —like the Greek shard of Amyntas, which was the kind of machine by which everything got moving." And, if that were not enough, we have evident parallels between the death of Ayesha (the She of the title) and the death of Saruman. Perhaps it would be well to set them out here.

Haggard's description of the death of Ayesha may be the less familiar of the two:

> Smaller she grew, and smaller yet, till she was no larger than a monkey. Now the skin had puckered into a million wrinkles, and on her shapeless face was the mark of unutterable age. I never saw anything like it; nobody ever saw anything to equal the infinite age which was graven on that fearful countenance, no bigger now than that of a two-months' child, though the skull retained its same size. . . . I took up Ayesha's kirtle and the gauzy scarf . . . and, averting my head so that I might not look upon it, I covered up that dreadful relic.

Beside this may be set Tolkien's description of the death of Saruman:

> Frodo looked down on the body with pity and horror, for as he looked it seemed that long years of death were suddenly revealed in it, and it shrank, and the shrivelled face became rags of skin upon a hideous skull. Lifting up the skirt of the dirty cloak that sprawled beside it, he covered it over, and turned away.

The parallel is not exact, but it is certainly highly suggestive. Nor do I think I would be stretching a point to bring in, as additional evidence, the predominant importance of caves in both Haggard and Tolkien. In *King Solomon's Mines*, the Don is found dead in a cave on the way, the dead kings are enthroned in the cave, and the travelers are very nearly entombed there as well. In *She* the secret fire of immortality, which destroys Ayesha, is likewise in a cave—and, of course, both fire and cave have their parallels in Orodruin. And Moria, Shelob's lair—all those dark places where "the flowers of symbelmynë come never to the world's end"—testify eloquently to what is at least a noteworthy similarity between the two. (Freudians may find a different explanation; I prefer mine.)

Perhaps it would also be worth recalling here that Haggard was drawn to Africa, where he had been secretary to the Governor of Natal, because of its mystery, its age-old past, and even (though not so strongly) the majesty of its languages. Given this evidence, I think we will not be far wrong if we assign to Haggard a chief place among Tolkien's literary forebears.

Next among them—and here we may be on more tenuous grounds— we find G. K. Chesterton, between whose works and Tolkien's "On Fairy Stories" we can trace a set of connections, including some Tolkienian passages with a remarkably Chestertonian ring. Let me give you some examples of what I mean. Andrew Lang once remarked that the taste of children "remains like the taste of their naked ancestors thousands of years ago." Tolkien began his response by saying, "But do we really know much about these 'naked ancestors' except that they were certainly not naked?" When Max Muller claimed that mythology was a "disease of language," Tolkien made this reply:

> Mythology is not a disease at all, though it may like all human things become diseased. You might as well say that thinking is a disease of the mind. It would be more near the truth to say that languages, especially modern European languages, are a disease of mythology.

Either response could have been written by Chesterton, and the first, in fact, echoes a passage in *The Everlasting Man*.

Finally, I would challenge readers who do not recognize it to tell me whether Tolkien or Chesterton wrote the passage which is my third example:

> We may put a deadly green upon a man's face and produce a horror; we may make the rare and terrible blue moon to shine; or we may cause woods to spring with silver leaves and rams to wear fleeces of gold, and put hot fire into the belly of the cold worm.

In fact, the quotations are from "On Fairy Stories" (from the *Tolkien Reader*). Nevertheless, we do not know whether Tolkien read the early Chesterton of *The Man Who Was Thursday* or *The Napoleon of Notting Hill*. On the available evidence we can only say that it seems highly likely and on that basis look briefly at what Chesterton was trying to do, and what it was that he succeeded in doing.

Haggard in ordinary life was a sufficiently prosaic Englishman (an expert on English agriculture) and sought in his books to portray the romance of what everyone could see was romantic. Chesterton, on the other hand, was anything but ordinary (witness the fictional portrait in John Dickson Carr's Gideon Fell), and I think it not coincidental that he sought to portray the romance of what everyone could see was prosaic: "We feel it is epical when man with one wild arrow strikes a distant bird. Is it not also epical when man with one wild engine strikes a distant station?" It is true that Chestertonian paradox can grow wearying, but the root of his love for paradox lies in the not at all paradoxical belief that the wide world is really a remarkably interesting place after all.

How, then, might this have influenced Tolkien in *The Lord of the Rings*? Most directly, I believe, in the very character of the Hobbits. As Chesterton's Father Brown is short and round and the essence of the Norfolk flats, so Bilbo Baggins is short and round and the essence of an English shire. Perhaps the Battle of Bywater is not unlike the battles in *The Napoleon of Notting Hill*. Of course, at these points Chertertonian paradox was touching something deep in the paradoxical character of England, and Tolkien could certainly have touched it entirely without Chesterton's intermediation. But I do not think he did.

Third among the authors Tolkien read—and here I claim an unfair advantage in the game of *Quellenforschung*—was Algernon Blackwood. The evidence I have seen lies in an entry in the original (but not the edited and published) version of the "Notes on the Nomenclature of *The Lord of the Rings*," in which Tolkien traces his use of "the crack of doom" to an unidentified story by Blackwood. Now for our purposes it is unimportant whether the source of Tolkien's Crack of Doom (in Orodruin) was indeed something Blackwood wrote; what is important is that Tolkien could not have thought it was if he had not read (and been influenced by) Blackwood. I suspect there may be confirmatory evidence for the reading (and the influence) in the character of Old Man Willow, though he is not so terrible as the willows in Blackwood's story of that name.

Blackwood's narrator writes of the "acres of willows, crowding . . . pressing upon the river as though to suffocate it, standing in dense array mile after mile beneath the sky, watching, waiting, listening. . . . Their serried ranks, growing everywhere darker about me as the shadows deepened . . . woke in me the curious and unwelcome suggestion that we had trespassed here upon the borders of . . . a world where we were intruders, a world where we were not invited to remain." And a little later "the note of this willow-camp became unmistakably plain to me: we were interlopers, trespassers; we were not wanted. The sense of unfamiliarity grew upon me." And finally (in a passage with Entish—or perhaps Huornish—connotations), "They first became visible, these huge figures, just within the tops of the bushes—immense, bronze-coloured, moving. . . . I saw them plainly and noted, now I came to examine them more calmly, that they were very much larger than human, and indeed that something in their appearance proclaimed them to be *not human* at all. . . . I saw their limbs and huge bodies . . . rising up in a living column. . . ."

The style is different, of course, and yet I catch in Blackwood something I catch in Tolkien but in few others—perhaps at night in the wildwood in *The Wind in the Willows* also (yet those willows are friendlier). I mean a sense of man (or Hobbit) as interloper in the woods, of the trees as sentient entities, and of something neither tree nor human—nor yet, as with Saki, clearly Pan. And in the same volume ("The Glamour of the Snow" in *Strange Stories*) I find passages that could be glosses on the experience with Caradhras.

Here the hero of the story (not the same as in "The Willows") tried to turn away in escape, and so trying, found for the first time that the power of the snow—that other power which does not exhilarate but deadens effort—was upon him. The suffocating weakness that it brings to exhausted men, luring them to the sleep of death in her clinging soft embrace, lulling the will and conquering all desire for life—this was awfully upon him." And then, as he escapes, "For ever close upon his heels came the following forms and voices with the whirling snow-dust. He heard that little silvery voice of death and laughter at his back. Shrill and wild, with the whistling of the wind past his ears, he caught its pursuing tones; but in anger now. . . ."

I am not suggesting here that Blackwood is Tolkien's source for the character of Old Man Willow or for the snowstorm at Caradhras; he could be, I suppose, but it is not in this that his importance lies. What I am suggesting is that the cast of Blackwood's mind, as revealed in these passages, is surprisingly like the cast of Tolkien's mind. It does not much matter whether the snow at Caradhras comes from Tolkien's alpine experiences or from Blackwood's. It matters considerably that they saw the snow in much the same way.

Indeed, it matters enough that we should ask what Blackwood was doing in his stories. The answer is that he was creating the modern story of the supernatural—not the pure ghost story of M. R. James or the story of the un-dead that found its best-known expression in Bram Stoker's *Dracula*, but the story in which (if I may be forgiven a paradox of my own) nature itself is in a way supernatural. To be sure, Blackwood wrote ghost stories and stories of the un-dead, and he wrote stories that did not concern the supernatural at all, but what he added to English literature was a sense of mystery and unreliability underlying ordinary things. Blackwood's vision was of the treachery of natural things in an animate world: call it their mystery if you will, but the mystery has a sinister touch.

It is hard for us to re-create any world-view, especially the view of a world in which we have not lived, but there is little doubt that the generations of England who were brought up on Haggard, on Chesterton, on Blackwood—and on Stevenson, Conan Doyle, G. A. Henty, even Saki—were brought up as romantics, in the common sense of that word. While it is not easy to define romanticism in that common sense, we may at least note that ghost stories and stories of the un-dead make their first appearance in modern English literature with the Romantics, unless of course one wishes to count *Hamlet* as a ghost story. In any case, that these generations, and their romanticism, died in the trenches of the Great War is a truism. Like other truisms it is both true and overlooked, as it seems to be overlooked that Tolkien fought in that war and began his first epic of Middle Earth while convalescing.

It should be emphasized that the Edwardians of whom I am speaking were all of them storytellers. Their poetry—one thinks of Masefield or Kipling—was narrative poetry, even if it was not a narrative of princes and prelates. To a greater extent than in most of Victoria's reign, their natural form of narrative was the short story (it is worth recalling that only by an exercise of almost undiluted romanticism did Conan Doyle, in *The Hound of the Baskervilles*, succeed in writing a satisfactory novel about Sherlock Holmes). But their short stories in many cases, and their novels in some, were installments in a continuing story. I have elsewhere called these Edwardians "world-creators," and I am not sure how important it is that their worlds were created monthly in *The Strand* rather than in the three-deckers of Trollope's age. After all, Dickens published his novels in parts, but they are still novels, and (witness the Baker Street Irregulars) the world of Sherlock Holmes is still one world for all that it was created story by story over the years. The important point is that what were being told were stories—not tone-poems, not Dunsanian lyrics, not Mervyn Peak's word-pictures (though they may be first-rate of their kind), but stories.

All this should give an idea, albeit a sketchy one, of what kind of information exists to make up our first set of clues. It must be admitted that the information is not abundant. We have Tolkien's own word for it that he was neither as voracious nor as attentive a reader as his friend Lewis, and of course Lewis wrote that "no one ever influenced Tolkien—you might as well try to influence a bandersnatch." (Someone more adept than I at the intrica-

cies of Carrolliana may know why a bandersnatch would be particularly difficult to influence.) Even so, no writer, when young, is immune to influences,
and it is certainly reasonable for us to use such clues as we have to try to
determine who Tolkien's influences were.

Our second set of clues is, alas, equally sparse. One reason is that critics
in general (despite Lewis's lead in his *Experiment in Criticism*) have not
addressed themselves to most works of literature with the question in mind,
"How is this book being read?" Another reason, at least as important, is that
criticism of Tolkien has generally begun *de novo* with Tolkien, just as most
criticism of science fiction seems to begin *de novo* with the field of science
fiction, as though no other fiction had ever been written. But to this
approach to Tolkien *de novo* there are at least two exceptions that may be of
use in our inquiry, both of them provided by English critics. The particular
writers they pick as Tolkien's compeers are not, as it happens, the ones I
would pick, but this may only mean that their taste in Edwardian literature
differs from mine. Even if they are not entirely on the right track, I am
convinced at least that the track they are on begins from the right place.

Mr. Colin Wilson suggests a relationship between Tolkien and Jeffrey
Farnol. Now to say that Jeffrey Farnol is widely overlooked in histories of
English literature is to overstate the notice taken of him, but as Mr. Wilson
points out, his picaresque novels were enthusiastically circulated among the
members of Tolkien's generation. I do not myself believe that Tolkien read
the novels of Jeffrey Farnol, but I emphatically do believe that Mr. Wilson
reads Farnol's novels and Tolkien's three-decker for much the same reasons.

Similarly, Mr. Brian Aldiss compares Tolkien to the late P. G. Wodehouse. Now this is curious. Mr. Aldiss is a scholar of science fiction and
fantasy, and his discussion of Tolkien occurs in his history of science fiction.
Yet for a comparison he goes to an author who did not write science fiction
(though he may have written fantasy), and who would not generally be
considered to place high on the list of "authors comparable to Tolkien."
Upon consideration, I can see more reasons than were initially apparent for
the comparison—Wodehouse was, after all, a world-creator, and of a very
English world at that—but linking the two still has a certain oddness to it.
Oddness aside, it provides us with the evidence that Mr. Aldiss reads Tolkien
at least for some of the reasons he reads Wodehouse.

My own contribution here may be at least as odd. I might reasonably
make a general case for the parallel between Tolkienian "scholarship" and the
"scholarship" devoted to the arcana of Sherlock Holmes—thus suggesting
that some readers turn to Tolkien for the same reason that others turn to
221B Baker Street. I have already discussed the parallels between Tolkien and
Rider Haggard, and could easily claim I read one for largely the same reasons

I read the other. But I find by self-analysis that—in some moods at least—I read Tolkien as I read Saki (H. H. Munro).

That is a fact. What to do with it is a problem. Presumably I should be able to find an undercurrent of Tolkien's vision in Saki or an undercurrent of Saki's vision in Tolkien, or else find that I am particularly attracted to the Edwardian world-view exemplified by both. For the first, I cannot imagine that Tolkien enjoyed Saki: their humor, if not poles apart, is at least extremely dissimilar, and Tolkien lacks Saki's cruelty. Certainly any connection between Frodo Baggins and Clovis Sangrail is not obvious, nor—to put it mildly—is Comus Bassington the avatar of Gandalf the Grey. Admittedly, both Saki and Tolkien were Tories, and my own mind has that cast, but I would prefer for the moment to leave that line of thought aside as a possible red herring (or perhaps, in the circumstances, a blue herring?). I suspect that my turning to Saki, Mr. Aldiss's turning to Wodehouse, and Mr. Wilson's turning to Jeffrey Farnol have in common principally the fact that each of us is turning to the first (or close to the first) Edwardian author with whom we came in contact. I should note here that Mr. William Ready has observed the Edwardian nature of *The Lord of the Rings*, but he shuns what I welcome. Still, this is useful confirmatory evidence.

Those who have followed me thus far may think it odd, if not remarkable, that I have managed to discuss the sources and analogues of *The Lord of the Rings* without turning to the *Elder Edda* or *Beowulf* or any of the other commonplaces of the discussions generally heard on the literary genesis of Tolkien's work. But those are properly the subject of another inquiry: they are part of the influence of Tolkien's professional life on his imaginative life (though not the most important part). This, by contrast, is a look at the influence of other imaginative writers on Tolkien's imaginative life, so far as that influence affects the form of his work. By the nature of things (at least according to the "bandersnatch" theory), the *terminus ad quem* of this inquiry more or less antedates the *terminus a quo* of the other.

I have noted Tolkien's statement that his first response on reading a medieval work was to want to write a modern work in the same tradition. If that was true throughout his life, and not only of medieval works, then it is certainly proper to look at the kind of stories he read to see what kind of stories he was trying to write. I could wish I had in front of me the earliest manuscript of *The Silmarillion* as a check on my speculation, but failing that I have *The Lord of the Rings*, as well as a set of clues on the authors Tolkien read, and a set of clues made up of readers' reactions to Tolkien.

From these clues I would argue, with some confidence, that in *The Lord of the Rings* Tolkien set out to write an adventure story of the Rider Haggard sort, with overtones of G. K. Chesterton and undertones of Algernon Blackwood (to take only the authors mentioned here), an adventure story in what may be called the Edwardian mode. I would like to argue—anticlimax or not—that this "adventure story in the Edwardian mode" was precisely a "pre-existing form of literary creation" with its own set of expectations to excite and fulfill, and its own diverse powers. And I would like to spend some time examining the form.

The Edwardian adventure story might be of the "I have before me as I write" sort (to borrow Peter Fleming's phrase), in which a particular object associated with the adventure leads the author into his book. It might be a fictional travelogue, or at least a travel story, beginning with some such phrase as "It's eighteen months or so ago since I first met Sir Henry Curtis and Captain Good, and it was in this way." But however the story began, in general it would, like Conan Doyle's *The Lost World*, be framed in familiarity.

This is, in many ways, the mode of the fairy tale, though we do not always recognize it because the woodchoppers and petty kings with which the tales begin are, as Professor Lewis pointed out, as remote to us as the dragons and witches to which the tales proceed. But this is not quite the mode of the fairy tale, for the fairy tale begins "once upon a time," while the Edwardian adventure story begins in rooms in Oxford in the late 1880's, or rooms in Baker Street in the same decade, or with a Fleet Street journalist's assignment to interview an eccentric professor, or with an English poet in Saffron Park in the London of the Edwardian age. In economist's jargon, these beginnings are "time-specific."

In this adventure story odd and inexplicable things happen, not in Oxford or Baker Street or Saffron Park, but in the land of the Amahagger, or on Dartmoor, or on a lost plateau in South America, or in a kaleidoscopic adventure across a Europe of enchanted scenery and stock characters—the Europe, one might say, of a dream. In no case is characterization the chief concern of the story. Holly and Job in *She*, Malone and Lord John and Summerlee in the *Lost World*, Homes and Watson themselves, the Council of Days in *The Man Who Was Thursday*—all are types: the "true but ugly," the "faithful servant," and so on. That they sometimes, as with Holmes rise to the dignity of archetypes takes them further yet from the novel of character.

In a sense, even if it is a paradoxical sense, in many of these stories it is the character of nature, and not the characters of any of the actors, that is, as the French would put it, "realized." That is why Blackwood's "The Willows" follows naturally in the Edwardian mode: there is no real effort at characterization (the author's companion is a stolid Scandinavian), except at the characterization of the willows themselves. And the character that nature bears in these stories is not altogether a good one. (I suspect, by way of personal aside, that this is one of the attributes of Saki's work that appeals to me: there is a fey quality to "The Hounds of Fate" and "The Stag" and a thoroughgoing supernaturalism to "Gabriel-Ernest," standing in remarkable contrast to the world of Reginald or Clovis Sangrail. For comparison one might look to Badger's house on the one hand, and the Piper at the Gates of Dawn on the other.)

It should particularly be noted that the adventurers in the Edwardian adventure story are, in general, not solitary. They may indeed be "we few, we happy few," but (if only so that one may tell the story of the others), they are at least two in number—Holmes and Watson, for example. They are likely to be more than two: indeed, the characteristic Edwardian adventure story is that of Sir Henry Curtis, Captain Good, Allan Quatermain, and Ignosi, or of G. E. Challenger, Lord John Roxton, Edward Malone, and Professor Summerlee—the band of (very different) brothers. And the narrative is in the first person, even if it involves that first person's bringing in parts of the story of which he had no firsthand knowledge. That is, there is a convention that the story should be told by those whose story it is. In general, the narrator is the most ordinary member of the band of adventurers (Allan Quatermain, Edward Malone, John Watson), and the tone of the narration tends to be self-depreciating.

This tone, and the first-person narration, mark the Edwardian mode as something quite apart from the mode of the fairy tale or (*pace* Edmund Wilson) from the school story—though the school story does perhaps represent a separate but related development from the Victorians. I suppose this Edwardian mode of the adventure story had its origin in the travel journals and first-person newspaper accounts that were conspicuous features of the English and American literary landscape in the second half of the nineteenth century. The names of Richard Burton and H. M. Stanley come immediately to mind, followed by the war correspondent W. H. Russell and the American John Lloyd Stephens, whose *Incidents of Travel in Central America, Chiapas, and Yucatan* is one of the finest examples of this Victorian literature of exploration. It should, however, be pointed out that the self-depreciating tone comes in later, and may have its origins in the tradition of the *pukka sahib*— stiff upper lip, British understatement, and all that—that is in part the legacy of the Duke of Wellington. In any event, the Edwardian adventure story would appear to be a case of art imitating life.

One could, I suppose, distinguish between this travel literature and the derivative literature of Rider Haggard or Conan Doyle, on the grounds that one is more interested in the traveling and the other in what lies at the end— the object of the quest—thus making *King Solomon's Mines* or *She* into a quest story. But I am not sure this would be profitable. The Edwardian adventure story was indeed a story of Englishmen abroad in the wide and mysterious world, but what they were looking for was not so much the Holy Grail or the Golden Fleece as—whatever excuse may have been provided by Maple White or the Shard of Amyntas—the wide world itself. (It is worth noting that the best of Blackwood's stories take place on the Danube or in Canada or in the Alps.) And I find this parallels *The Lord of the Rings*: it does not seem to me that Frodo sets out on a quest much more than Bilbo set out on one in *The Hobbit*. Certainly Frodo and Bilbo, though they are Hobbits, are Englishmen, and to them the "back again" in the subtitle of *The Hobbit* is as important as the "there."

As I have said, the actors in these Edwardian stories were stock Englishmen, most of them. Mostly they returned to England and their workaday lives, if they survived at all. It is not my purpose here to point out in detail how *The Lord of the Rings* conforms to the Edwardian mode, only to suggest its conformity, but perhaps another example of that mode would not be amiss. The example that comes most quickly to mind (though it is late, having appeared in 1923) is John Buchan's *Huntingtower*, in which the character of the Scottish businessman is so Tolkienian that one would almost assume that Tolkien took time off from *The Year's Work in English Studies* to read Buchan. Buchan, admittedly, was Scottish, while the Shire is "forever England"—but that is not an insuperable difference.

The quite ordinary Englishmen (or, occasionally, Scots or Irishmen) who set off on their travels in these Edwardian adventure stories do more than merely see strange sights and have strange adventures: they sense a mysterious character indwelling in the world itself, or at least in that part of the world in which the adventures take place. The story may be of their triumph over nature (as with *The Lost World*), or it may be of their escape from it ("The Willows"). It may be, in its later and lesser form, a story of romance and a mysterious Russian princess (as with *Huntingtower*). Or the mystery may be—and frequently is—that of the past mysteriously alive in the present. This is the case with *King Solomon's Mines*, *She*, *The Lost World*, much of Chesterton, and the very idea of the ghost story, whether by Blackwood or M. R. James or whomever. In fact, from the number of examples I can call to mind, this might be taken as a hallmark of the Edwardian mode. To be sure, others have felt the lure of the past: it is a part of the nature of romanticism, and it was a Victorian, not an Edwardian, who wrote (if he wrote nothing else worthwhile) the great line "A rose red city half as old as time." But the past alive in the present is a recurring motif in the Edwardian adventure story nonetheless.

The framework of the story, even in Haggard's time, is "there and back again." The "back again" is skimped, and it would appear, in part, a convention necessitated by the first person narrative: the narrator has to return home in order to tell his story (though Haggard did find a way around this in *She*). By Blackwood's time—as a result, I suppose, of the short-story form—the framework largely disappears, and we are left with the real kernel of the story, which in Blackwood is the mystery (or the "supernaturalism") of nature. (Chesterton dropped the first-person narrative, while retaining the viewpoint of the first-person narrator, who likewise must return home to tell the story.)

It may be objected that I have taken three disparate authors and parceled them together very oddly, and that an "Edwardian mode" that over-looks Baron Corvo on the one hand or Henry James on the other is scarcely worth discussing seriously. Now I could look at either of these and find something of the sense of the past I have been discussing here, just as I could find it in Bram Stoker. But what have I, and what has Tolkien, to do with feigned autobiography in the manner of *Hadrian VII* or novels of character in the manner of *The Ambassadors*? The ancestry of the adventure story in its Edwardian mode is to be found in Scott and the Dickens of *A Tale of Two Cities*, as well as in Burton, Stanley, John Lloyd Stephens—the list is almost endless. It has its late Victorian affinities in G. A. Henty—and as in Henty's novels, where boys who make their way without benefit of birth are frequently found to have had that benefit all along (but to have been stolen or orphaned as very young children), the Edwardian adventure story is frankly aristocratic in its conventions, as was the Edwardian world from which it came.

That *The Lord of the Rings* is an exemplar of this Edwardian mode is at the root of the adverse reactions by such readers as William Ready or Edmund Wilson. In a way—and here Mr. Aldiss is quite correct—its basic presuppositions are those of P. G. Wodehouse, though Tolkien's knowledge of political reality was far superior to Wodehouse's (on which see Dr. Plank's essay on "The Scouring of the Shire"). I am not here concerned with the literary value of Edwardian adventure stories (except to note that Lewis's test in his *Experiment in Criticism* should convince us that they have a value). But Tolkien's adverse critics have in fact been concerned with that value, to the extent of denying that it exists. I am not here concerned with such questions as whether the aristocratic—or the Tory—view of things is the right one. But Tolkien's adverse critics have in fact been concerned with that question, and have come up with an unequivocal answer, unequivocally expressed. What the adverse critics have not been concerned with is what I am concerned with here: using my scattered evidence on sources to find out what kind of work Tolkien is likely to have been writing.

Certainly this adventure story in the Edwardian mode is a prime candidate to be considered the pre-existing form to which *The Lord of the Rings* was designed to contribute. At the very least, a formal comparison of *The Lord of the Rings* with various exemplars of the mode should prove to be enlightening. While not making the formal comparison here, I might suggest the lines along which it could be made. Take Conan Doyle's *The Lost World* as an exemplar. In this story the four travelers come together more or less by accident—or by the machinations of Professor Challenger (who is not with them for the entire journey). *The Lord of the Rings* has, of course, nine travelers, who come together more or less by accident—or partly by Gandalf's intent (and Gandalf does not make the entire journey with them). The four travel to unknown lands, seeking a way up (and then a way down) a mysterious plateau—involving, on the way down, travel through a cave. The Nine Walkers likewise travel to unknown lands, with Frodo and Sam seeking a way up (through Shelob's cave). The four are types: sportsman, Irish rugger, desiccated (but tough) professor, eccentric omnicompetent. The Nine likewise are types: master and man, enthusiastic but fallible assistants, warrior, king-in-exile, elf, dwarf, and the eccentric omnicompetent, Gandalf.

Further parallels are easy enough to discover. Nature—in the form of prehistoric animals and even (perhaps) the ape-men—attacks the four. Nature—in the form of Old Man Willow or the snow at Caradhras—attacks the Nine. The four come safely through to the triumph; eight of the Nine Walkers do likewise. The story of the four is told by the most "ordinary" of the group, Edward Dunn Malone (but, ordinary or not, "there are heroisms all around us"). Similarly, the story of the Nine is told by Frodo, whom David Miller has called "the common lens for heroic experience"—ordinary on the surface if not beneath it. The very attraction of the lost world is the past alive in the present on the mysterious plateau. And certainly the continually sounding theme of *The Lord of the Rings* is the past alive in the present: the Ring, Gandalf, Galadriel, Elrond, the sword reforged, the Barrow Wights—to list examples is to list nearly everything in the book.

I have elsewhere suggested that after the Great War there was a division in the Edwardian inheritance between the storytellers and the world-recreators—between Edgar Rice Burroughs and Angela Thirkell, the pulp writers and the country-house novelists. One might almost say the division was between those who were chiefly interested in the "there" and those who were chiefly interested in the "back again." I still think that this is true, and that, as I also suggested, Tolkien brought the long-sundered branches of the Edwardian line back together again—for which reason he, more than P. G. Wodehouse, deserved the title of "the last Edwardian." But I am not sure how much emphasis this merits here. Though the Shire's Tory quality is unmistakable, its idylls include no country houses, and my present concern is not with the Edwardian inheritance so much as the Edwardian mode of

The Lord of the Rings—with the fact that whatever the mode in which others were writing. Tolkien was writing an Edwardian adventure story.

It may be introduced as an objection that the Edwardian mode tended at least toward shorter novels, and in its final form toward the short story. Moreover, the speed of its writing, as well as the pace of its action, was almost journalistic. Haggard wrote *King Solomon's Mines* in six weeks, and Conan Doyle cranked out Sherlock Holmes at high speed for monthly publication. Chesterton wrote prodigiously, hastily—one might say, gargantuanly. But Tolkien wrote a three-decker novel and he took forty years to write it, if one counts from his beginning *The Silmarillion*, or twenty-five years, if one counts from the time he began the story of Bilbo Baggins. I think we will find, however that the variation in the basic form represented by *The Lord of the Rings* was determined by Tolkien's professional life, and its period of gestation determined the same way. That is to say, what differentiates Tolkien from other writers of Edwardian adventure stories generally would be properly treated in a discussion of the influence of his professional life on his imaginative creation, with the root of the difference lying in the love of language that led him to philology as his life's work.

But that, as Aristotle taught us the formula (long before Kipling), is another story. To be exact, it is the story of the philologist's world, and not the Edwardian mode, of *The Lord of the Rings*. To write it requires some knowledge of what a philologist does and how his mind works. To write what I have written here so far has required only a knowledge of what it was Tolkien read in the first ten years of this century, or may have read—a far easier requirement, and made easier yet for me by the fact that I was brought up on the same books. To me this game of *Quellenforschung* has been a game of auld acquaintance, and doubly enjoyable on that account.

But it has been, I hope, instructive to the reader besides being entertaining to me. And its value, I think, is clear: we will be armed against a tendency to attack (or defend) Tolkien on the wrong grounds if we can determine what the proper grounds are—that is, what *The Lord of the Rings* is intended to be. To go back for a moment to Professor Lewis's example, it is necessary to know what the corkscrew or the cathedral is designed to do before we can say it is well- or ill-designed: once we know what the purposes are, the prohibitionist may attack the corkscrew or the Communist attack the cathedral. And here it is important that we realize one thing: the attack of the prohibitionist or the Communist is not an attack on how well the corkscrew or the cathedral works. The better the corkscrew works, the less the prohibitionist will like it. The more men pray in the cathedral, the more the Communist will seek to shut it down. The greater the success of *The Lord of the Rings* as an adventure story in the Edwardian mode, the more those who dislike adventure stories in the Edwardian mode will seek to denigrate and depreciate it.

In part, the critical dislike of this mode is merely an example of the critical dislike of adventure stories of all kinds, a point which Professor Lewis illustrated in his essay "On Stories" and which I need not illustrate here. But the dislike runs deeper for this mode than for others, and I suspect that there are those who enjoy *Don Quixote* or *The Three Musketeers* who do not enjoy the Edwardian adventure story any more than they enjoy the *Chanson de Roland*, with its good Christians and bad infidels ("Paiens ont tort et chrestiens ont droit"). The different modes of the adventure story appeal, I believe, to somewhat different—perhaps very different—audiences, and it would be a mistake not to distinguish among these modes.

The particular characteristics of the Edwardian mode that seem to cause the most trouble for the critics are those that apparently form the substratum of almost all popular Edwardian literature: the aristocratic view, the black-and-white morality, the lack of interest in character development (certainly more extreme in this mode than in others), the movement of "there and back again," the emphasis on "we few, we happy few" (related to, but not altogether the same as, the aristocratic view), the fascination of the past alive in the present, the undercurrent of mystery (or even malignity) in nature. If one looks at the chief forms of the adventure story a few years into the last quarter of the twentieth century, he will find not these but the morally ambiguous: the hard-drinking and hard-wrenching private eye, the solipsistic James Bond, the not-so-good sheriff and not-so-bad outlaw. If all these are part of the current mode of the adventure story, we could reasonably expect to find the Edwardian mode disliked.

Now the evidence of Mr. Wilson and Mr. Aldiss (and in conversation I have found others who support his linking of Tolkien and Wodehouse), as well as my own aberration in the direction of the world of Clovis Sangrail, should make it clear that there are some readers who enjoy the Edwardian character of *The Lord of the Rings*, for all that Mr. Wilson seems a little uncomfortable in his position and Mr. Aldiss speaks of "the counterfeit gold of an Edwardian sunset." But we must be careful not to claim greatness for Tolkien merely because we are enamored of the Edwardian mode, just as those who dislike it should be careful not to deny him greatness because they are not so enamored.

And yet, I can hear my readers saying to themselves, "This is all very well, but how can he speak of the Edwardian mode of the adventure story in the same terms in which Lewis spoke of something so far beyond it as the secondary epic? Surely it is a little odd to speak of Tolkien in terms that have been reserved for Vergil or Milton. Surely he has lost his sense of proportion." But a brief explanation should allay such misgivings.

It may indeed be the case that an epic is a greater thing than an adventure story; that does not mean that a given epic is greater than a given adventure story. I could also point out that Milton's "Epic following Nature" is very like an adventure story—perhaps, indeed, it would be well to note this as a corrective to the view that an adventure story is an inferior thing. Moreover, if a critical system is well drawn up, it should be applicable not only to Vergil and Milton but to the writers of three-deckers (let us say Tolkien and Trollope) as well. And there remains the corrective supplied in Professor Lewis's *Experiment*: if the work is capable of "good" reading (and especially of re-reading), then we had best be wary for dismissing it out of hand, or indeed at all. After all, popular literature (*vide* Shakespeare in his age) is not necessarily bad, and there is a genuine critical approach embodied in the assertion, "I don't know much about art but I know what I like."

Admittedly, we are too close in time to *The Lord of the Rings* to judge its place in literary history. Yet we are not close enough in time, it appears, to judge accurately what it is supposed to be. Tolkien disliked the idea that anyone might write a critical study of his work while he was alive, both because he was a private man not welcoming fame and because he thought it wrong that someone should spin theories about what he had written without checking those theories with him. One appreciates his point, but one must also recognize that it has made criticism of his work more difficult: just as one would have enjoyed a talk with Lewis's ancient Athenian, if not his dinosaur in the laboratory, one would like to have spoken with the last Edwardian.

I suspect more may be recovered than I have recovered here. Haggard and Chesterton and Blackwood were not the only authors the young Tolkien read, and Mr. Wilson and Mr. Aldiss are certainly not the only critics to have examined Tolkien's work in ways that are useful for this kind of endeavor. But I would strongly urge those who seek more information to follow this path. Certainly enough evidence exists to show that *The Lord of the Rings* is an adventure story in the Edwardian mode. And whether we believe it to be as sublime as the cathedral, or as mundane as the corkscrew, or somewhere in between in merry middle-earth, it should be worth something to us to have some idea what it is.

D A V I D   L .   J E F F R E Y

Recovery: Name in The Lord of the Rings

Students of Tolkien have often noted that while Tolkien denies allegorical intention in *The Lord of the Rings*, the trilogy does seem to have a few allegorical features. Among these are relatively archetypal items such as Gollum's (Sméagol's) Cainlike murder of his brother Déagol in the story's ur-past, the tree symbolism analogues, the fall of Sauron on March 25 (which Tolkien certainly knew as the date of the Feast of the Annunciation) and also, as I hope to clarify, the name and characterization of Aragorn himself. Typically, these elements have been regarded, in respect of Tolkien's testimony, as part of the writer's richly allusive characterization.

The other notable component of the allusive texture of the trilogy is one Tolkien does not deny: the countless evocations of old Germanic and Gaelic mythology along with traces of their original languages. It has been observed already that the Ring, and Faramir and Éowyn, are to be found in thirteenth-century German literature, that Isildur's story may be read in the *Poetic Edda* and *Nibelungenlied*, and that the speech of the Rohirrim is very close to Old English. (It is actually, in some respects, even closer to Old Norse.) Typically, these elements have also been regarded, in tribute to Tolkien's scholarship, as deliberate attributes of the writer's richly allusive philological style.

It seems to me that both philological allusion and what sometimes

From *Tolkien: New Critical Perspectives*, edited by Neil D. Isaacs and Rose A. Zimbardo. © 1981 by The University Press of Kentucky.

appears to be allegory (but which in Tolkien ought to be called, as he calls it, "Recovery") are intrinsic and fundamental expressions of Tolkien's subcreative method. Philology and allegory both offer ways of looking back. Tolkien is, most of us would agree, heartily interested in looking back, and it is in keeping with this interest that by retrospective and synthetic definition he should offer us access to an understanding of his subcreation's force: "To ask what is the origin of stories (however qualified),"he says, "is to ask what is the origin of language and of the mind."

Again, in contextualizing his "cordial dislike" for "allegory in all its manifestations," he asserts that he "much prefer[s] *history*, true or feigned, with its varied applicability to the thought and experience of readers." I should like to offer the simple observation that for a medieval philologist the natural confluence of history, language, and personal thinking comes at the point of *name*, and that once one has understood what this means in *The Lord of the Rings*, the appreciation of what formerly appeared to be rich allusion is likely to be heightened to a new appreciation as the trilogy's most basic vocabulary.

In relating the origin of stories to the origin of language and the mind Tolkien suggests how it is that "Secondary Belief" must be the arena of a subcreation's engagement, and thereby doubly demonstrates how fundamental to his art is his acceptance of a traditional Christian doctrine of Creation. Yet his work resists Christian allegory. In acknowledging that in traditional one-to-one (text-to-text) terms allegory is not to be found in *The Lord of the Rings*, R. J. Reilly has offered a description of the allusive, numinous elements as "inherent morality," and related that to "the sense of a cosmic moral law" as found in C. S. Lewis and George Macdonald. One supposes that it is these same numinous elements that have led enthusiasts to speak of the trilogy as a "personal theology," "like a Bible," or as containing "all the necessary materials for a religion." The same elements, and fairly enough, lead Patrick Grant to a sustained Jungian analysis of the archetypal patterns in Tolkien's characters, and to an interpretation of the trilogy's allusive texture as metaphorical and mythic in the Jungian sense, rather than, in any received sense, allegorical. These approaches seem to me to be responding to the right patterns, and I should like to contribute to an affirmation of their perceptions from a philological point of view.

What does Tolkien mean when he avers that he prefers "history" to allegory? Here we need to remember Tolkien's familiarity with the perspective of medieval writing, of writing as subcreation. For a medieval writer, writing is always an analogous activity, a repetition in history of patterns first translated in Creation, and in the Garden of Eden. In the medieval view all writing that is true will inevitably, even in the world of fallen fantasy, exemplify. The medieval writer believes that except in primary Creation, and in the Incarnation, nothing happens for the first time. The men and events of the Old Testament prefigure those of the New, and the lives of the Fathers and the saints repeat the pattern laid down from the beginning. History patterns: the medieval view is a view of representative history, of history *sub speci aeternitatis*. Or history as poetry.

In quite traditional vocabulary, then, it is possible to see that Tolkien's medievalism makes available insights into subcreation (and Secondary Belief) parallel to those afforded by the more recent vocabulary of Jung. I say "parallel," not "coeval," because Tolkien, like Lewis and Barfield, submits his appreciation of archetypes to a traditional acknowledgment of creation. As Patrick Grant puts it, "Lewis's criticism that Jung offers a myth to explain a myth can be met only by assertion: there is a myth that is true, and fundamental." In everything he writes, but particularly clearly in *On Fairy-Stories*, a fundamentally true creation is Tolkien's working premise. From out of the world of fallen fantasy, as he calls it, students (or writers) gather leaves. But this, though secondary, is far from invidiously reductive or simply repetitious:

> Who can design a new leaf? The patterns from bud to unfolding, and the colours from spring to autumn were all discovered by men long ago. But that is not true. The seed of the tree can be replanted in any soil. . . . Spring is, of course, not really less beautiful because we have seen or heard of other like events: like events, never from world's beginning to world's end the same event. Each leaf, of oak and ash and thorn, is a unique embodiment of pattern, and for some this very year may be the embodiment, the first ever seen and recognized, though oaks have put forth leaves for countless generations of men.

Leaf is pattern. Yet since even fallen leaves are not authorized by men, in the pattern of story the focus is not on the leaves as allegories but on the art of their ingathering. Or to put the same thought in another way, where the medieval writer would say that allegory was not so much a way of writing as a theory of history (in which men and events signify, as do words), for Tolkien the activity he calls "Recovery" (as of leaves) likewise exemplifies a view of history.

The term "Recovery" presupposes that something has been lost. The idea, Tolkien tells us, "includes [the] return and renewal of health," and here his chthonic vocabulary reminds us that his doctrines of creation and subcreation consistently interpret the matrix of art as "the fantasy of fallen Man."

The Lord of the Rings is a work of art which develops an acute sense of *fall*, the dissipation of the strength and power of Lothlórien, a Lothlórien largely recalled in mysterious and powerful utterances of its ancient tongue. Lothlórien, though diminished, is even yet a place with a different sense of time, a place of *light* and "no stain," characterized by a garden, by harmony, and by a mysterious tree.

But there came a time, as Glóin puts it, "that a shadow of disquiet fell upon [his] people." The power of the Dark Lord is shown in estrangement, a separation of men from men, men from elves, and elves from each other. And we are told that the elves that fell, fell by "their eagerness for knowledge, by which Sauron ensnared them." We see, too, that the knowledge by which Sauron ensnares, symbolized by Orthanc, is very different from the kind of knowledge desired by the elves when they first made the elf-rings, not as weapons of war, or conquest. "Those who made them," Elrond says, "did not desire strength or domination or hoarded wealth, but understanding, making, and healing, to preserve all things unstained." The elves of old, in a sense, were proto-recoverers. And Recovery, in every sense in *The Lord of the Rings*, seems within the pale of belief because the universe is, if diminished, not totally corrupted. We are shown that the language of the elves still has the power to "recover"—to still Shelob, the watchers, the Nazgûl. That is, it is language that most powerfully preserves the traces, the pattern in the leaf of the world's first forest. The great opposition in *The Lord of the Rings* is an opposition between a Recovery of old elven wisdom and a present obtrusiveness of the knowledge of Orthanc. It is expressed as a struggle between the language of elves and the gobble of orcs.

Language makes possible Recovery. For a medieval philologist there is a rich and multivalent sense in which language is itself allegory. Or at least the modern philologist recognizes this view of language in the medieval writers he studies. To express the idea in the simplest terms, we might say that for a medieval writer language had central value because it mediates between mankind's two appreciations of reality: history and dream. (One could describe the two aspects of medieval reality in other terms, of course, e.g., time and eternity, nature and grace, memory and desire, etc., and in the end each would come to mean much the same thing.) Between history and dream comes language. For a medieval Christian, following Saint Augustine, language provides a paradigm for all human understanding, seeming, as it does, to express timeless truth through an utterance in time. *Verbum caro factum est* models, in the Word, the relationship of God to the world. But Christian reality contains both appreciations. It is neither "the Platonic dream of disembodied logos, an intellectual reality totally divorced from the world, nor an unintelligible [historical] nightmare irredeemably lost in the world." In medieval Christian reality, God's word is eternal, external, from the beginning. History is a kind of continuous writing of the unfolding of God's word in time, until, as in the words of Isaiah's vision, "the heavens shall be folded together as a book."

We see then that the primary book, like the primary creation, remains under the authorship of God. All literature, for the Middle Ages, forms a present gloss on an absent text, or, in Dante's words, "shadowy manifestations of the vision of God's Book." Yet shadowy or not, fallen or not, in a logo-centric perspective, text like language itself lives as a mediator, as a conjoiner of realities, and Tolkien affirms this medieval view of language emphatically, both in historical terms and as a personal perspective in his *Beowulf* essay. But as a medievalist and a philologist Tolkien also knew that the very closest and most faithful mediation of language—especially between present and shadowy past—comes in the Recovery made possible by the meaning of *names.*

Aragorn is a name compounded from elements that are highly evoca-tive for a philologist who has studied European languages of the last millen-nium. The first syllable, *ar*, is one of the most pregnant monosyllabic words in the Old English language and it is found with cognate meaning in many other Indo-European languages (e.g., Gk *arêtê*; OIr *ara*; Goth *áirus*; OSw *êru*; ON *árr, éru, æru*; OHG *êra*). It is glossed in early texts in four ways, three of which are correlative: as a person, as a quality of character, and as a personal action. When *ar* denotes a person it is glossed as *nuntius, apostolus, angelus minister*, as in "ba com dryhtnes *ar* of heofonum," ("then came the messenger of the Lord from heaven). When it signifies a quality of character the glosses are *honor, dignitas, gloria, magnificentia, honestas, reverentia*, as in "sie him *ar* and onweald in rodera rice" ("may he have glory and power in the kingdom of heaven"), or in "ióva us ba *ar*, be be Gabriel brohte!" ("reveal to us the glory which Gabriel brought to you"), or in "bringaõ nu drihtne wlite and *ar*," ("offer the Lord glory and honour"). When *ar* indicates a personal action, the glosses read *gratia, misericordia, beneficium, favor*, as in "cymeõ him seõ *ar* of heofnum," or in "bam be *ar* seceõ, frofre be fader on heofnum."

While the middle syllable of Aragorn could be thought of as a kind of possessive infix, much more likely the last two syllables should be taken together as *agorn*, alluding to OE *agan* (to possess), and to the OE verb *agangan* (to pass by unnoticed, but also to surpass; to travel quickly; to come forth; to come to pass): "geseah he wunder on wite *agangan*" ("he saw a miracle come to pass"), "aer his tid *aga*"; "ba *agangen* was tynhund wintra fram . . ." "Wyrd ne cubon, . . . swa hit *agangen* wearõ eorla manegum" *Beowulf*, 1234.

It is in the context of all of these associations, too, that we begin to acquire a fuller understanding of the name Arwen, the elven lady who

Aragorn loves and for whom he works and waits. The second syllable of her name, *wen*, is related to OE *wyn* ("joy"), yielding therefore "the joy of *ar*." But the form *wen* (as opposed to *wyn* in *Éowyn*), though it is related to "joy"—"hearpan *wyn*, gomen glēobeames"—also has the meanings "prospect," "conviction," "belief," and "expectation," as in "Him seo *wen* geleah" (Gen. 49, 1446; *Beowulf* 2323). It is also used in the sense of "faith," "in the fullness of time," or faith in Providence.

We see then that Aragorn has a name charged with meaning which even in its application of character history, is an incarnation of the tale's dream structure. But we see something more: that the encounter of history and dream finds in name, if not in plot, an interpenetration that must recall the Incarnation, that is indeed a recollection or "Recovery" of the meaning of that event. Yet association with biblical language is "accidental," tacit rather than explicit, in that Tolkien has chosen to anchor his referential language beneath the conscious structure of other mythic formulations (biblical or Germanic) in the subconsciously meaningful deep structure of Western language itself. The weightiest register of Strider's full name lies in the access of its roots to a language spoken before any of the contending tongues of Middle-earth in which his name still means, at a time when all language was much closer to one.

The register of deep meaning in Tolkien's names helps, I think, to guide us away from a bifocal view of some events which might otherwise be too lightly construed as allegorical in the traditional sense. Yet even as we recall these events we can at least appreciate how they might easily evoke interpretations both allegorical and archetypal: Aragorn comes to the great battle out of the Paths of the Dead and from the sea. He is the exiled king who returns. It is suggested by Pippin that he is related to Gandalf; he is the elf-man, the one by whom that which was long ago separated and estranged is now joined—he speaks of Elrond as "the eldest of all our race," he takes the elf-name Elessar (ON "one who appears in another manner"), and he marries at last an elven lady who is his perfect complement, and who represents the recovery of a joy which overcomes his eros-longing (*Ar*-wen, "the joy of *ar*").

Appropriately then, as symbol of an old wound healed, he is the king who heals, the "Renewer." He employs, symbolically, the *athelas* (OE "spirit of the King, or God"), breathing on the wounded, creating and restoring their health. As Faramir (ON *fara*, to travel) awakens, he speaks:

> "My lord, you called me. I come. What does the king command?"
> "Walk no more in the shadows, but awake!" said Aragorn. "You are weary. Rest a while, and take food, and be ready when I return."

"I will, lord," said Farmir. "For who would lie idle when the king has returned?"

The reign of Aragorn, and that of his heirs, is to be dominion over all Middle-earth, "unto the ending of the world." He ushers in a New Law of mercy, and a New Age: it is no longer the Third Age of Middle-earth. Symbolically, there is a new tree. And though Aragorn dies, his death is not a cause for despair—in fact his coming is meant to banish despair. His final speech is that which promises the transformation of history in the book: "But let us not be over-thrown at the final test, who of old renounced the Shadow and the Ring. In sorrow we must go, but not in despair. Behold! We are not bound for ever to the circles of the world, and beyond them is more than memory. Farewell!"

Measured against the backdrop of events, we see even more clearly that Aragorn's name is, philologically speaking, incarnational. Language remembers much, and in the perspective provided by names the quasi-allegorical characterization in parts of *The Lord of the Rings* can be seen, mythologically, archetypally, and philologically, as a pattern of "recovery." Characterization and action become a kind of gloss on the name. Or we could say that Tolkien's subcreation, in respects both psychological and philological, constitutes, in a manner analogous to medieval writing, a present gloss on an absent text.

This idea could, I think, be extended much further in the whole work. For example, the sensitive handling of Éowyn's love (OE *eow*, "thou," *wyn*, "joy") for Aragorn, which he must restrain in favor of Arwen, can be interpreted through a comparison of the meaning of their names in relation to his own. This sort of speculation and etymologizing is a game, to be sure, but just such a philological entertainment as is consistent with the language-making of the whole trilogy, and it is natural to the character of mind demonstrated by this philological and medievalist author at every other turn, from his lectures on *Beowulf* to his notes on *Sir Gawain and the Green Knight*.

That Tolkien is trying to achieve much more with the idea of Recovery than the mere calling up of individual Indo-European languages is made evident in his selection of language elements which are still powerfully evocative for our residual collective memories because, in key names from Aragorn to Legolas to Mordor, the morphology and lexicology is so close to roots that the names are open to understanding in all the tongues of Middle-earth. The function of philological recovery, as of the recovery of history, is here much more than the surface illusion of being conversant in strange tongues: it is a participatory inculcation in an ancient depth of language, of word, and of name still accessible to us all through the subliminal, often unacknowledged, but persistent half-conversance which we share—despite that first dark tower.

Much has been written about Tolkien's eucatastrophe and anagogy, and I will not indulge myself by adding my own *peroratio* to those insights. But I do think it fair to conclude by suggesting that what Tolkien would have us catch sight of in the "sudden glimpse" of the good fairy story's eucatastrophe is as much an incarnational reality as his Eucharistic (Christian), historical, and philological terminology implies, and that its narrative realization, as secondary belief, is the realization in story of a primally powerful Word, one which as Word, comprises both aspects of reality—history and dream. "Recovery," as he says, "is a regaining—regaining of a clear view." Since now, in the world of fallen fantasy, we see through a glass darkly, we need, as he says, "to clean our windows" to see "things as we are (or were) meant to see them . . . as things apart from ourselves." The virtue of incarnational language is that, in it, subject and object reacquire their integrity and are not forever confused. In the making of his subcreation and in the response it evokes, Tolkien invites us to see subcreation in Adam's terms, as *naming*, and yet to see the meaning of name in *The Lord of the Rings* as the very pattern in the leaf, the leaf of the world's first forest as the leaf of the world's first book.

ROSE A. ZIMBARDO

The Medieval-Renaissance Vision of
The Lord of the Rings

In the course of this paper I will be talking about a vision of cosmic harmony—the great *discordia concors*—that was celebrated in English literature until the mid-seventeenth century, when men—even poets, who should have known better—discarded that image, as Tolkien's friend, C. S. Lewis, tells us, and, in the spirit of Saruman, set up their own reason as their god and launched us into the dark ages from which we are still struggling to emerge. It is for that reason that I cannot label the imaginative vision that shapes *The Lord of the Rings* as either "medieval" or "Renaissance"; Lewis was, to my mind, quite right in arguing the falsity of such a distinction.

What has always interested me about *The Lord of the Rings* is its title. So sensitive was Tolkien to language, so fully aware that to "name" a power is to give it life and even to become subject to it, that he surely did not name his trilogy for Sauron, the Dark Lord, and, as surely, the rings of his title are not to be identified with the terrible Ring of his tale. Who then is the Lord of the Rings whom the title and the tale celebrate, and what is the nature of the rings that he holds?

As we all know, Tolkien was a scholar as well as a teller of tales; the conception of artistic "imitation," or the way that tale imitates truth, that he held is that which dominates the thought of the period he studied. His conception is quite different from most post-eighteenth-century conceptions

From *Tolkien: New Critical Perspectives*, edited by Neil D. Isaacs and Rose A. Zimbardo. © 1981 by The University Press of Kentucky.

of artistic imitation, which, by attempting to shape art to the dimensions of what can be empirically known, diminish the function of art, narrow the conception of the "nature" that art imitates to the confines of human experience, and confuse "realism" with reality. For Tolkien's conception of artistic imitation we must go back to the Renaissance commonplaces that associate the creative artist with the Creator, that make his arena "the Globe," and that consider a work of art a design that, as Sidney says in *An Apologie for Poesie*, "shewes such formes as nature, often erring, would shew" if she could. This esthetic conception originates in the thinking of the late medieval commentators. As Hugh of St. Victor puts it: "This entire perceptible world is as a book written by the finger of God, that is created by divine power, and individual creatures are as figures within it, not invented by human will (arbitrio), but instituted by Divine authority (placito) to make manifest the invisible things of God."

Conversely, for the medieval-Renaissance artist, a book is a design of figures moving in an interrelation that "makes manifest the invisible things of God"; it is an imitation of the world, and, like the world, it manifests the nature of the Creator. The Lord of the Rings that Tolkien's trilogy celebrates is God, the Creator; the rings that he holds are the concentric circles of all created life that stretch from the well-balanced individual soul of each creature to the farthest reaches of the cosmos—to sound what the Renaissance called "the music of the spheres." Because Tolkien attempted to revive the medieval-Renaissance conception of artistic imitation, he could slough off as irrelevant the criticisms of those reviewers who faulted him for not having "realistic characters" and could be impatient with others who labeled his work an "allegory," as though, to his mind, this whole world and all of us in it were not an "allegory" of sorts.

Two principles govern the visionary world of *The Lord of the Rings*: the twin principles that the Renaissance called "permanence in mutability" (the idea that we find in Spencer's *Cantos of Mutabilitie*) and *discordia concors*, the idea that the harmony of the whole of creation depends upon the variety within, and the balance among, each of its parts. The time scope of *The Lord of the Rings* implies vast reaches beyond the "last battle" to which the narrative confines itself. The age of wizards, elves, dwarves, men, and hobbits that we see is unique in itself (and insofar as it *is* unique, it must pass); but it is also a recapitulation of ages that have been, as the songs of the elves reminds us, and it is also a preparation for ages to come. The temporal order that *The Lord of the Rings* implies is in itself a ring—the ring of endless renewal.

Each age must pass, but in every age, if the inhabitants of the world set right the balance of a time that may seem in their eyes to be "out of joint," if they capture the past in poetry—as the elves do—and if they plants seeds for coming generations, they can insure a new birth and can thereby contribute in their turn of time to the cycle of endless renewal. Each creature, each generation, each species must pass, because each is subject to the law of mutability, but their passage insures the birth of new ages. All forms of life are subject to change, but in that change nothing is lost. Gandalf the Grey goes through death and reemerges as Gandalf the White. The idea is perhaps best expressed by Golding, the Renaissance translator, who tells us in the introductory epistle to his translation of Ovid's *Metamorphoses:*

> Of this same dark Philosophie of turned shapes, the same
> Hath Ovid into one whole masse in this book brought in
> frame.
> Foure kinds of things in this his work the Poet doth
> conteyne.
> That nothing under heaven doth ay in stedfast state
> remayne.
> And next that nothing perisheth; but that each substance
> takes
> Another shape than that it had . . .
> Then sheweth he the soule of man from dying to be free.

The temptation that the "One Ring" (and its terrible significance is that it is the *"One"* Ring, or the Ring of Oneness) has for Galadriel is the temptation that is presented to the powerful in every generation from the necromancer of the middle ages to the cryogenist of our own—to make *my* time all time, to make *my*self or *my* people immortal by freezing the cycle of regeneration to my own needs.

Galadriel's wisdom is sufficient to the test; she knows that her people must in their time "go West" and pass into another dimension of being in order for the seeds they have planted and the songs they have made to pass into the hands of a new age of creatures and thereby, curiously, to enter "the artifice of eternity"—the greater time that poetry imitates. Because she loves her people, and all living things, she knows that the only alternative to passage through time is enslavement in it. As she tells Frodo, who offers her the Ring, if she were to use it she would cease to be Galadriel, the soul of Lothlórien, and would become the "Terrible Queen," another Sauron, however good her original intention might seem to her to be. Galadriel's greatness rests upon her ability to see herself and her people as one part in a greater harmony that embraces them. It is by denying herself for the good of the whole that she preserves the integrity of her particular note in the harmony.

The structure of *The Lord of the Rings* shapes that harmony, the *discordia concors* that the world is when, in rightful balance, it reflects the greater, cosmic harmony. Tolkien uses the metaphor as it appears in Renaissance poetry and thought, where, as John Holland reminds us, it was "interpreted in the old Pythagorean way as intervals produced by stopping a monochord" rather than in our modern conception of "the ordering of simultaneously sounding musical tones, taken as a 'package.'" The image of the rightly balanced world appeared in the emblem books as a "well-tuned lyre," the emblem of Concord. Each note is separate, each unique, and the differences among them, as well as the distances between them are essential to the harmony that they produce. That is why we have in *The Lord of the Rings* so many different creatures. That is why we have creatures whose natures are antithetical—like dwarves who live beneath the ground and work in metals, and elves who lie above the ground and work in song—and who would war with each other if they were not held in proper alignment by the greater harmony, the ring of *discordia concors*, that together they comprise.

The distances between them—from "high" wizards to "low" hobbits—is equally vital to Tolkien's musical metaphor. Those sloppy readers who have accused him of expressing "aristocratic," or even "fascistic" political attitudes in his work are, once again, reading in the spirit of nineteenth-century naturalism. After all it is the hobbits, the lowly provincials whom the seemingly wise Saruman and Sauron have been too self-absorbed to notice and whom only the truly wise Gandalf never underestimates, who emerge as the heroes of the work. They are heroes because each maintains his own, and respects other, individual integrity, and because of their inclination to fellowship. In right balance, when the unique integrity of each part is preserved and when each part is in rightful alignment with all other parts, the world is a well-tuned lyre. That balance can be broken, however, and the lyre unstrung if any part within it refuses to recognize that it *is* a part within a greater whole, if any creature forgets the "ring" of *caritas* and falls victim to *cupiditas*, the desire to make himself his only good. It is pity for Gollum that saved Bilbo in the past; it is Frodo's pity for Gollum, his own dark doppelgänger, that preserves Gollum for the final part he has to play. In fighting the Gollum in himself and subduing it, Frodo (i.e. Frodo/Gollum) is able at last to drop the Ring of Oneness—of falsely defined individuation—into the Crack of Doom. But, like Sir Gawain, he must bear the scar of this dubious conquest even after his quest has been completed.

The moral import of Frodo's quest is as old as the story of Lucifer's fall, and as new as today. We are each of us "Ring-bearers," for the smallest but most important of the "rings" that the great Lord of rings holds is each creature's idea of self. A creature may succumb to the power of the "One Ring," the delusion of false individuation—the dark desire that lurks within each of us to make all time and all other creatures subject to our own wills. In that case his "self" becomes a shadow, a perverse parody of self as it was originally created. Like Lucifer, or Milton's Satan, longing to be "himself alone," to be self-willed and self-generative, he falls into false self-love; he becomes "a motion unregenerative" (*Paradise Lost*). His will becomes convoluted, and barren; he can only create shadowy parodies, grotesque imitations of the good.

Sauron is never personified in the book, but appears only as an eye. That eye is the emblem of false self-reflexive consciousness. Sauron is the power, a possibility implicit in free will, to turn away from the whole of creation to the contemplation of self as our only reality. True self, rightful identity, can only be found in fellowship. The resolution of the book, the reunion of the fellowship that has saved the world from Sauron and made possible *The Return of the King*, depends upon a recognition by each of its members that, as Shakespeare puts it:

> Then is there mirth in heaven
> When earthly things made even
> Atone together
>
> > (*As You Like It*, V, iv, 109–11)

with a pun that makes atonement dependent upon attunement.

The comic/cosmic resolution of the trilogy is Tolkien's answer to the question of how each separate entity, each self, maintains its unique and independent identity and is yet part of a whole greater than it is. The answer is not a "blending"; it is only in Mordor that all creatures are reflections of the One, who is himself only an eye contemplating its own empty image. Nor can we live in the Ovidian "golden world" of unthinking innocence that is ruled by Tom Bombadil and Goldberry, the ancestral nature god and goddess, who nourish our lives as they nourish the perennial lives of flowers, but who cannot comprehend the burden of self-conscious individuation that each of us must bear (Tom Bombadil, as Gandalf tells us, would forget the "One" Ring, or lose it).

The question, then, is how does a creature atone "the penalty of Adam." Separated from the world of unthinking nature, conscious of self, and forced to act, how does any "Ring-bearer" maintain the delicate balance between losing the "One" Ring and falling victim to its pull? Conceiving of the self as both an entity and a part, Tolkien tackles the problem of the "guilt of individual existence" as Karl Jaspers defines it: "Guilt in the larger sense is identical with existence. The idea, already found in Anaxamander, recurs in Calderon [and, we might add, in the *Gawain* poet, in Spenser, and in Shakespeare] although in a different sense—that man's greatest guilt is to have been born. This is revealed in the fact that my very existence causes misery [as Frodo's existence causes Gollum's] . . . whether I act or not, merely by existing I infringe upon the existence of others. Passive or active I incur the guilt of existence. A particular life is guilty through its origin." And, curiously, Tolkien, like the medieval and Renaissance artists in whose tradition he was working comes to the same conclusion that was reached by the modern philosopher. The "guilt of individual existence" can only be atoned when it is assumed and when the quest to be relieved of the burden is seen as part of a larger design

Frodo must assume the burden of the Ring and must journey, not as he first thought from the comfortable, insulated Shire to the boundaries of the familiar world, the Last Homely House only, but beyond that to the very Crack of Doom. He must take that journey, not knowing where it will lead him and never fully aware of its importance in the greater plan, the outcome of which is not understood even by Gandalf the White. His only companion at last is Sam Gamgee, the very emblem of love and service to the other, the agent of *caritas*.

Frodo, the "Ring-bearer" as we are each of us Ring-bearers, is both Everyman and the Hero. His journey is what the medieval commentators upon Virgil called the epic "journey to wisdom." On his journey he must encounter many threats, from the simple desire to "disappear" and forget the demand that has been made of him, to the primal terror of death that he meets in the barrow, to the inferno where he loses his guide to the Balrog—an evil to men more ancient than the moral evil that Sauron represents—to the cave of the terrible Shelob, Tolkien's versions of the Black Mother-Goddess of the ancients, to the Crack of Doom. But along the way he also encounters greater and greater manifestations of healing good—all of them images of fellowship from the initial insistence of Merry and Pippin, creatures like himself, upon risking themselves to accompany him, to the Fellowship of the Nine, creatures of varied natures who are bound by a common cause, to Lothlórien, where Galadriel gives him a glimpse of the larger, cosmic fellowship and the gift of a starlight that cannot fail however deep the present darkness.

At the very end of his journey he is accompanied by Sam, his simple, loving, "other self," and Gollum, his darker image, and there he must make a choice that proves him both good and vulnerable. He has come, against all odds, to the Crack of Doom. He has fought the power of the Ring of self to his utmost strength. But at the end he cannot willingly give it up any more than Sir Gawain can submit to the Green Knight's axe stroke without flinching, for the self is our only known life. It is here, when all that *can* be done has been done, that Providence intervenes. One strand in Frodo's destiny, his "unreasonable" charity to Gollum, never recognized either by him or by us as important, proves to be his salvation. Just as we cannot know the full design in which our particular journey is a thread, so neither can we know the full importance of any step in the journey until we have come to its end. The quest has taken place within a larger context. In the "last battle" all creatures of the Good—from the ents who bring the most ancient force of life to destroy Saruman's tower of technology, to the Kings of Men, to the eagles, the horses, and, of course, the heroic hobbits—must fight Sauron the Dark Lord of the Eye (which is also the "I") and the whole army of Shadows—shadow Kings, orcs, who are shadows of elves and dwarves, shadow Riders on shadow distortions that are neither eagles nor horses, which his power has created to mock and confuse them. Each of the forces of good conquers in the same way as Frodo, the Ring-bearer, conquers: by meeting to the best of his ability the demands of the way he has chosen, preserving his unique integrity, and serving the needs of the All while never really knowing the whole of its design.

The many journeys, which are really one journey, end back in the Shire, for in Tolkien, as in medieval-Renaissance epic, all journeys end in new beginnings. But just as each of the travelers has gone through his particular trial and been transformed, has lost himself to find himself, so too the Shire must be destroyed to be rebuilt. It could not remain an Edenic "golden world." In the literary tradition Troy had to fall for Rome to be founded, and Britain is Brutus's "second Rome"; so too the Shire had to fall to become part of the new Jerusalem, a small but highly honored province in the territory of the King.

KATHARYN W. CRABBE

The Quest as Legend:
The Lord of the Rings

When *The Hobbit* was so well received by the children's market, Allen and Unwin immediately approached Tolkien with the suggestion that he write a sequel—"More about Hobbits." Though Tolkien had continued to write about Middle-earth, and though he did want to publish more of his fantasies with Allen and Unwin, he did not have any more hobbit stories; but he agreed to try. As he began to write the story of Bilbo's nephew, one of the "nephews and nieces on the Took side" mentioned at the end of *The Hobbit*, Tolkien found himself becoming more and more interested in other characters—the elves and Elf-friends, wizards, those "masters of lore and good magic" who with Gandalf had succeeded in driving "the Necromancer from his dark hold in the south of Mirkwood," and, of course, the Ring.

Thus, although Tolkien began to write his sequel to *The Hobbit* in 1936, and although his publishers hoped it would be another children's book, *The Lord of the Rings*, Tolkien's second full-length work of fantasy, did not appear until 1954–55, and then its proper audience was not immediately apparent. It is an epic fantasy in three volumes, each volume containing two books, which traces the adventures of Bilbo's nephew, Frodo, and his friends as they struggle to beat back and destroy the evil Sauron and to restore peace to Middle-earth.

The Lord of the Rings is, without doubt, the most impressive and most

---

successful of Tolkien's full-length works. Although it is long, it does not sprawl; rather the plot advances steadily and the subplots are integrated into the main plot neatly. The number of characters is large, but each one has a vivid and memorable existence for the reader. Most important, although the theme of *The Lord of the Rings*, like that of *The Hobbit*, is the unending struggle of good and evil, in the later work Tolkien has managed to make that basic dialectical struggle complex and interesting by daring to entertain the idea that a range of goods as well as a range of evils is possible in the world.

Volume one of the trilogy is *The Fellowship of the Ring*. In it, Bilbo's ring is revealed to be the "One Ring" of the ominous verse, "One Ring to rule them all, One Ring to find them, / One Ring to bring them all and in the darkness bind them." At Gandalf's urging, Frodo, his two friends, Pippin and Merry, and his gardener, Sam Gamgee, undertake to deliver the ring to Elrond, the Master of Rivendell. The journey is filled with dangers, including attacks from strange, formless, black-cloaked riders, one of whom wounds Frodo with a Morgul (*black-arts*) knife.

At Rivendell, Frodo is healed and the company discovers that uprisings of evil have sent representatives of all the "Free Peoples of the World" to Rivendell for counsel. When it is decided that the Ring must be destroyed and that Frodo must carry it to Mount Doom and throw it in the volcanic fires, the Fellowship of the Ring forms to accompany him. It comprises the four hobbits, Frodo, Sam, Pippin, and Merry; two men, Aragorn (the rightful king) and Boromir (the son of the Steward of Gondor); an elf, Legolas, son of the King of Mirkwood; a dwarf, Gimli, son of Glóin; and the wizard, Gandalf.

Beset by forces of evil in the forms of nature, monsters, and Orcs, the fellowship experiences the deaths of Gandalf and Boromir before Frodo and Sam strike off on their own; Pippin and Merry are captured by Orcs; Aragorn, Legolas, and Gimli set off to rescue them.

Volume two, *The Two Towers*, tells of the reunion of Pippin and Merry with Aragorn, Gimli, and Legolas; the return of Gandalf (now called "The White"); and the alliance of the fellowship with the men of Rohan just as the forces of evil begin the siege of Gondor, seat of Aragorn's kingdom. Meanwhile, Frodo and Sam, found in the wastes by the creature from whom Bilbo took the Ring in *The Hobbit*, force Gollum to guide them to Cirith Ungol, the spider's pass, a less heavily guarded entrance to Mordor. Frodo is wounded by the giant spider, Shelob, and is captured by the Orcs.

Volume three, *The Return of the King*, recounts the heroic actions of men, elves, dwarves, and hobbits at the siege of Gondor, the acceptance of Aragorn as King of Gondor, and the assault of his armies on Mordor. Paralleling the military epic is the lonely trek of Frodo and Sam to Mount Doom, where Gollum suddenly reappears, snatches the Ring, and falls with it into the volcano. The heroes are reunited, evil is cast out of the kingdom, including the Shire where it has lately flourished, and the last of the fair folk, the elves, leave Middle-earth, taking Frodo and Bilbo, the Ring-bearers, with them. The reign of men begins.

The first difference one notes in moving from *The Hobbit* to *The Lord of the Rings* is the tone. The trilogy is not uniform in tone (Tolkien himself observed that the tone of Book One was very different from the rest), but it immediately sounds far more serious than *The Hobbit*, and the level of diction and the level of seriousness increase steadily as the locus of the story moves away from the Shire and its domesticity toward the stateliness of Rohan and the glory of Gondor. To understand how the tone of each work is appropriate is to begin to understand some of the essential differences between the two.

Structurally, as Randel Helms points out, *The Lord of the Rings* is *The Hobbit* writ large in that both works participate in the vision of the whole life of man as a quest. That quest, however, is marked for all men by two great events: the coming of adulthood, with all the rights and privileges pertaining to it, and the coming of death. To borrow the paradigm developed by Joseph Campbell, author of *The Hero with a Thousand Faces*, there is one heroic life, and quest stories differ only as to how they make use of different parts of it. *The Hobbit* clearly makes use of only the first half of the cycle, ending with the hero's passage into maturity. As a story of the beginning of a full and fulfilling adult life, the specifics of which we are left to imagine for ourselves, and as the tale of a young hobbit with his life before him, it is appropriately sunny, even comical, in tone. *The Lord of the Rings*, however, takes the hero completely through the cycle to the point of his essentially sacrificial death. Its somber tone is appropriate to the story of inevitable decline and death. In fact, the only time *The Lord of the Rings* sounds at all like *The Hobbit* is when Pippin and Merry, in the early chapters, indulge in some youthful foolishness. Even Sam, who is often seen as a vehicle for comic relief, is identified as serious from the early stages of Book One by his reverence for elves.

As the nature of the transitional event toward which the plot moves differs in seriousness, so does the social status of the characters. Bilbo is an ordinary hobbit, comfortable, but surely not aristocratic—not, in fact, extraordinary in any way. It is the function of his story to show how the most ordinary young hobbit may "have more to him than anyone suspects." The dwarves with whom he travels are also identified as ordinary folk. The party travels in weatherstained cloaks, regards the adventure as a commercial enterprise, and, unable to find or afford a hero, settles for a burglar instead.

The Lord of the Rings, however, selects its personae from the higher social orders. By virtue of Bilbo's fortune and his status as Elf-friend, Frodo's social and moral position is higher than Bilbo's was at the opening of *The Hobbit*. The backgrounds of Pippin and Merry are traced in the Prologue in such a way as to establish their status as descendants of some of the first families of the Shire.

Similarly, while the elves of *The Hobbit* are silly, capricious, and given to singing nonsense rhymes, such as "tra-la-la-lally, come back to the valley," the elves of *The Lord of the Rings* are glorious, responsible, and poetic. Much has been made of Tolkien's evolving ideas of the nature of elves, and by the time the first group of elvish travelers appears in *The Lord of the Rings*, driving off the black riders with their hymn to Elbereth, it is clear that we are dealing with a race in whom the attributes of divinity are legion. The appearance of the Elf-Lord, Glorfindel, whom Frodo sees for a moment at the ford "as he appears on the other side," Elrond's status as acknowledged leader of all the free people of Middle-earth, and Galadriel's mystical insights in Lothlórien all succeed in mirroring the seriousness of the tone in the depiction of the elves.

The third race of heroes, men, also is represented by higher social orders in *The Lord of the Rings* than in *The Hobbit*. While it is perhaps true that Bard foreshadows the character of Aragorn, his part in *The Hobbit* is small. *The Lord of the Rings*, on the other hand, gives over half of its space to the affairs of men, the quest of Aragorn and the matter of Gondor, in which the descent of men from the nearly mythic men of Númenor is central.

As Tolkien widened his focus in *The Lord of the Rings* to include the affairs of kings of men as well as hobbits, he simultaneously changed the nature of the quest in another way. *The Hobbit*, with its steady focus on Bilbo and his development, is a singularly good example of a quest story that is primarily concerned with personal or individual issues. Though some mention is made of issues that involve whole societies, especially in the recognition of one's duty to mankind and the vision of the responsibilities of a leader to his people, the central thematic and structural concern is Bilbo's growth and development, and through him, individual human growth and development. *The Lord of the Rings*, however, though it is still concerned with the individual struggle as depicted in Frodo, is much more a social work, reflecting ideas about broad issues of social roles and responsibilities and cultural attributes. This social vision is one reason languages become so important in the latter work—languages both reflect and create cultures; and the life of a culture depends on its language: "Each language," wrote Waclaw Lednicki, "represents centuries of tragic efforts on the part of human beings to find an adequate expression for their feelings and thoughts about the universe. Indeed, every great language is a unique mirror of the landscape, of the air, of the sky—of all the natural surroundings in which it has developed."

When we have observed that *The Lord of the Rings* differs from *The Hobbit* in being more serious in tone, in representing a higher social order, and in addressing social rather than personal issues, we have described a set of differences that contains three of the important distinctions between fairy tales and myths. The two forms have much in common, to be sure—the vision of life as a quest; the basic dialectical structure that sets a world of happiness, security, and peace against a world of humiliation, loneliness, and pain; and a cyclical pattern that depicts a movement from the bright world into the dark one and back again. However, myth is typically more majestic, more spiritual, more concerned with life as it *ought* to be lived rather than as it *could* be. Bruno Bettelheim has observed that "A myth, like a fairy tale, may express an inner conflict in symbolic form and suggest how it may be solved—but this is not necessarily the myth's central concern. . . . [In myths] the divine is present and is experienced in the form of superhuman heroes who make constant demands on mere mortals. Much as we, the mortals, may strive to be like these heroes, we will remain always and obviously inferior to them."

In *The Lord of the Rings*, then, we have a story that bridges the gap between fairy tale and myth. Though both elves and wizards and super-human heroes are present, they are not quite central; instead, the story focuses on the fortunes of men and hobbits. Yet, the tone, the importance of social issues, and the hierarchical social structure marks the work as one which aspires toward the status of myth. This medial position of the trilogy is reflected in Tolkien's treatment of good and evil, and the function of language.

In calling *The Hobbit* a fairy tale, one says something about the quality of the heroism in it—that the hero, Bilbo, is a low-mimetic hero—one not significantly better than we in kind or degree. But in *The Lord of the Rings*, we seem also to be reading the kind of story that deals with the doings of gods and godlike men. This shift in focus from the ordinary to the extraordinary does not result so much from a change in the conception of hobbits, who are still the beings most like us, as it does from Tolkien's decision to create a structure that brings men into the center of the action. When we speak of the men of *The Lord of the Rings*, we speak, without a doubt, of godlike men, those high-mimetic heroes who are beyond us in both kind and degree. The emergence of these heroes in Tolkien's second work mirrors his growing preoccupation with his own myth of a golden age. Yet *The Lord of the Rings* is not itself a golden age story; it is the story of a lull in the decline of a world that already looks back to a golden age and mourns its lost grandeur and nobility. Aragorn, for example, is the last of the Kings of the Númenórean line, that is, the last of men directly descended from the three houses of men that came into the world when the elves still lived in Middle-earth, and the last in whom the high blood has not mingled with that of other, lesser races.

But even in Aragorn, the noblest of men, Tolkien traces some falling off since the golden days. The kings of Númenor were, we learn, descended from Eärendil the Mariner, who, having chosen to cast his lot with the elves (the first-born) is immortal. His son Elros, first king of Númenor, having chosen to stay with men, was granted "a great life-span . . . many times that of men." But as his descendants grew suspicious of the Eldar and began to persecute those who wished to remain Elf-friends, and as their fear of death grew, their life-spans shortened. So the death of Aragorn comes when he has lived only "a span thrice that of the Men of Middle-earth."

The Steward of Gondor, Denethor, and his son Boromir, illustrate another degree of falling away, the result of mixing with men of lesser blood. What remains longest among the men of Gondor from their Númenórean heritage is their physical being—men of high blood are always "tall men and proud with sea-gray eyes." But in only a few do the spiritual attributes of the original men live on as they live in Aragorn. Thus Pippin's shock of recognition when he first sees Faramir: "Here was one with an air of high nobility such as Aragorn at times revealed, less high perhaps, yet also less incalculable and remote: one of the Kings of Men born into a later time, but touched with the wisdom and sadness of the Elder Race."

The differences between Boromir and Faramir is an expression of the difference in what they have inherited from their Númenórean past. Boromir has inherited the bearing and the appearance—the physical attributes—only. But Faramir has also the lore and wisdom of his past for he has studied the "ancient tales," and he loves his city "for her memory, her ancientry, her beauty, and her present wisdom." It is not only knowledge of the past but reverence for it and understanding of it that set Faramir apart, and that knowledge, reverence, and understanding are his links to the golden age.

The men of Middle-earth, then, though they are not as godlike as they once were (Faramir says, "We are become Middle Men, of the Twilight, but with memory of other things"), are by virtue of their inheritance, symbols of an order of mankind above us. The reader's perspective is more nearly that of Merry, who agrees that hobbits "can't live long on the heights" but adds, ". . . at least, Pippin, we can now see them, and honour them."

Thus, though they are high-mimetic heroes, the men of Middle-earth, as they are depicted in *The Lord of the Rings*, are not divine. Indeed, as Aragorn's death (described in the Appendix) and the deaths of Denethor and Théoden show, the inevitability of man's death is one of the most important facts of his existence. The heroic men of the trilogy occupy a medial position between the everyman hero, the Bilbo of *The Hobbit*, and the divine heroes of the golden age.

In the heroes of men in *The Lord of the Rings*, we can see a whole hierarchy of heroic possibilities. In the men of Rohan, we see man as a purely physical hero, the warrior who was in such short supply in *The Hobbit*. The Rohirrim are "fair to look upon," and "love war and valour as things good in themselves, both a sport and an end." The power of the idea of the warrior hero is so great that, though it is an unpopular notion in our own time, it actually moved Tolkien to unite the image of warfare with that of creativity: In the battle of Pelennor fields, the men of Rohan "burst into song, and they sang as they slew, for the joy of battle was on them, and the sound of their singing that was fair and terrible came even to the city."

The men of Gondor, also brave, strong, and physically adept, add to the image of the warrior hero a spiritual quality that moves them up the heroic ladder. The difference is the admiration the men of Gondor have for "more skills and knowledge than only the craft of weapons and slaying" which, if we look to Faramir as an example, means being "a lover of lore and of music" and a seeker after wisdom. By exemplifying a hero who values the spiritual life of a culture as well as its physical life, Faramir links the Rohirrim to Aragorn, King of the Númenóreans.

Aragorn, with his transcendent beauty revealed at moments such as the Council at Rivendell, the visit to Cerin Amroth in Lothlórien, or the coronation in Gondor, and his spiritual strength revealed by his ability to turn the palantir away from Sauron and by his command of the oath-breakers, tops the hierarchy of heroes of men. Not only does he protect, as the Rohirrim, and preserve, as the stewards of Gondor, he also *creates* (literally, re-creates), bringing both physical and spiritual life to the people and to the land.

His first appearance as a healer occurs even before he is revealed as the king in exile, when he ministers to the wounded Frodo, victim of a black rider and his "morgul-knife." He treats the wound by bathing it with a water in which he has steeped *athelas*, "a healing plant that the Men of the West brought to Middle-earth." With the same *athelas* he treats the less serious wounds of Sam and Frodo after the escape from Moria and the death of Gandalf.

It is not until Aragorn enters the city of Gondor, in the echo of the old saying, "The hands of the King are the hands of a healer," that the common name of athelas is revealed—"kingsfoil . . . the country folk call it in these latter days." And the rhyme of the old wives foretells its virtues:

> When the black breath blows
> and death's shadow grows
> and all lights pass,
> come athelas! come athelas!

> Life to the dying
> In the king's hand lying!

As the wounded heroes in the Houses of Healing are called back to life by the baptismal bathing with *athelas*, so the land and the city are brought back to life with trees and fountains, likewise suggesting a renewal of fertility.

As king, Aragorn unites all the heroic qualities to become the most heroic of men: "Ancient of days he seemed and yet in the flower of manhood; and wisdom sat upon his brow, and strength and healing were in his hands." However, his own position as intermediary is made clear by his consistent consciousness that he must be instructed by others, such as Elrond and Gandalf, who, more than he, seem attuned to the voices of beings beyond the world, whose existence seems to be wholly spiritual. Though the heroes of men approach the divine, they are human, not superhuman, and they see, as we do, that yet another level of heroism and another level of heroes must have preceded them.

Among the hobbits, Frodo is no more a traditional hero than Bilbo was before him. He is neither stronger than most men, nor braver than most. He is reluctant to take risks and is terrified by the implications of the Ring. Nor is he finally strong enough to resist its power.

But the heroic qualities Frodo does possess, though of less dramatic proportions than those of high-mimetic heroes, are sufficient to the task given him. Despite his fear, he has an unwavering commitment to the quest once he has undertaken it. He is selfless in his love for his companions. He is able to feel pity for even the tormented Gollum and the fallen Saruman, and he is willing to accomplish by sacrifice what he cannot hope to accomplish by strength. Most important, he is capable of carrying on when there is no hope.

Frodo's commitment to the quest in unquestionable. His understanding of the necessity for the quest begins with his conviction that what is good must be preserved and protected, and idea to which Tolkien returns, again and again: in Frodo's willingness to sacrifice himself for the Shire; in Bilbo's commitment to his "Translations from the Elvish"; in Faramir's desire to study the archives of Gondor under the tutelage of Gandalf; in the histories compiled by Pippin and Merry; and in the Red Book of Westmarch, kept by Sam and handed down through Elanor. A reverence for the past and its values is among the first of Frodo's virtues and an important motive for his quest.

Second among his heroic attributes is the willingness to sacrifice himself to preserve those things he values. His agreement to carry the ring into Mordor and probable destruction is a triumph of the will to serve over the will to live. During the council at Rivendell, Frodo is conscious only of his fear of the Ring and of the evil it represents. He is nearly as surprised as anyone else when he hears himself say, "I will take the ring . . . though I do not know the way."

In fact, despite the continual subconscious longings to give in to the power of the Ring, symbolized by his hand's continual straying toward it, Frodo never gives up his conscious decision to offer himself as a sacrifice until he stands at the crack of Doom. When at that moment the subconscious will to live and to assert power breaks through the conscious desire to sacrifice himself to destroy power, the result is symbolically the sacrificial death required, though the body sacrificed is that of Frodo's alter-ego, Gollum. Frodo has finished his spiritual quest by that time, however; he has completed his task and is ready to die, though Sam, who has much living to do yet, hopes on, saying, "I don't want to give up yet. It's not like me, somehow, if you understand."

From this point to the end, Frodo is essentially an inactive hero. Like Oedipus, in the course of saving his world he has become unable to be a part of it, so he remains only long enough to complete his share of the Red Book and thus to make possible the ritual re-creation of his sacrifice. As he tells Sam,

> I tried to save the Shire, and it has been saved but not for me.
> It must be so, Sam, when things are in danger: some one has to
> give them up, lose them, so that others may keep them. But you
> are my heir: . . . and you will read things out of the Red Book
> and keep alive the memory of the age that is gone, so that
> people will remember The Great Danger and so love their
> beloved land all the more.

But it is not only Frodo who is self-sacrificing and apotheosized. Of the other high-mimetic heroes, both Gandalf and Aragorn sacrifice much for the greater good. For Aragorn the sacrifice is appropriately one that only a ruler can make—to hold his own claims to happiness and well-being in abeyance until he can provide for his subjects. His sacrifice is therefore his long and lonely life as an outcast Ranger and his enduring love for Arwen Evenstar. Gandalf, like Frodo, is called upon for a sacrifice in a more circumscribed context. Like Frodo, Gandalf must offer his life, and like Frodo, he is willing to do so. Though the apotheosized Gandalf returns from his fall into the bottomless pits of Moria, his sacrificial offering of himself to save his friends from the Balrog is none the less heroic. Nor is Boromir's defense of Pippin and Merry from the Orcs less heroic because it fails, culminating in their capture and his death.

A third defining characteristic of the Tolkien hero is a courage that transcends mere physical bravery. From the first moment Frodo hears of the enemy and his connection with the Ring, he is afraid. At home in The Shire he is afraid and lonely and extremely conscious of the power of the enemy. At the parting of the paths that marks the breaking of the Fellowship, Frodo says to Boromir, "I know what I should do, but I am afraid of doing it, Boromir, afraid." And, of course, the effect of the Nazgûl is to strike fear into the hearts of men. But like Frodo, those men are heroes who feel the fear, acknowledge it, and then do what they must do despite it. In Middle-earth, the shame is not in losing hope but in letting despair immobilize one, as it does Théoden, Lord of Rohan, or in letting it turn one to the service of the dark, as Denethor, Steward of Gondor.

Instead of giving in or giving up to despair, Tolkien's heroes must continually move forward. Thus, though Aragorn moans that without Gandalf the fellowship has no hope of succeeding in its mission, he also says, "We must do without hope." And Sam, guarding the sleeping Frodo on the plains of Gorgoroth, suddenly realizes that if they do reach Mount Doom, they have no chance of returning: "But even as hope died in Sam, or seemed to die, it was turned to a new strength."

In *The Lord of the Rings*, then, Tolkien's heroes are only in part traditional conquering heroes. They are preeminently suffering heroes who persevere. The status of the heroes as sufferers is psychologically, if not logically, connected to the next great characteristic of the Tolkien hero—his mercy. On the one hand, the heroes' mercy is part of the ethic that "The hands of the King are the hands of healing," because the essence of mercy is the invitation to reenter the good; that is, to reenter spiritual life or to escape spiritual death. This must be the significance of Gandalf's response to Frodo's judgment that Gollum deserves death: "'Deserves it! I daresay he does. Many that live deserve death. And some that die deserve life. Can you give it to them? Then do not be too eager to deal out death in judgement.'"

Mercy, in a Christian sense, refers specifically to the heavenly reward that might be given to one who has not earned it and cannot be expected to give recompense for it. From the point of view of the merciful, showing mercy means not paying one by what he deserves, thus giving kind and compassionate treatment to one who has no reason to expect it.

Here and in *The Hobbit*, the motive for mercy is pity, the hero's ability to feel and understand the pain and suffering implicit in the failure to be the best one can be. That is, pity is evoked by an awareness of the suffering of others, and in Middle-earth, suffering is inevitable. Physical pain, but also spiritual pain, is always possible and nearly always present, and no one is immune—not Gollum, who is ravaged by desire for the Ring; not Saruman, whose quest for power leads him to exile and thence to death; not Denethor, whose pride and love for his son leads him to death; not Frodo; not Gandalf; not Aragorn; not even Galadriel and Celeborn can escape suffering.

But to be able to pity others who suffer distinguishes the heroic from the villainous. In fact, Tolkien was no doubt making use of the philological fact that *pity*, in the general sense of "a feeling of compassion" did not exist as separate from its specific religious sense of *piety* until well after 1600: until then the ability to feel pity was a mark of piety.

Like Bilbo, who has been damaged so little by the Ring because he began his ownership of it with pity and mercy, Frodo finds reason to show compassion to Gollum. But unlike Bilbo, Frodo finds the motive for mercy in the commonality of his experience with Gollum's. Bilbo, we recall, was struck by the differences between the dark loneliness of Gollum's life and the sunny domesticity of his own. But by the time Frodo meets Gollum in *The Two Towers*, he too has felt the pain of loss and the burden of the Ring and is thus able to feel pity for the wretched creature.

Similar to Frodo's treatment of Gollum is Gandalf's treatment of the fallen Saruman when he offers Saruman the freedom to leave Orthanc, and Treebeard's release of Saruman after the defeat of Sauron. Aragorn's mercy is illustrated in his treatment of the army he leads to the Black Gate. When the horror of the evil overcomes the army of the King, Aragorn counsels,

> "Go! . . . but keep what honour you may, and do not run! And there is a task which you may attempt and not be wholly shamed. . . . "
>
> Then some being shamed by his mercy overcame their fear and went on, and the others took new hope, hearing of a manful deed within their measure that they could turn to, and they departed.

There is an existential side to all of these instances of heroic mercy, for in *The Lord of the Rings* mercy seems to mean the refusal to accept any being's less than perfect state as his essential nature. Justice would pay each according to what he has done; mercy pays him according to what he might do—according to the ideal. That is, those who are not a part of Mordor are not evil because they were created to be evil but because they have failed to live up to the level of goodness inherent in them. In a sense, the act of mercy works to preserve the free will of the receiver, giving him the chance to become the better being that is within his capability. Thus mercy is an essentially creative act—it leaves the possibilities for a recreation of the self open as does any healing process. As the hero shares with a divine being the quality of mercy, he shares with him his creative power.

Finally, the heroes of *The Lord of the Rings* are selfless in their love for their companions. This quality, like the others, is expressed differently in the different characters, according to their mimetic level. It is for love of the Shire and for love of mankind (the Free Peoples) that Frodo undertakes the quest. But it is his selflessness that leads him away from the company above the Falls of Raumos, for he is loath to lead them further into danger. This selflessness is matched, however, by Sam's unwavering determination not to let his master go on alone. Sam, as Frodo's servant and as a being with free will, exhibits a selflessness that yields perseverance unmatched by any of the abject slaves of Sauron, and in doing so illustrates the superiority of love freely given over force, no matter how strong.

This caring for the health, safety, and happiness of others is simply a less elevated version of the more godlike concern of Aragorn, in whom it is revealed that "The hands of the King are the hands of the healer."

As is true of the concept of heroism, the ideas of the nature of good and evil are markedly more complex in *The Lord of the Rings* than in *The Hobbit*. So great is the richness and extent of the trilogy that in it the moral issue is not simply good versus evil, but goods versus evils. Tolkien's view of the universe here is that it is not simply dualistic but pluralistic, and there is room in a pluralistic world for a multitude of goods and evils.

On the positive side, the trilogy presents a range of goods, represented by the members of the fellowship. The range may be described as a hierarchy, although it is a hierarchy of kinds, not degrees, ranging from the earthly to the divine. Gandalf the Grey, later Gandalf the White is a representative of a good that suggests knowledge of the whole of experience and that actively opposes the evils it sees, from the most elemental (the Balrog, against which only Gandalf has any power) to the merely human (Wormtongue). His breadth of vision and his range of power suggest that this is a force for good that might well be called divine.

A more limited (because more human) range of good is represented by Aragorn, King of Gondor, whose power over the natural or elemental evils is indicated by his power of healing, and whose immersion in the more earthly aspects of heroic conduct, as when he rides into battle with the sword of Isildur gleaming before him, marks him as a hero of men. Where Gandalf's importance on the field of physical battle is primarily symbolic or psychological, Aragorn's is both symbolic and practical, as is appropriate for the last true son of the West and the betrothed of Arwen Evenstar, daughter of Elrond Half-elven.

As Aragorn's good is to Gandalf's, Boromir's is to Aragorn's. Boromir, a descendant of the Stewards of Gondor who have through the years become less like the Númenóreans and more like ordinary men, is in every way a physical hero. He is himself stunningly attractive—tall, strong, well-proportioned, and well-spoken. He is chiefly distinguished by his physical prowess—though he is ultimately overpowered, he kills legions of Orcs before succumbing. But his spiritual ties are more limited than those of Gandalf or of Aragorn. When he blows the horn of Gondor at need, only his brother and his father hear it. His fate does not have the cosmic implications of the fate of a Gandalf or an Aragorn.

Boromir's goodness is, then, limited to an active goodness. He is brave, he is adept, and he is a great warrior. But he is limited in his ability to understand the nature of the evil he must oppose. Like Gandalf and Aragorn, he has seen the evil of the Dark Lord face to face, but he has failed to understand it as anything more than a physical evil—a force that, in his view, simply must be met by greater force. His continued insistence that he would use the Ring for good, and should thus be give it serves only to illustrate his failure to understand that evil has its own existence and will not be transformed by anyone.

Though Boromir can be described as limited in goodness because, having seen, he only partially understands the nature of the evil that threatens his world, the hobbits are even more limited than he. The innocent folk of The Shire are, until the Black Riders appear, utterly unaware of the evils that stalk their borders. Yet in the course of the quest, Frodo comes to an understanding of the totality of the moral world, both the good side and the evil, that rivals Gandalf's perception. The equality of the perceptions of the two is perhaps most poignantly suggested in the image of the two of them riding, together with Bilbo and the elves, to the Grey Havens to sail into the sunset. But the hobbits who never leave the Shire also grow in their knowledge of good and evil when Sharkey and his men take over the Shire and transform it until Frodo can truly, say, "Yes, this is Mordor." Tolkien suggests that the hobbits' ignorance of evil is part of their vulnerability to it.

As a pluralistic world has room for multiple goods, it also has room for multiple evils, ranging from the simple greed and envy of the Sackville-Bagginses to the conscious and unmitigated malice of Sauron. At intermediate points are betrayal by the quisling Bill Ferny of Bree, the warped hatred of Gollum, the inbred violence and perversions of the Orcs, and the elemental evil of Shelob and the Balrog. As the hierarchy of goods ranged from the human to the divine, the hierarchy of evils ranges from the human to the demonic. And the most demonic evil is Sauron.

Evil, as Tolkien conceives of it in *The Lord of the Rings*, is not unique in its forms or attributes: Like other evils in the western tradition, Sauron is *dark*—he is variously the Dark Lord, the Dark Power, or the Power of Darkness. His ancient home is the Dark Tower of Mordor, the Land of Shadows, and his messengers are the Dark Riders. The very uttering of his language is enough to cause a shadow to pass over the sun, and the years of his domination are called the Black years.

As it is reflected in Sauron, evil is closely allied with a quest for power. Here the notion of power goes beyond the simple acquisitiveness of *The Hobbit* to include the ultimate control—control over being. Sauron's power, or the power he seeks, is a power that parodies the power of the creator. Rather than create, Sauron will destroy; rather than set free, he will enslave; rather than heal, he will harm. The desire of Sauron to make everything in Middle-earth less than it is capable of being is clear in his repeated threats to "break" captives, in the ruined and desolate lands that were once fertile and productive, and in the Orcs and trolls, his parodies of men and dwarves (or as Treebeard would have it, of elves and ents).

Sauron's title, *The Lord of the Rings*, also suggests the enduring quality of evil, the quality that makes a final victory impossible. Though Sauron was "vanquished" when Isildur, the patriarch of Aragorn's line, cut the Ring from his finger, and though Sauron was caught in the wreck of Númenor and "the bodily form in which he long had walked perished," evil cannot be completely destroyed. It can be temporarily defeated; it can be set back; in the vision of *The Lord of the Rings*, it cannot be finally removed from the world.

In addition to being enduring, the evil of *The Lord of the Rings* is insidious. That is, the Ring as an extension of Sauron and thus as an embodiment of evil corrupts those who lust after it, those who accept it only from good motives, and those who take it knowing nothing of its nature, as the compulsion of Gollum, the fall of Boromir, the inability of Frodo to complete the quest, and the "stretching" of Bilbo all show.

Tolkien suggests, then, that every man contains the seeds of evil and that the seeds may be brought to germination by exposure to evil. Thus Gandalf, Aragorn, Faramir and Galadriel reject the Ring because though each of them has power of his own, they each know that even with the best intentions they could not control the Ring and change it from a power for evil to a power for good. That is, the Ring is not evil simply because it is powerful; it is inherently evil because it was born of evil, and it cannot therefore be made good, even by Gandalf or Galadriel.

The insidiousness of evil makes Tolkien's version of the sacrificing hero even more poignant and moving than its archetype. Frodo's danger is not simply a danger to his physical life, with the assurance of a reward in another world; he risks his spiritual life as well, for the very proximity to the Ring that will allow him to save the world threatens to make of him the source of its destruction. That is, on the edges of the cracks of doom the Ring succeeds in making of Frodo a hobbit Sauron. He claims the Ring, and it is taken from him as it was taken from Sauron at the end of the Second Age, by the severing of his finger.

This pairing of Frodo with Sauron not only suggests the dual nature of man, it also suggests just how close Frodo has come to becoming the enemy he has offered his life to defeat. The ultimate defeat, then, in *The Lord of the Rings* is not simply to lose the battle with evil, but to become incorporated into it.

That such a danger exists (and its presence is equally clear in the lives and fates of Denethor, Wormtongue, and Saruman, all once good men who fell away from the good and became the servants of Sauron) suggests that Tolkien is working with a notion of man as a creature "strong enough to stand, but free to fall."

In developing the idea that the Ring is inherently evil, and in exploring the notion that good men may *become* evil, Tolkien has moved beyond the idea that evil is a simple absence of good. Though the capabilities for good and evil coexist in some characters, evil has for Tolkien a real and independent existence. The eschatological view of *The Lord of the Rings* is thus not one which foresees the conversion of evil to good, but one which sees that evil must conquer or be conquered.

The conception of evil as a force that has being of its own raises in all mythologies the question of the origin of evil, and Tolkien's mythology is no exception on this point. Most of the reflections on the origin of evil in *The Lord of the Rings* occur in the Appendices to the trilogy where it appears that even during the First Age there was an enemy (Morgoth) who poisoned the two trees that gave light to the land of the Valar and who stole the Silmarilli, the jewels in which the light of the two trees was preserved. Hence, evil entered Middle-earth before the elves. It is, then, coeval with the world. Evil was able to act among the Eldar because of the familiar weaknesses of character—e.g., pride and willfulness.

After the defeat of Morgoth, his servant Sauron appeared to be the plague of men. As pride and self-will were the weaknesses of the Eldar, fear of death was the weakness that brought men low and brought to an end the Second Age. Evil is thus a hydra-headed monster that takes whatever form the time requires.

Although Frodo, Aragorn, Gandalf, and Sam are the heroes of *The Lord of the Rings*, there is a sense in which the trilogy is Sauron's—he is the Lord of the Rings, and as the embodiment of evil, he is the force that initiates and perpetuates the action. But his importance to the trilogy extends beyond simple matters of plot to include more complex matters of theme, for he provides the work with a central image of evil and with the beginnings of a theory of the origin of evil.

Sauron's evil is directly opposed to Aragorn's heroism—rather than healing men, he would "break" them. The Mouth of Sauron who meets the armies of Gondor at the Black Gate tells them that Frodo's fate shall be to "endure the slow torment of years, as long and slow as our arts in the Great Tower can contrive, and never [to] be released, unless maybe when he is changed and broken, so that he may come to you, and you shall see what you have done." The motif of breaking or deforming is consistent with Sauron. Théoden's counselor, Wormtongue, is a snake who was once a man, a queer twisted sort of creature, and by the time of the Scouring of the Shire, a being who crawls like a dog. Similarly, Gollum was once an inquisitive and curious being "of hobbit-kind," but under the influence of the Ring he became mean-spirited, wretched, as the Ring began to "[eat] up his mind." When Sauron does create, he can only counterfeit. Treebeard the Ent tells Pippin and Merry, "Trolls are only counterfeits, made by the Enemy in the Great Darkness, in mockery of Ents, as Orcs were of Elves."

Parallel to the destruction or breaking of the creatures of Middle-earth, the destruction of the earth itself is a dramatic manifestation of evil. To follow Saruman is to follow death, to be sure, but Tolkien's images of death are most powerful when they depict the destruction of the land, the source of life itself. Again, the cultivated fertility of The Shire with its flower gardens ("snapdragons and sunflowers, and nasturtiums trailing all over the turf walls and peeking in at the round windows"), its meadows and hedges, contrasts with the wild beauty of Ithilien "the gardens of Gondor now desolate," which, as it "had only been for a few years under the dominion of the Dark Lord . . . was not yet wholly fallen into decay," but it contrasts even more vividly with the lands that have been long under his sway. The Brown Lands near the border are desolate, "long formless slopes stretching up and away toward the sky; brown and withered they looked, as if fire had passed over them, leaving no living blade of green: an unfriendly waste without even a broken tree or a bold stone to relieve the emptiness."

Nearer Mordor, desolation becomes hell. North of the Black Gate "[t]he gasping pools were choked with ash and crawling mud, sickly white and grey, as if the mountains had vomited the filth of their entrails upon the lands about." And inside Mordor the plains of Gorgoroth, which Sam and Frodo cross on the last leg of their journey to Mount Doom, are equally hellish: " . . . what from a distance had seemed wide and featureless flats were in fact all broken and tumbled. Indeed the whole surface of the plains of Gorgoroth was pocked with great holes, as if, while it was still a waste of soft mud, it had been smitten with a shower of bolts and huge slingstones. The largest of these holes were rimmed with ridges of broken rock, and broad fissures ran out from them in all directions."

The contrast between fertile growth and sterile destruction is further developed in the two images of restoration that close the trilogy. Aragorn's ascent to the top of Mount Mundolluin after he has been crowned reveals "the towers of the City far below them like white pencils touched by the sunlight, and all the vale of Anduin was like a garden, and the Mountains of Shadow were veiled in a golden mist." Less elevated but equally important is the work of restoration Sam accomplishes in the Shire after Saruman has cut down trees, installed smoke-belching and pollution-producing machines, built rows of cheap and nasty houses, and generally tried, as one Shiredweller puts it, "to make the Shire into a desert." Like the good gardener he is, Sam replants the Shire and, we are told, "tried to restrain himself from going round constantly to see if anything was happening." When trees accomplish twenty years' growth in one, when the air is full of "richness and growth," and when all the children are born fair and strong, the Shire has plainly been restored.

If the nature of evil in Middle-earth is that it is eternal and that it is insidious and thus widely threatening, if the attractions of evil are such that neither men nor wizards, dwarves nor hobbits are immune, we may wonder what factors constitute the weaknesses of evil. Why, in short, does evil fail in Middle-earth?

As W. H. Auden pointed out, the greatest weakness of evil is a lack of imagination—" . . . for, while Good can imagine what it would be like to be Evil, Evil cannot imagine what it would like to be Good." From Galadriel to Sam, those in the service of good can imagine what would become of them if they tried to use the Ring. Indeed, the portrait of Frodo being pulled further and further into the darkness as he begins to be unable to call on memories of the good provides the reader with imaginative access to Tolkien's idea of what it is to be evil. He begins to see what it would be like not to be able to imagine good. Sauron simply cannot imagine that anyone could resist using the Ring and so is unlikely to suspect that anyone would ever try to destroy it.

Everywhere we look in *The Lord of the Rings*, we see evidence of the lack of imagination of evil, most clearly in the inability of evil to perform the basic imaginative act: creation. It is said, for example, that Orcs are either men broken to Sauron's will or beings created as parodies of dwarves or elves. It is further said that Orcs and trolls do not even have languages of their own, " . . . but took what they could of other tongues and perverted it to their own liking." Even the One Ring, which was made by Saruon, could be made only after he lured the elvensmiths of Eregion into his service and learned their secrets. And, paradoxically, the smithies and furnaces of Isengard, with their iron wheels revolving and their hammers thudding, like the poorly built houses and the mills that belch smoke and stench in the Shire, are more represented as symbols of destruction than of creation.

One may thus be tempted to set up or to postulate some dialectical split between the natural and the artificial that will parallel a split between goods and evils, but Tolkien's version of reality is not quite that simple. It is true that machines are identified with evil in *The Lord of the Rings*, from the smithies of Isengard to the horrible catapults with which the Orcs throw the severed heads of the slain into the citadel of Minas Tirith, to the battering rams that break down the gates of that city. However, it is also true that elves and dwarves are makers or artisans, making for Minas Tirith gates "wrought of mithril and steel" as well as mail, swords, and shields. So it is not simply that to make, construct, or fashion flies in the face of nature. What, then, makes the difference between the tainted efforts of Saruman and Sandyman and the admirable efforts of the elves and dwarves?

Certainly a central point of differentiation is the aesthetic sensibility—even the most functional items made by dwarves and elves, swords, say, or the rope that Sam carries across the wastes, are made beautifully. The helmets and shields of the men of Gondor and Rohan are elaborately styled and decorated and the elven cloaks, like the ropes, are "strong, silken to the touch, [and] grey of hue." The arts and crafts of the elves unite them with nature and celebrate the implicit sacredness or magical quality of nature through the workmanship. The cloaks the travelers are given in Lórien are "grey with the hue of twilight under the trees . . . ; and yet if they were moved, or set in another light, they were green as shadowed leaves, or brown as fallow fields by night, dusk silver as water under the stars." And the paddles of the elven boats have "broad leaf-shaped blades." The secret of the beauty, and hence the positive qualities of the arts of the elves, is explained by the leader of the group that gives the cloaks to the travelers: "Leaf and branch, water and stone: they have the hue and beauty of all these things under the twilight of Lórien that we love; for we put the thought of all that we love into all that we make."

Thus the differences between the mechanic arts of the Free Peoples and those of the servants of the Dark Lord are two: the Free Peoples create in evocation or celebration of nature, in a preindustrial attitude which sees the world as essentially integrated (with people as part of nature), while the servants of Sauron create in an industrial mode which intends to distinguish among parts of the world by setting some elements above others (Sauron above creatures, machines above natural forces). Moreover, the Free Peoples produce from love while Morgul production arises from hatred.

The attitude reflected in the Morgul arts is one that celebrates distortion in nature. The livery of the Orcs of Barad-dûr, for example, is marked by a red eye, and the guard of the Tower of Cirith Ungol bear "a Moon disfigured with a ghastly face of death." And in contrast with the heroes' dwarfish mithril mail and elven cloaks, the Orcs wear "long hairy breeches of some unclean beast-fell, and a tunic of dirty leather."

Many writers on Tolkien have commented on the nostalgia of *The Lord of the Rings*, the sense of longing for an earlier time when man was closer to nature and society was less industrialized, when the unity of the world was more apparent. It is perhaps not surprising that these qualities and this time are closely associated with the elves, and the elves, their attitudes, their values, and their ways are closely bound up with the idea of good in *The Lord of the Rings*.

In contrast to evil, good in *The Lord of the Rings* is preeminently natural. Elves are known as The People of the Forests as dwarves are known as The People of the Mountains. The Tower Guard of Osgiliath takes for its crest a pair of white wings, and the men of Rohan ride to the sign of the White Horse. Aragorn's banner combines earth and air in the device of seven stars and one white tree. Thus the symbols of the powers for good in the trilogy are contrasted with evil not only by the contrast of black with white, but also by the contrast of the natural (trees and stars) with the human (the Red Eye of Barad-dûr and the White Hand of Saruman).

Good is also connected with nature in the trilogy by its character as a creative, life-giving force. First among the instances of this must be the folk wisdom of Gondor, "The hands of the King are the hands of a healer." This proverb unites the ideas of goodness, heroism, and creativity in the single symbol, *athelas.*

The chief characteristic of the *athelas* is its fragrance, which is its atmosphere-changing property. To the wounded, the fragrant steam is refreshing and strengthening, driving out both physical and spiritual pain. To them, and those about them, it calls up earlier, happier times and the strength that accompanies such memories. It clears and calms their minds; it lightens their hearts, it smells like "a memory of dewy mornings of unshadowed sun in which the fair world in Spring is itself but a fleeting memory," or it smells as if "a keen wind blew through the window, and it bore no scent, but was an air wholly fresh and clean and young, as if it had not before been breathed by any living thing and came new-made from snowy mountains high beneath a dome of stars, or from shores of silver far away washed by seas of foam," or "like the scent orchards, and of heather in the sunshine full of bees."

Jane Nitzche in *Tolkien's Art* rightly observes that the three responses to the *athelas* reflect the renewal of the three human faculties, rational, appetitive, and sensitive. However, it is equally significant that the three victims of the great battle wake to impressions of those things that are most important to them. For Faramir, the image of "some land of which the fair world in Spring is but a fleeting memory" is appropriate because it evokes the pervasive myth of the golden age, to which he has always felt allegiance, though to his father's sorrow. For Éowyn, the image of unbreathed air and high stars is appropriate because it represents the purity for which she has pined during the long years she has felt her life and that of her race being defiled by the works of Wormtongue. Placed next to the elevated images associated with Éowyn, those associated with Merry strike the reader as distinguished by their domesticity. The evocation of orchards, heather, and bees is an evocation of the rural paradise that is the Shire.

What this tailoring of sense impressions to the greatest joys of the three wounded warriors suggests is that *athelas* heals by helping people to be more fully themselves. To be well is to be individual, which is to be free. Thus, though Aragorn creates Faramir, Éowyn, and Merry (in the sense that he is responsible for their rebirths), he creates them to be free, to be themselves, not to be bound to him.

Though the idea of healing is prominent in Tolkien's conception of the good, it is also associated with other kinds of creative or life-giving behavior. A great deal of the creativity associated with the good is linguistic, including Bilbo's ballad of Eärendil, all the heroic myths of the Eldar, and, as Frodo and Sam remind us, the creation of the story of *The Lord of the Rings*. Such joy in the uses of language is also reflected in the delight in names and naming felt by the elves and men, as, for example, Aragorn, son of Arathorn, Isildur's heir, Elessar, the Elf-stone and the Renewer, Strider of the house of Telcontar. The practice of naming and renaming continually reaffirms the existence of the good and, in that sense, continually re-creates it. Tolkien contrasts this practice with the tendency not to name evil at all if it can be helped, particularly on the part of Faramir, for to name is to create.

Closely related to linguistic creativity is the question of the kinds of information sources that can be trusted. Though supernatural sources of information are available (the palantíri), like the Ring's power, the usefulness of their information varies according to the characteristics of the user. Thus Denethor's use of the palantír drives him to despair and Saruman's seduces him to evil, for even the stones of Westernesse may be turned to the service of evil.

What is worthy of trust, then, is the creative and the individual—the literature and lore of the ancient days and the intuition of the individual. From the literature and lore of the ancient days come history, motivation, and prophecy, and though the stories may be dismissed (as by Ted Sandyman) or misunderstood (as by the Master of the Houses of Healing), they speak true to those who listen. From individual intuition comes a sense of where the public and the private dreams overlap and why, therefore, the myths of the ancient days are important and true.

The trustworthiness of traditional and intuitive knowledge is a part of the larger value of respect for the past. Respect for the old tales and the refusal to assign them merely to the nursery or to the "cracked" is an attribute of both pragmatic and absolute good. On the pragmatic level, the usefulness of the information gained from the traditional sources is clear. From the old books Gandalf has learned the secret of the Ring. From the advice of the ancient seer, Aragorn is reminded to ride the Path of the Dead.

But it is not only, or even primarily, for such immediately pragmatic purposes that reverence for the past is valued. More significantly, and more generally, the literature and lore of the ancient days of Middle-earth, like the literature and lore of our own world, reflect the continuities of earthly human existence. The point is not that the story of Beren and Lúthien Tinúviel is recapitulated in the story of Aragorn and Arwen Evenstar, but that, for example, Beren's quest for the Silmaril, his love of Lúthien, his suffering for her sake, and his heroic death invoke not just the sorrows and joys, the triumphs and defeats of Aragorn, but of all the children of earth, as Sam realizes: "Beren now, he never thought he was going to get that Silmaril from the Iron Crown in Thangorodrim, and yet he did, and that was a worse place and a blacker danger than ours." For Sam as for all of us, myths exist as myths because they say something to the human spirit, something that remains worth saying even though the meaning, not just the story, is ages old. And therein lies the connection between the theme of the nature of good and evil and the uses of language in *The Lord of the Rings*.

As Tolkien expanded his thinking about the nature of heroes and heroism from *The Hobbit* to *The Lord of the Rings*, and as he grew subtler in his thinking about good and evil, he also enlarged the role of language in his imaginative world. One can see in *The Lord of the Rings* the same kind of use of wordplay as Tolkien enjoyed in *The Hobbit*, though the riddles, puns, and proverbs are more serious in tone and more heroic in purpose. Tolkien goes beyond the mere linguistic fun of *The Hobbit* to reflect in his history of Middle-earth the interpenetrations of language and culture. He constructs languages for the people of his imaginative world and then investigates what those languages suggest about the cultures from which they come. The magnitude of his achievement is clear when we consider that in undertaking this task of philological investigation of an imaginative world, Tolkien hardly misses a beat in the progress of the narrative. One rarely feels that the professor has stepped out of his role as a fantasist to lecture, at least until one reaches the appendices.

In *The Hobbit* Tolkien used proverbs to increase the sense of reality with which the reader meets the imaginary world. In *The Lord of the Rings* he goes further, using proverbs to build the sense of the familiar, but also to create a sense of the individuality of cultures. The proverbs, as groups, refer to Anglo-Saxon and Middle English sources, but they have the effect, even for readers who do not recognize the references, of lending a solidity to the projection of Middle-earth. A culture that has its own folk-wisdom, whether it is the same as ours or only parallel to it, is a culture that seems to make sense, to have coherence, to operate by rules of some kind—in short, to seem real.

In general, there are two possible uses for proverbs in literature: they may be intended to instruct or to entertain. It is unlikely that Tolkien's intent in *The Lord of the Rings* is to instruct, because he often amuses himself and the reader by creating situations in which obvious statements of traditional wisdom are set in opposition, as when Elrond reminds the nine walkers of their freedom to reject the quest at any time:

> "Faithless is he that says farewell when the road darkens," said Gimli.
> "Maybe," said Elrond, "but let him not vow to walk in the dark, who has not seen the nightfall."
> "Yet sworn word may strengthen quaking heart," said Gimli.

Like the classic opposition, "He who hesitates is lost," and "Look before you leap," Gimli's exchange with Elrond suggests the limitations of the partial truths of proverbs as guides to action.

If Tolkien's purpose in using proverbs is not simply to instruct, then it is likely to be to entertain, and Tolkien's entertaining uses of proverbs are many and varied. He uses proverbs to cap climaxes or to emphasize situations, as when Aragorn's entry in to the city of Gondor is met with "The hands of the King are the hands of a healer," or when Faramir reveals that he is Boromir's brother with "Night oft brings news to near kindred." He uses proverbs seriously, as when Aragorn applauds Pippin's using his brooch from Lórien as a trail marker during his capture by the Orcs, saying, "One who cannot cast away a treasure at need is in fetters." Or he uses them humorously, as when Gandalf says of Barliman Butterbur, "He can see through a brick wall in time (as they say in Bree)." But most of all, he uses proverbs to heighten the sense of identity of a single character or group.

Barliman's string of platitudes, "It never rains but it pours, as we say in Bree" and " . . . there's no accounting for East and West, as we say in Bree" is perfect as a representation of the conversation of a man who is too busy to concentrate on what is before him. This sort of nearly meaningless utterance is only probable in a kind of semiconscious conversation that prepares us for a shock of recognition instead of a simple shock when Barliman reveals that he has forgotten to send Gandalf's warning letter to Frodo.

On the other hand, the serious, thoughtful, almost stately character of the men of Rohan is reflected in the phrasing of their proverbs: "Where will wants not, a way opens" or "Oft evil will shall evil mar." There is about these proverbs an archaic feeling, in part the result of word choice (*oft, froward*) and in part a function of Tolkien's having rendered a familiar thought in unfamiliar syntax, such as "Need brooks no delay, but late is better than never."

The reader's tendency to identify most closely with the hobbits is strengthened by the similarity of their traditional wisdom to our own. Sam's "Where there's life there's hope" and his "Handsome is as handsome does" are familiar in word, phrase, and meaning, whereas a proverb like Gandalf's "The burned hand teaches best," while familiar in sentiment, is probably better known in its "Once burned, twice shy" form.

It would not be precisely true to say that there is less wordplay in *The Lord of the Rings* than in *The Hobbit*. It does seem to be true, however that the proportion is smaller. Proverbs are still abundant and seem to be used toward a multitude of literary ends, including the development of character. Actual riddles are much less in evidence, though the sense of the world as a riddle, or an enigma, is much more pervasive here than in the earlier work. Similarly, puns are much less apparent here, though it may be only that they are subtler, as when Goldberry recognizes Frodo as an Elf-friend by "the ring in your voice."

But of central interest to any discussion of language in *The Lord of the Rings* is the trouble Tolkien takes to develop his technique of using differences in language to differentiate among races, and, in many cases, to suggest the character of the various races. Each of the major groups of *The Lord of the Rings* has its own language, and even the nonphilologist perceives how the language reflects the racial character of its speakers. One should note, however, that the language of the trilogy purports to be a translation in all cases; thus the reader is driven to the extensive appendices to find Tolkien, "the translator's," explanation of the nature of the original languages and the decisions he found necessary for the translation.

Hobbits, for example, speak what is called the Common Speech. Their vocabulary is generally simple and unexotic, as is their sentence structure, although the educated among them speak more formally, causing nearly all who meet them to comment on their verbal charm, as when Beregond tells Pippin ". . . strange accents do not mar fair speech, and hobbits are a fair-spoken folk." Hobbits, it seems are a race of chatterers, who " . . . will sit on the edge of ruin and discuss the pleasures of the table, or the small doings of their fathers, grandfathers, and great-grandfathers, and remoter cousins to the ninth degree. . . . " For them, that is, language is fundamentally a social tool. They are great talkers, great storytellers, and, at least among the more admirable, great lovers of poems, songs, and stories. Bilbo's translations from the Elvish and his Red Book may be anomalous, but Sam's love of stories of elves and his memory of the old nonsense rhyme about "oliphunts," as well as Frodo's tendency to be moved to poetic expression when he leaves home or when he meets Goldberry, suggest that as language users, hobbits have more to them than first meets the ear.

More indication of the hobbits' characteristic uses of language is to be found in the narrator's commentary on the habitual humming and singing of the hobbits. He observes that hobbits "have a way" of singing, " . . . especially when they are drawing near to home at night." And at the same time as he establishes the basically domestic and social nature of hobbit language use, he points out the unusual qualities of Frodo, Sam, and Pippin, who sing not of supper and bed, but of the joys of the open road.

Hobbits consider conversation one of the chief joys of social life, as is demonstrated by Merry's desire to sit and talk herb lore with Théoden, King of Rohan; they also appreciate the social character of literary utterance, for the folk in the Prancing Pony enjoy a bit of a song as much as the folk of Elrond's haven of Rivendell, though the celebration of "brown beer" in Frodo's song about the man in the moon is much less elevated in subject matter and diction than Bilbo's ballad of Eärendil, which is, in turn, less elevated than the Elven hymn, "A Elbereth Gilthoniel." The elves of *The Lord of the Rings* speak one of two languages: Quenya (High-Elven) or Sindarin (Grey-Elven). By the time of *The Lord of the Rings*, Quenya is only a literary rather than a social language, and thus appears only in songs such as "A Elbereth Gilthoniel." But the elves of Rivendell and the elves of Loth-lórian and Mirkwood, whether descended from the High Elves or the Grey Elves, speak a variety of Sindarin.

Whether Quenya or Sindarin or Common Speech, the language of the elves is much more formal than the colloquial diction of the hobbits. For example, translated, the Common Speech as the elves speak it is a language without the informality of contractions—elves say *cannot* rather than *can't*. The faintly archaic character resulting from this formality suggests the elves' racial age, for they are the firstborn who were created in the First Age, before men and dwarves came into the world. Thus for Elrond to speak of his "sire" or to "deem" a doom appropriately dates him. Similarly, Celeborn's observation that "Oft it may chance that old wives keep in memory word of things that once were needful for the wise to know" as much suggests a respect for the past, with his choice of words and the way he orders them, as with the sentiment he expresses. In this way Tolkien creates for the reader some sense of the degree of formality of the Sindarin, the Elvish tongue spoken in Middle-earth.

The vocabulary of the elves is easily perceived as the most musical of the languages of Middle-earth, largely because of the high proportion of liquids (*l*'s and *r*'s) and of vowels that are sounded in the front of the mouth. These features give the language a quickness and sparkle that is accentuated by the tendency of Elvish words to be polysyllabic and to feature sequences of unaccented syllables. As Tolkien describes the language in the appendices, "Where the last syllable but one contains (as often) a short vowel followed by only one (or no) consonant, the stress falls on the syllable before it, the third from the end." That is, words with pronunciation patterns like that of *slippery* or *listening* are prominent in the language, and the characteristic linking of unaccented syllables gives the language the impression of speed.

The pure musicality of the language he had invented was one of its chief charms for Tolkien, who saw how the shapes and sounds of even an unknown language could work on the imagination to produce images and effects. It is the same phenomenon that leads people to say that the word *Schenectady* sounds like a railway switching yard. The connection is not at all a matter of meaning; it is purely one of the suggestion of the sounds. And this is the phenomenon Frodo experiences as he listens to the music of Rivendell for the first time:

> At first the beauty of the melodies and the interwoven words in the Elven-tongue, even though he understood them little, held him in a spell, as soon as he began to attend to them. Almost it seemed that the words took shape, and visions of far lands and bright things that he had never yet imagined opened out before him.

Indeed, the speech of the elves abounds in those effects that we generally call *musical*—a repetition of vowel and consonant sounds, and use of onomatopoeia in words such as *sighing* and *whispering*.

Another musical language of Middle-earth, though one in which the tempo is much slower, is Entish. The language of the Ents is characterized by the translator as "slow, sonorous, agglomerated, repetitive, indeed long-winded; formed of a multiplicity of vowel shades and distinctions of tone and quality." It is a perfect expression of the being and character of a race that prides itself on never being "over-hasty." The sonority and the agglomeration and repetition are clearly reflected in the Entish version of the Common

Speech that Fangorn speaks. The long-windedness by comparison with the speech of other races is perhaps best suggested by the very long lines of the song Fangorn sings as he carries the two hobbits through his forest: "In the willow-meads of Tasarinan I walked in the Spring." The fifteen syllable lines of this song are exceeded in length only by the sixteen syllable lines of the war song the Ents sing on their way to Isengard: "To Isengard! Though Isengard be ringed and barred with doors of stone." The line lengths alone illustrate the translator's assertion that Ents are "indeed long-winded."

As the languages of various races distinguish among them, the languages of various "nations" distinguish among men. Most distinctive are the men of Rohan, who speak a language that seems to be derived from Old English. John Tinkler has shown how many of the untranslated words spoken by the men of Rohan, could be Old English words. For example, he suggests that *Éothéod*, reported by the translator to be the earliest name for the people of Rohan, is a combination of *eoh* (Old English "horse") and *theod* (Old English "nation or people"). Similarly, the names of Théoden's and Éomer's swords are Old Englsih names: Théoden's *Herugrim* is in Old English, "very fierce, cruel, sharp" and Éomer's *Guthwine* is "friend in battle."

The translator also notes that when the hobbits first heard the men of Rohan speak, they thought they could understand or recognize a few of the words here and there. That is, their relation to the language of Rohan is about what ours would be to the language of a long lost colony of Anglo-Saxons. Yet the language is not inaccessible to the reader who lacks a knowledge of Old English. Our understanding of the importance of horses to the men of Rohan and the ubiquitous presence of the prefix *Eo* in Éomer, Éomund, Éowyn, Éored, Eothain, coupled with Gimli's first epithet to Éomer, "horse-master," is enough to suggest the etymology Tolkien was illustrating for us. Similarly, one need not know that the Old English *mearh* means "horse" or "steed" to see the meaning of the Rohan word *mearas* when it occurs in context: "That is Shadowfax. He is the chief of the Mearas, lords of horses."

As the men of Rohan resemble Anglo-Saxons in language, they resemble them in culture. They are a race in which the heroic code takes precedence over all else, who "love war and valour as things good in themselves, both a sport and an end." They sing of past greatness in terms of "the helm and the hauberk" and the old songs that celebrate the old heroes. And Théoden's joy in being recalled to himself after years of being undermined by Grima (Wormtongue) is not, as we might expect, a song of rebirth in nature, but a call to battle: "Arise now, arise, Riders of Théoden!" Indeed, there is little in the songs of the Rohirrim to suggest any relationship with the world beyond a constant and heroic struggle to maintain life.

The men of Gondor and others of the Númenórean line have in common with the Rohirrim a gravity and an old-fashioned way of speaking that suggests their high origins as well as their antiquity. But unlike the Rohirrim, they celebrate "more skills and knowledge than only the craft of weapons and slaying." The songs of Gondor not only celebrate the past, but preserve the wisdom of it, even beyond the recognition of learned men of the present generation, as for example in the rhyme about *athelas*.

That the old songs of Gondor should preserve wisdom beyond the understanding of the present generation is fully appropriate, because the city itself, like the Stewards who rule it, is the last preserve of the strength and wisdom of the Númenóreans, the Men of the West. And, as Faramir's observation on the differences between Gondor and Rohan suggests, it is important that the two rhymes of Gondor, the *athelas* rhyme and Boromir's riddle, "Seek for the Sword that was broken," both focus on a reawakening process without celebrating the martial arts. Indeed this difference in thematic concern points up the appropriateness of Éomer's observation that Boromir was more like a man of the Mark than like a man of Gondor.

Finally, there is the unique case of the language of Tom Bombadil. Bombadil is "Master of wood, water, and hill," "oldest and fatherless," and will be "last as he was First." He is a kind of Adam before the fall, a natural man able to "sing" to all of nature, and a link to the golden age. His status as a natural man is reflected not only in his power over Old Man Willow and Barrow-Wights, but also in his marriage to Goldberry, the River-daughter, who is described in terms reminiscent of a water nymph: Her hair "ripples," and her gown is "green as young reeds."

Bombadil's songs are a mixture of nature imagery and nonsense. The nonsense lines with their bouncy rhythm reflect the careless happiness of an innocent nature, but Tom is not limited to this naive role as his ability to sing control over Old Man Willow and his stories of "evil things and good things, things friendly and things unfriendly, cruel things and kind things" shows.

The songs, and indeed Bombadil's normal discourse, are composed of lines which function either as single units with heavy use of assonance and alliteration preserving the unity or as two-line units, marked by strong caesura and rhymes. Whether the basic unit is the single line or the couplet, each line is marked by a strong caesura or midline pause. There does not seem to be a pattern of number of syllables or number of stresses before or after the pause, but the pause itself is unmistakable, and links Bombadil to the alliterative tradition in Old and Middle English poetry, and by analogy, to the ancient cultural past of Middle-earth (in contrast with the elves, who would be more nearly analogous to the cultural past of, say, Rome and the Latin language). Bombadil's lines fall naturally into two parts:

I had an errand there:	gathering water-lilies
gathering leaves and lilies white	to please my pretty lady,
the last ere the year's end	to keep them from the winter,
to flower by her pretty feet	till the snows are melted.

Not only do Bombadil's songs lead back to an historical past, his other utterances allude to a mythic past when the natural mode of discourse was song—this is another reference to the golden age when all of humankind and nature communicated. So Tom sends the hobbits to bed, saying,

Some things are ill to hear	when the world's in shadow.
Sleep till the morning light,	rest on the pillow!
Heed no nightly noise!	Fear no grey willow!

Bombadil's language and his use of it not only locate him morally by associating him with the other natural goods in the work, but also help to locate him historically and geographically in Middle-earth. He is thus one of the best examples of what it can mean to say *The Lord of the Rings* is philologically inspired.

In contrast to the lilt and flow of the language of the elves, the friendly informality of the hobbits' language, and the stateliness of the languages of Rohan and Gondor, the language of the Orcs, the Black Speech of Barad-dûr, looks and sounds dark and horrid: Its alien appearance is emphasized by its use of suffixes to mark grammatical function (durbatuluk), its use of hyphenated forms (Saruman-glôb), its jaw-breaking clusters of consonants (Uf-thak), and its frequent use of vowels that are pronounced with the tongue well back in the mouth (Lugburz, Nazgûl). The language looks and sounds as though it were cut out of wood, and so clicks and thuds into place instead of flowing.

When the translator writes in the appendices that "Orcs and Trolls spoke as they would, without love of words or things; and their language was actually more degraded and filthy than I have shown it," he directs our attention to the perversions of language reflected in the example of an Orc proverb, "Where there's a whip, there's a will, my slugs." He contrasts the Orc's brutality and their tendency to see the world as covered with their own slime with the simple optimism and determination of the common "Where there's a will, there's a way" and the more grave and determined "Where will wants not, a way opens" of Rohan. In his note, the translator also recalls to us Shagrat's harangue: "'Curse you, Snaga, you little maggot . . . he knifed me, the dung, . . . I'll put red maggot holes in your belly." To listen to Orcs talk is to hear a language that draws most of its imagery from the process of death and decay.

The physical ugliness of the language, which mirrors the moral depravity it expresses, is represented by Tolkien's giving Orc speech, whether it is the Black Speech or the Orcish corruption of Westron, configurations and pronunciations that are unfamiliar and harsh to the eyes and ears of speakers of English. His two chief devices in creating a sense of the ugliness of the language are the use of clusters of consonants in combinations we find unusual and unpronounceable, such as the *zg* in "Nazgûl" or the *bh* in "bubhosh," and the use of the back vowels, vowel sounds that are made with the tongue pulled back in the mouth, such as the *u* in "buck" or the *o* in "glob." The combination of harsh consonants and back vowels makes the language sound harsh and grating, while the clustering of consonants in unusual combinations, the use of the circumflex and hyphenation of words ("Burzum-ishi" or "Saruman-glôb") combine to make it look equally ungainly. If the Orcs can be said to have a culture, something of its nature as the antithesis of the orderly, the organic, the creative, and the worshipful can be perceived from the extraordinary ugliness of their language.

Thus, the language, and particularly the songs of Middle-earth, clearly serve to establish the uniqueness of each people of that world. Thematically and formally, they allude to a variety of languages and cultures from our world, from the Old English sparseness of the Rohirrim to the romantic ballads of the elves. However, the most formal and most elevated style is reserved for the great Eagle who brings the news of victory at the Dark Gate to the city of Gondor:

> Sing now, ye people of the Tower of Anor,
> for the realm of Sauron is ended for ever,
>   and the Dark Tower is thrown down.

The reverberations of form and content here are biblical, with particular reference to the psalms. The image of a savior-king who will return to rule the faithful and the promise of a return to life by "the tree that was withered" have Christian reverberations that again reinforce the sense of elevation, the high importance of the song, as does the identity of the messenger, for in medieval Christian iconography, the eagle was the symbol of St. John the Evangelist, who is noted for his contemplation of the divine nature of Christ, and quoted for the opening line of his gospel, "In the beginning was the Word. . . . "

Thus, though it is possible and even practical for a reader with no particular philological background to comprehend and appreciate the uses to which Tolkien puts languages in the *Lord of the Rings*, it is by no means true that he "uses a remarkably plain variety of everyday midtwentieth century

English." In *The Lord of the Rings*, Tolkien used languages to delineate cultural attitudes, to expose racial personalities, and to lead the reader to an understanding of or a feeling for the quality of consciousness of the various groups. His achievement is that he did so without interrupting the flow of his epic story, without sacrificing action to exposition or character to stereotype.

Chronology

1892	John Ronald Reuel Tolkien, called Ronald, is born on January 3, the first son of Mabel Suffield Tolkien and Arthur Tolkien.
1894	Ronald's brother, Hilary Arthur Reuel, is born.
1896	Arthur Tolkien (father) dies of rheumatic fever in Africa.
1900	Mabel and her sons become Catholic. Ronald enters King Edward's School.
1904	Mabel Suffield Tolkien (mother) dies in November. Father Francis Morgan is designated the boys' guardian.
1910	Awarded a scholarship to study Classics at Exeter College, Oxford.
1913	Transfers from Classics to English, with emphasis in philology, and formally studies Old Norse.
1914	Gets engaged to Edith Bratt.
1915	Takes a First Class degree in English from Oxford. Enters the army.
1916	Marries Edith Bratt. Participates in the Battle of the Somme. Is invalided out of the army in November.
1917	Begins to write tales later known as *The Book of Lost Tales*. First son, John, is born.
1918	Joins the staff at the Oxford English Dictionary.

1920　Appointed Reader in English Language at Leeds University. Begins poems known as *Lays of Beleriand*. Second son, Michael, is born.

1924　Appointed Professor of English Language at Leeds. Third son, Christopher, is born.

1925　Publishes an edition of *Sir Gawain and the Green Knight* with E.V. Gordon. Is named Rawlinson and Bosworth Professor of Anglo-Saxon at Oxford University.

1929　Daughter, Priscilla, is born.

1930　Completes full draft of *The Silmarillion* (printed in *The Shaping of Middle-Earth*, 1986).

1932　C.S. Lewis reads a manuscript of *The Hobbit*. Tolkien at work on an expanded *Silmarillion* and continues to publish poems and articles.

1936　Delivers lecture, "Beowulf: The Monsters and the Critics," before British Academy. *The Hobbit* is accepted for publication.

1937　*The Hobbit* is published.

1938　*The Hobbit* is published in the U.S. and receives *New York Herald Tribune* award as best children's book of the season.

1939　Delivers lecture "On Fairy-Stories" at St. Andrews University.

1945　Named Merton Professor of English Language and Literature at Oxford University.

1948　*The Lord of the Rings* is completed.

1949　*Farmer Giles of Ham* is published.

1954　The first two volumes of *The Lord of the Rings* (*The Fellowship of the Ring* and *The Two Towers*) is published.

1955　The last volume, *The Return of the King*, is published.

1959　Retires from Oxford University.

1962　Publishes *The Adventures of Tom Bombadil*, a collection of poems.

1964　*Tree and Leaf* is published.

1965　Tolkien Society of America is founded.

1967　*Smith of Wootton Major* is published.

1971   Edith Tolkien dies, aged eighty-two.

1972   Receives honorary doctorate from Oxford University and is honored by the Queen.

1973   Dies on September 2 at age eighty-one.

Contributors

HAROLD BLOOM is Sterling Professor of the Humanities at Yale University and Henry W. and Albert A. Berg Professor of English at the New York University Graduate School. He is the author of over 20 books, including *The Anxiety of Influence* (1973), which sets forth Professor Bloom's provocative theory of the literary relationships between the great writers and their predecessors. His most recent book, *Shakespeare: The Invention of the Human* (1998), was a finalist for the 1998 National Book Award. Professor Bloom is a 1985 MacArthur Foundation Award recipient, served as the Charles Eliot Norton Professor of Poetry at Harvard University in 1987–88, and has received honorary degrees from the universities of Rome and Bologna. In 1999, Professor Bloom received the prestigious American Academy of Arts and Letters Gold Medal for Criticism.

HUGH T. KEENAN is a literary scholar and critic who has published several articles on fantasy fiction including an original essay on J. R. R. Tolkien for the collection *Tolkien and the Critics: Essays on J. R. R. Tolkien's* The Lord of the Rings.

BURTON RAFFEL has written, translated and edited many volumes of work. His publications include *The Art of Translating Poetry*, *Poems and Prose from the Old English*, and he was coeditor and translator of *The Essential Horace: Odes, Epodes, Satires, and Epistles*.

RANDEL HELMS has taught Critical Writing at the University of California. His publications include *Tolkien's World*.

HUMPHREY CARPENTER studied at the University of Oxford, where he met J. R. R. Tolkien. He has worked as a producer for the BBC and was responsible for Tolkien programs. In addition to a biography on Tolkien, he is co-author of *A Thames Companion*.

JANE CHANCE NITZSCHE is a professor of English at Rice University, where she teaches old and middle English and women's studies. Her publications include *The Genius Figure in Antiquity and the Middle Ages*.

JARED LOBDELL was the editor of *A Tolkien Compass*, and for eight years was a book reviewer for *National Review*. He has taught at several colleges including Carnegie-Mellon University in Pittsburgh.

DAVID L. JEFFREY has been a professor of English and the department chairperson at the University of Victoria. His publications include *People of the Book* and *A Dictionary of Biblical Tradition*.

ROSE A. ZIMBARDO has taught in the English department at the State University of New York at Stony Brook. She has collaborated in the editing of two collections of essays on Tolkien including *Tolkien and the Critics: Essays on J. R. R. Tolkien's* Lord of the Rings.

KATHARYN W. CRABBE has been the Associate Dean of Undergraduate Studies at the State University College in Geneseo, New York. She has written widely on Children's literature and is the author of *Evelyn Waugh* in Frederick Ungar's Literature and Life Series.

Bibliography

Auden, W. H. "Good and Evil in *The Lord of the Rings*." *Tolkien Journal* 3 (1967): 5–8. Reprinted in *Critical Quarterly* 10 (1968): 138–42.

———. "At the End of the Quest, Victory." *New York Times Book Review* (22 January 1956): 5.

———. "The Quest Hero." *Texas Quarterly* 4 (Winter 1961): 81–93.

Beatie, Bruce A. "*The Lord of the Rings:* Myth, Reality, and Relevance." *Western Review* 4 (Winter 1967): 58–59.

Becker, Alida, ed. *The Tolkien Scrapbook*. New York: Grosset and Dunlap, 1974.

Bettelheim, Bruno. *The Uses of Enchantment: The Meaning and Importance of Fairy Tales*. New York: Alfred A. Knopf, 1976.

Blissett, William. "Despots of the Rings." *South Atlantic Quarterly* 58 (Summer 1959): 448–56.

Campbell, Joseph. *The Hero with a Thousand Faces*. New York: Pantheon, 1949.

Carpenter, Humphrey. *Tolkien: A Biography*. London: George Allen and Unwin, 1977. Boston: Houghton Mifflin, 1977. New York: Ballantine Books, 1978.

Crabbe, Katharyn F. *J. R. R. Tolkien*. New York: Frederick Ungar, 1981.

Evans, Robley. *J. R. R. Tolkien*. New York: Warner, 1972.

Giddings, Robert, ed. *J. R. R. Tolkien: This Far Land*. London: Vision, 1983.

Grotta-Kurska, Daniel *J. R. R. Tolkien: Architect of Middle Earth*. Philadelphia: Running Press, 1976.

Hall, Robert A., Jr. "Tolkien's Hobbit Tetralogy as 'Anti-Nibelungen.'" *Western Humanities Review* 32 (1978): 351–60.

Hammond, Wayne G., and Christina Scull. *J. R. R. Tolkien, Artist & Illustrator*. Boston: Houghton Mifflin, 1995.

Hayes, Noreen and Robert Renshaw. "Of Hobbits: *The Lord of the Rings*." *Critique* 9 (1967): 58–66.

Helms, Randel. *Tolkien's World*. Boston: Houghton Mifflin, 1974.

Hillegas, Mark R., ed. *Shadows of Imagination: The Fantasies of C. S. Lewis, J. R. R. Tolkien, and Charles Williams.* Carbondale: Southern Illinois University Press, 1979.

Irwin, W. R. "There and Back Again: The Romances of Williams, Lewis, and Tolkien." *Sewanee Review 69* (1961): 566–78.

Isaacs, Neil D. and Rose A. Zimbardo, eds. *Tolkien and the Critics.* Notre Dame, IN: University of Notre Dame Press, 1968.

Kocher, Paul H. *Master of Middle Earth: The Fiction of J. R. R. Tolkien.* New York: Houghton Mifflin, 1972.

Manlove, C. N. *Modern Fantasy: Five Studies.* Cambridge, England: Cambridge University Press, 1975.

Mathews, Richard. *Lightening from a Clear Sky: Tolkien, the Trilogy, and* The Silmarillion. San Bernardino, CA: Borgo, 1978.

Lobdell, Jared C., editor. *A Tolkien Compass.* LaSalle, IL.: Open Court, 1976.

Nicol, Charles. "Reinvented Word." *Harper's* (November 1977): 95.

Nitzsche, Jane Chance. *Tolkien's Art: A Mythology for England.* New York: St. Martin's Press, 1979.

Norman, Philip. "The Prevalence of Hobbits." *New York Times Magazine* (January 15, 1967): 3.

Petty, Anne C. *One Ring to Bind Them All: Tolkien's Mythology.* Tuscaloosa: University of Alabama Press, 1979.

Purtill, Richard. *Lord of the Elves and Eldild: Fantasy and Philosophy in C. S. Lewis and J.R.R. Tolkien.* Grand Rapids, MI: Zondervan, 1974.

Sale, Roger. "England's Parnassus: C. S. Lewis, Charles Williams, and J. R. R. Tolkien." *Hudson Review* 17 (1964): 203–25.

———. *Modern Heroism: Essays on D. H. Lawrence, William Empson and J. R. R. Tolkien.* Berkeley: University of California Press, 1973.

Salu, Mary and Robert T. Farrell, eds. *J.R.R. Tolkien, Scholar and Storyteller: Essays in Memoriam.* Ithaca: Cornell University Press, 1979.

Shippey, T. A. *The Road to Middle-Earth.* London: George Allen and Unwin, 1982.

Spacks, Patricia Meyer. "Ethical Pattern in *Lord of the Rings.*" *Critique 3* (1959): 30–42.

Thomson, George H. "*The Lord of the Rings:* The Novel as Traditional Romance." *Wisconsin Studies in Contemporary Literature* 8 (1967): 43–59.

West, Richard C., *Tolkien Criticism: An Annotated Checklist.* Kent, Ohio: Kent State University Press, 1970.

Acknowledgments

"The Appeal of *The Lord of the Rings:* A Struggle for Life" by Hugh T. Keenan from *Tolkien and the Critics: Essays on J. R. R. Tolkien's The Lord of the Rings*, edited by Neil D. Isaacs and Rose A. Zimbardo. © 1968 by University of Notre Dame Press.

"*The Lord of the Rings* as Literature" by Burton Raffel from *Tolkien and the Critics: Essays on J. R. R. Tolkien's The Lord of the Rings*, edited by Neil D. Isaacs and Rose A. Zimbardo. © 1968 by University of Notre Dame Press.

"Frodo Anti-Faust: *The Lord of the Rings* as Contemporary Mythology" by Randel Helms from *Tolkien's World* by Randel Helms. © 1974 by Randel Helms.

"1925–1949(ii): The Third Age" by Humphrey Carpenter from *Tolkien: A Biography* by Humphrey Carpenter. © 1977 by George Allen & Unwin (Publishers) Ltd.

"*The Lord of the Rings*: Tolkien's Epic" by Jane Chance Nitzsche from *Tolkien's Art: A 'Mythology for England'* by Jane Chance Nitzsche. © 1979 by Jane Chance Nitzsche.

Index